DATE DUE

C4

DEMCO, INC. 38-2931

D1570545

The
CYBRARIAN'S
WEB 2

An A–Z Guide to Free Social Media Tools, Apps, and Other Resources

Cheryl Ann Peltier-Davis
Foreword by David Lee King

 Information Today, Inc.
Medford, New Jersey

First printing

The Cybrarian's Web 2: An A–Z Guide to Free Social Media Tools, Apps, and Other Resources

Copyright © 2015 by Cheryl Ann Peltier-Davis

Publisher's Note: The author and publisher have taken care in the preparation of this book but make no expressed or implied warranty of any kind and assume no responsibility for errors or omissions. No liability is assumed for incidental or consequential damages in connection with or arising out of the use of the information contained herein.

Many of the designations used by manufacturers and sellers to distinguish their products are claimed as trademarks. Where those designations appear in this book and Information Today, Inc. was aware of a trademark claim, the designations have been printed with initial capital letters.

Library of Congress Cataloging-in-Publication Data

Peltier-Davis, Cheryl Ann.
 The cybrarian's web 2 : an A–Z guide to free social media tools, apps, and other resources / Cheryl Ann Peltier-Davis ; foreword by David Lee King.
     pages cm
 Includes bibliographical references and index.
 ISBN 978-1-57387-512-7
 1. Web sites—Directories. 2. Free computer software—Computer network resources. 3. Libraries and the Internet. I. Title.
 ZA4225.P44 2015
 025.0422—dc23

2015000244

Printed and bound in the United States of America

President and CEO: Thomas H. Hogan, Sr.
Editor-in-Chief and Publisher: John B. Bryans
Project Editor: Randall McClure
Associate Editor: Beverly M. Michaels
Production Manager: Norma J. Neimeister
Indexer: Candace Hyatt

Interior Design by Amnet Systems
Cover Design by Dana Kruse Stevenson

infotoday.com

To Andre and Antonio

Contents

Foreword

Last autumn, Cheryl Ann Peltier-Davis asked me if I'd be interested in writing the foreword to her new book. When she told me what it would be about, I jumped at the chance.

Why? Because *The Cybrarian's Web 2* is a *really* useful, at-your-fingertips resource covering some cool online tools, apps, services, and resources.

Let's say you are a new librarian (or you're not so new, but the web is still—let's be honest here—slightly foreign to you at times). Your supervisor suddenly gives you a small project; maybe your assignment is to research social news aggregators. Now, you know next to nothing about social news aggregators—in fact, you actually haven't heard the term "social news aggregators" before—you just know the supervisor wants you to find something to help her track local and national news on her iPad.

Okay, then. What do you do next? If you're like most of the modern world with easy access to the web, your next stop is your best friend (or should I say "frenemy") Google. You sit down and start randomly typing in search strings. You'll probably search for things like:

> ➤ Online news alerts

> ➤ iPad news apps

> ➤ iPad news trackers

Hopefully, you'll find some potentially interesting articles to skim through, and perhaps some articles will be from iPad app blogs or computer tech sites like *Macworld* and *PC Magazine*.

Eventually, you will find something that points you in the right direction because you are a good librarian. You'll complete the project—after lots of searching, reading, skimming, and possibly playing around with random iPad apps. But guess what? There's an easier way: You can keep *The Cybrarian's Web 2* on your desk—and in your library, right? (Buy two copies!) Just picking this handy book up, you can find information on four social news aggregators in the space of a minute.

Each of these social news aggregators has a chapter devoted to it. Coverage includes an overview and description of the tool or service along with useful features and current trends.

It gets even better. After the overview comes a "How Cybrarians Can Use this Resource" section, detailing how the resource fits into a librarian's arsenal of tools.

Wow.

And that's just the four tools focused on social news aggregation. *The Cybrarian's Web 2* provides an in-depth look at 61 tools, apps, and resources. I'm a *huge* geek who's very familiar with the modern web, and I'm familiar with about 40 of them. *The Cybrarian's Web 2* is as current as it is useful.

That's actually why Cheryl wrote the book. To help *you* and *me*. Her goal is "to assist the library community in the discoverability and use of these resources." While her first volume of *The Cybrarian's Web* (2012) focused on tools that many of us now know, like Facebook, Twitter, and WordPress, this second installment focuses on some lesser-known but still extremely useful tools that can help librarians in the workplace and beyond.

I have to say, I now have some homework to do. I need to check out most of the nifty tools Cheryl covers that I haven't yet discovered—like Aurasma, an augmented reality service; BrandYourself, an online brand reputation service; and Popplet, a visualization tool.

Who knew all these tools were out there? Cheryl Ann Peltier-Davis, that's who. So join me, and let's read on and learn.

David Lee King
davidleeking.com

Acknowledgments

This second volume would not have been possible without the support and assistance of my cybrarian friends and colleagues. My inspiration is drawn from your dedication and commitment to adopt and use leading-edge tools that sustain libraries for present and future generations. I am also inspired by the developers of the resources covered in this book, whose timely innovations provide the groundwork required for the extensive research that went into writing this work.

I want to thank the reviewers who posted insightful evaluations and comments on the first volume and the many requests for work on a second iteration. Thanks also to David Lee King for his advice and willingness to write the Foreword for *The Cybrarian's Web 2*. I extend my gratitude and acknowledge the very thorough review of the first draft of this manuscript by my colleague and friend Arlene Batson-George, who voluntarily took time out from her busy schedule to meticulously go through each chapter.

Thanks to Randall McClure, editor extraordinaire, who brought extensive knowledge, extreme patience, and generous support to the project. I also wish to thank John B. Bryans, Editor-in-Chief and Publisher at Information Today Books, for his ongoing encouragement and enthusiasm for my work.

Lastly, thanks to my two sons, Andre and Antonio, and source of inspiration Antonio Caraballo, for their support and understanding during the long hours I spent in researching and writing this book. I could not have accomplished this task without your help, and I hope it inspires you to follow your dreams, to believe that nothing is impossible, and perhaps to one day write on a subject about which you are passionate.

About the Website
www.cybrariansweb.com

In attempting to provide a useful annotated listing of internet resources, one of my challenges has been to ensure that the descriptions and strategies keep pace with the technologies themselves. To that end, I have created a companion website rich with web links to (and updates for) the 61 resources covered in the book, along with reviews of new resources, a link to my personal blog, and space for reader comments and recommendations.

Cybrariansweb.com is designed to help keep you current with developments in this highly dynamic and fast-moving information network we call the web. Please let me know what I can do to make it even better.

Disclaimer
Neither the publisher nor the author make any claim as to the results that may be obtained through the use of this website or of any of the resources it references or links to. Neither the publisher nor the author will be held liable for any results, or lack thereof, obtained by the use of this site or any of its links; for any third-party charges; or for any hardware, software, or other problems that may occur as the result of using it. This website is subject to change or discontinuation without notice at the discretion of the publisher and the author.

Preface

My intrigue with freely accessible resources on the web grew out of an insatiable fascination with tracking global trends in what I fondly refer to as the Free Content Online (FCO) numbers game. This time-consuming and sometimes arduous task is as intriguing as it sounds, as daily compilations of statistical data reveal the explosion of digital information online and the ease and speed at which this information is created, searched, and shared. For example, in 2012 Google indexed an estimated 50 billion webpages. Within the span of two years, this number increased to 67 billion pages, and, as any researcher who is willing to delve deeper into the numbers will discover, the majority of this content is freely accessible.

One can easily look at this statistical data, add the expansive range of freely available social media tools—blogs, wikis, social networks, and podcasts—and readily confirm one fact: there is limitless availability and access to free eresources for the typical searcher in this networked and interactive information environment. Unfortunately, this seemingly easy access to free econtent does not necessarily enhance the discoverability of these resources on the web.

The Cybrarian's Web 2 is my attempt to assist the library community in the discovery and use of these resources. It is not a work published in isolation; rather, it reflects a growing consensus—replicated in journal articles, books, conference papers, and reports—that we are entering an era when free resources are viewed as just as viable and valuable as commercial content. Within the pages of *The Cybrarian's Web 2*, there is also implicit acknowledgement that libraries and other organizations are still operating in a challenging economic environment where budget concerns mandate a proactive approach in re-evaluating existing acquisition and collection development policies, and combining this with efforts aimed at augmenting and enriching costly subscription collections with high-quality, free eresources.

Similar in purpose, organization, and content to the first volume, *The Cybrarian's Web 2* provides in-depth summaries and analysis of free resources on the web, focusing on the practical application and implementation of these resources in libraries and other work environments. Since the first volume was published, the rapid rate at which new social media tools, apps, and other resources have been developed and the use of these tools by libraries to market programs and services has mandated a slight change in the coverage of topics in this book.

While the first volume was written as a starter guide to social media tools, catering mainly to the needs of an audience with limited technological knowledge (for example, brief overviews and library use of popular tools such as Blogger, Delicious, Facebook, Twitter, Wikipedia and YouTube), *The Cybrarian's Web 2* focuses on lesser-known tools, along with trending concepts successfully implemented by libraries. Another major divergence, which will be immediately discernible to readers as they browse the table of contents, is the extensive coverage given to ebooks, ebook collections and services, and ebook reading devices. Given the popularity and widespread usage of this econtent within libraries and other communities, and the subsequent legal wranglings between libraries and publishers, it would be a disservice to the profession not to record the availability and accessibility of this group of unique resources.

The Cybrarian's Web 2 also focuses on innovative concepts and trends that are rapidly being mashed up and adopted in the library world. Readers will learn about these in succinct chapters that cover topics such as self-publishing, cloud storage and hosting, crowdfunding, mobile applications (apps), makerspaces, massive open online courses (MOOCs), social news aggregators, social media management services and visualization tools. Readers are also introduced to wearable technology in the form of Google Glass. Its inclusion as a separate chapter is not reflective of the product's popularity (sold out in one day), availability (exclusive availability initially to Glass Explorers only), and affordability to the average consumer ($1500 per headset), but is born of the necessity to sensitize the library community to the important issues it raises regarding patrons' data privacy, security, and safety and the critical role of librarians in advocating for our patrons' rights. Advocacy played a major role in Google's decision to halt the development and discontinue sales of the current version of Glass through its Explorer program and streamline efforts to develop a new and improved version.

Given the dynamic nature of most eresources on the web and the need to constantly monitor and update these resources, a companion website provides links to all the resources covered in this book. In hindsight, the launch of this companion website, which coincided with the publishing of the first volume, has proven to be a blessing in disguise, as it has provided an online forum for discussion and documentation of sites that have changed ownership, undergone radical alterations, or are now defunct.

I hope that this book, like its predecessor, continues to serve a wide cross section of readers in multiple communities supporting productivity, collegial collaboration, and self-development, and that readers discover its usefulness as a guide and learning tool to innovate, improve, and add value to library services in the digital age.

Cheryl Ann Peltier-Davis
Read–Learn–Experiment–Share

Introduction

In 2004, the term Web 2.0 was coined at the O'Reilly Media Web 2.0 conference. At the time, the term was considered revolutionary in identifying and giving credence to a second generation of web-based services—social networking sites, wikis, communication tools, and folksonomies—that emphasize online collaboration and sharing among their users. Now, some eleven years later, in an era dominated by mobile technologies that continue to transform the human enterprise in all sectors, there has been a notable shift in discussions on the continuing relevance of Web 2.0 technologies. Some writers have gone so far as to ask the provocative questions: "Is Web 2.0 dying?"[1] and "Is Web 2.0 becoming more and more a void (and an avoided) term?"[2] These questions have sparked a worthy debate, with proponents on both sides of the argument presenting convincing views.

Protagonists assert that Web 2.0 has indeed "lost its mantle as the most important internet paradigm"[3] and that momentum has shifted to the mobile revolution, justifying this assessment by citing the purchases by social media giant Facebook of the wholly mobile (that is, not web-based) photo-sharing app Instagram for $1 billion in April 2012 and the WhatsApp instant messaging service for $19 billion ($22 billion according to some sources) in February 2014. These investments have been widely viewed as an attempt by Facebook to make itself more relevant in a world that seems to be rapidly shifting away from Web 2.0, into a new world characterized as the "Age of Mobility."[4]

Current data certainly seems to support such a mobile shift, as the majority of consumers are now "spending more time in their mobile applications than they do browsing the web."[5] The Pew Research Center reports that 91 percent of American adults own cell phones and use their devices for much more than phone calls. Popular activities include texting, accessing the internet, sending and receiving mail, downloading apps, listening to music, and getting directions, recommendations, and other location-based information.[6]

Views supporting the sustainability and survival of Web 2.0 technologies and the development of the requisite symbiotic relationship in a mobile-driven environment can best be encapsulated in the following statement: "Web 2.0 is not really dead...but it is certainly in its twilight years."[7] It is safe to say that almost every website you visit on a computer or mobile device has some embedded component of Web 2.0 technology. Web 2.0 survival can be attributed in part to a dedicated base of users and their compulsive need to connect, communicate, and collaborate with family, friends, colleagues and communities, to find information, to be entertained, and to create content on their desktops and mobile devices.

This seemingly obsessive behavior has secured the longevity and profitability of established social networking sites such as Facebook (1.39 billion users), YouTube (1 billion users), Twitter (288 million users), and LinkedIn (332 million users), along with newer platforms such as Pinterest (70 million users), Instagram (300 million users), and Tumblr (420 million users).[8] This push towards online connectivity, communication, and consumer feedback has also ensured that embedded Web 2.0 technologies are now commonplace components in high-volume everyday sites managed by online media outlets.

The fact that Web 2.0 technologies are alive and well is also evidenced in a 2013 Pew report that finds "72 percent of online adults use social networking sites." Further solidifying the enduring nature of this phenomenon, the Pew researchers report that one of the more striking manifestations regarding the social networking population has been the steady growth in senior citizen users, whose numbers have tripled on social networking sites over the past four years. According to Pew researchers, 43 percent of internet users over age 65 used social networking sites in 2013, up from 13 percent in 2009.[9]

Given these realities, it is not surprising that the benefits of Web 2.0 technologies, which allow us to easily create, contribute, communicate, and collaborate with each other in new and exciting ways, are still being touted and experimented with in the library world and allied communities. According to the authors of "Libraries at the Epicenter of the Digital Disruption," "87 percent of respondents indicated that their libraries are using or offering social media experiences in one form or another ... and more than half of those surveyed are using social networking services as part of their outreach to patrons and constituencies."[10]

For this author, it seems clear that Web 2.0 technologies continue to provide the technological foundation required to develop social media tools on web-based and mobile platforms. As readers will discover in the chapters to follow, many of these tools and apps remain freely available online and have been successfully integrated into existing library services and other work environments.

Integrating Social Media Tools and Other Free Online Resources into Library Services—Benefits and Challenges

In the first volume of *The Cybrarian's Web*, I offered a list of immediate benefits for libraries using free Web 2.0 tools and other online resources.[11] These benefits included delivering value-added services to tech-savvy clients, expanding and enhancing library collections during an economic recession, building alliances with patrons, improving communications with staff, democratizing the web, and surviving in a technologically competitive landscape. While these benefits are still relevant and can be used to argue for the continued implementation of these resources, there are now additional research findings to support active implementation and use of free online content. Two noteworthy reports are the Taylor and Francis white paper *Facilitating Access to Free Online Resources: Challenges and Opportunities for the Library Community*, which "explores the issues relating to free online content discoverability from the perspective of librarians,"[12] and a recent IFLA Trend Report that identifies five high-level trends affecting the role and identity of libraries.[13]

Two key findings from Taylor and Francis support the adoption and integration of free online content into existing library services:

➤ Librarians and faculty alike agree that free online resources add value to the research process

➤ The vast majority of librarians believe that free online content is likely to become at least as important as subscription content in the future

Taylor and Francis also highlight inherent challenges encountered by librarians in identifying, selecting, cataloging, and providing timely access to this growing volume of free eresources. The value of this research to the library community lies in the areas delineated for improvement and innovation that facilitate the continuing access to free resources. Best practices include the following:

> ➤ Improving methods of providing permanent access and reliable archiving for free content

> ➤ Comprehensive indexing of quality free resources by discovery systems

> ➤ Developing trusted repositories linking to free content

> ➤ Improving user interfaces for accessing library-surfaced content

> ➤ Developing metrics for evaluating the impact of subscription and free content on institutional performance

The added observation within the IFLA Trend Report that "the global information economy will be transformed by new technologies" is particularly instructive to libraries and allied information centers. Implicit in this particular trend is an underlying call to arms for librarians and other information professionals to advocate for and become more adept at providing "information literacy skills such as basic reading and competence with digital tools" for their patrons, as "people who lack these skills will face barriers to inclusion within this [new technologies era] and in a growing range of [other] areas."[14]

Mounting evidence points to immediate benefits from integrating free or inexpensive econtent into existing services along with the push toward developing more consumer-oriented products. To this end, many libraries may choose to hasten the process of early adoption and implementation. It is important to note that when implementing any new product or service, a period of critical evaluation and review of factors such as current needs, communities to be served, and product effectiveness, combined with intense consultation of staff, clients, and vendors, is required. Developing an effective social media plan or strategy, with delineated objectives, target audiences, resources, training models, content curation tools, technical support, maintenance, and feedback strategies must also be incorporated into the planning process.[15] Only when these preliminary steps have been taken can a successful program or product be developed.

This book was written to jumpstart your research and implementation process. It can be used as a planning guide initially, then as a reference that supports the continual integration of social media tools and other free online resources into library services.

How The Book Is Organized

The Cybrarian's Web 2 shares the same goals as the first volume: to offer an "environmental scan" of available eresources and to methodically identify, select, and evaluate tools that information professionals can effectively introduce and integrate into their workspaces, communities, and even their personal lives.

Each resource covered in the ensuing chapters falls into one of several broad categories:

- ➤ Archiving/Note-taking tools
- ➤ Augmented reality services/Wearable technology
- ➤ Avatar creation services
- ➤ Barcode scanning and generator software
- ➤ Cloud storage/File hosting and sharing services
- ➤ Course management systems
- ➤ Crowdfunding platforms
- ➤ Digital libraries
- ➤ Digital publishing services
- ➤ Digital/Online learning services
- ➤ DIY collaborative workspaces
- ➤ Ebook collections and services
- ➤ Ebook reading devices
- ➤ Infographic creators
- ➤ Massive Open Online Courses (MOOCs)
- ➤ Microblogging/Instant messaging services
- ➤ Mobile applications (apps)

- Online reputation management services
- Photo and video sharing services
- Polling services
- Productivity tools
- Reference management services
- Self-publishing platforms
- Social bookmarking services
- Social media management services
- Social networking services
- Social news aggregators
- Video/Global conferencing services
- Video sharing services
- Visualization services
- Web and mobile reading applications
- Web/Wiki hosting services

The resources are arranged alphabetically to enhance readability and access. Two new appendices in this volume—tools by type of service and by mobile device availability—are designed to help readers easily find appropriate resources within these categories.

Each chapter is independent, enabling readers to jump immediately to those resources that most interest them. Resource information is organized as follows:

- Name of the resource
- Category (type of application)
- Static uniform resource locator (URL)
- Origin and development
- Features, functionality, design, and usability
- Suggestions for use by the library community
- Fun factoids or interesting snippets of information on the resource (FYI)

Cybrarians[16] will not want to miss the section in each chapter entitled "How Cybrarians Can Use This Resource." Here, I offer suggestions for use of a given resource in the work environment and provide examples of innovative library implementations. This section is valuable for anyone wishing to observe social media tools and apps at work in libraries. For library administrators, these examples will provide supporting evidence of the benefits of using tech tools to showcase innovative services and enhance the library's online presence.

I conclude the book with five appendices. Appendix I presents tips and teaching tools for cybrarians. Appendix II provides very brief summaries of all the covered resources. Appendix III is a list of referenced websites, and, as previously noted, Appendices IV and V list resources by type of service and by mobile device support, respectively.

Criteria Used in Resource Selection

Nearly all of the resources included in the book are free for cybrarians to use. Some have a minimal subscription fee attached to them, and this cost is disclosed to readers (though needless to say all pricing information is subject to change). Resources were selected based on independent review and analysis, with the following considerations weighing heavily in my decision-making process:

➤ Is the resource useful to librarians and information professionals? Can it add immediate value to current services provided? Can it be easily implemented by less tech-savvy users? Is it organized for ease of use?

➤ Is the resource well known and established? For example, is there constant chatter and buzz in blogs, eforums, and other discussion groups about its reputation?

➤ Does the resource suggest longevity as evidenced by the time since it was created and its current iteration?

➤ Has the resource received positive reviews from users?

➤ Is free technical support available for the resource?

➤ Is the resource supported on multiple platforms and on mobile devices?

Final Comment

As you navigate, explore, and gain a foothold in the ever expanding digital landscape, I hope *The Cybrarian's Web 2* will help you discover and experiment with free eresources and harvest all things innovative in order to develop information products and services that meet your and your clients' needs. As I have discovered since publishing the first volume, keeping up with eresources can be daunting, as new tools are continually being launched in a dynamic environment dominated by user-generated digital content. I urge you to assist in the task of identifying important resources for the cybrarian community by contributing to the book's companion website at cybrariansweb.com.

Notes

1. Ryan Alexander Hunt, "DIGIWRIMO Day 7—Is Web 2.0 Dead? Or Can it Even Die," IVRYTWR (blog), November 9, 2012, www.ivrytwr.com/2012/11/29/digiwrimo-day-7-is-web-2-0-dead-or-can-it-even-die.
2. Robin Wauters, "The Death of Web 2.0," *TechCrunch* (blog), February 14, 2009, www.techcrunch.com/2009/02/14/the-death-of-web-20.
3. Hamish McKenzie, "Web 2.0 Is Over, All Hail the Age of Mobile," *Pandodaily* (blog), April 27, 2012, www.pando.com/2012/04/27/web-2-0-is-over-all-hail-the-age-of-mobile.
4. Ryan Alexander Hunt. "Is Web 2.0 Dead? Or Can it Even Die."
5. Charles Newark-French, "Mobile App Usage Further Dominates Web, Spurred by Facebook," Flurry Insights (blog), January 9, 2012, www.flurry.com/bid/80241/Mobile-App-Usage-Further-Dominates-Web-Spurred-by-Facebook.
6. Maeve Duggan, "Cell Phone Activities 2013," Pew Research Internet Project, accessed January 16, 2014, www.pewinternet.org/2013/09/19/cell-phone-activities-2013.
7. Hamish McKenzie, "Web 2.0 Is Over, All Hail the Age of Mobile."
8. Figures based on December 2014 monthly active users statistics.
9. Joanna Brenner and Aaron Smith, "72 percent of Online Adults are Social Networking Site Users," Pew Research Internet Project, accessed January 16, 2014, www.pewinternet.org/2013/08/05/72-of-online-adults-are-social-networking-site-users.
10. Joseph McKendrick, "Libraries: At the Epicenter of the Digital Disruption: The Library Resource Guide Benchmark Study on 2013/14 Library Spending Plans," accessed January 21, 2014, www.comminfo.rutgers.edu/~tefko/Courses/e553/Readings/Libraries-At-the-Epicenter-of-the-Digital-DisruptionThe-Library-Resource-Guide-Benchmark-Study-on-2013-2014-Library-Spending-Plans.pdf.
11. Cheryl Ann Peltier-Davis, *The Cybrarian's Web: An A–Z Guide to 101 Free Web 2.0 Tools and Other Resources* (Medford, New Jersey: Information Today, 2012), xxi–xxv.

12. "Facilitating Access to Free Online Resources: Challenges and Opportunities for the Library Community: A White Paper from Taylor & Francis, May 2013," Taylor & Francis, accessed January 16, 2014, www.tandf.co.uk/libsite/pdf/ TF-whitepaper-free-resources.pdf.

13. "Riding the Waves or Caught in the Tide? Insights from the IFLA Trend Report," IFLA, accessed January 21, 2014, http://trends.ifla.org/insights-document.

14. Ibid.

15. "Getting Started with Social Media: A Guide for Nonprofit Organizations and Government Agencies," University of Illinois at Urbana-Champaign—University Library, accessed January 16, 2014, www.uiuc.libguides.com/social-media-for-nonprofits.

16. Cybrarian is a shortened form of *cyberlibrarian*, coined from the terms "cyberspace" and "librarian," to refer to a librarian whose work routinely involves information retrieval and dissemination via the internet and the use of other online resources. This definition is taken from the *ODLIS Online Dictionary for Library and Information Science* (www.abc-clio.com/ODLIS/searchODLIS.aspx).

1

Adobe
Productivity and Creativity Tools
www.adobe.com

Overview

Adobe Systems Incorporated is one of the leading computer software companies in the world. Established in 1982, the company has its main headquarters in San Jose, California, with major development operations based in Canada, Germany, India, Romania, Switzerland, and China. Historically focused on the development of multimedia and creativity software products, Adobe has tailored its recent software offerings to reflect changing user needs and an expanding and highly competitive computer software industry.

Adobe is best known to consumers for its free flagship products including the Portable Document Format (PDF), long regarded as the international standard and common medium for exchanging electronic documents, and the Adobe Reader software that allows users to view, print, and annotate PDF documents.

As a for-profit corporation, Adobe offers the majority of its standalone packages and suites to individuals, enterprises, and educational institutions at subscription costs. Productivity and creative software in this category include Acrobat (PDF creator, editor, and converter), Captivate (HTML5-based elearning), Connect (web conferencing), Dreamweaver (website and mobile app design), Illustrator (vector graphics and illustration), InDesign (page design, layout, and publishing) and Photoshop (image editing and compositing). All of these proprietary products are available for an evaluation or trial period of 30 days.

In addition to Adobe Reader, the company offers other freeware products (Adobe Digital Editions, Adobe Flash Player, and Adobe AIR) at no cost. These can be downloaded and used as productivity tools in the office and home environment.

Adobe Reader—free software
(www.adobe.com/products/reader.html)

Features

Adobe Reader is recognized as the global standard software for viewing, annotating, esigning, printing, and sharing PDF documents. Its popularity as a PDF file viewer is based on its versatility in opening and interacting with all types of PDF content, including forms and multimedia. The Adobe Reader app for mobile devices (iPads, iPhones, iPod Touch, and Android), available for download from Apple iTunes and Google Play, allows on-the-go access to PDF files.

Adobe Digital Editions—free software
(www.adobe.com/products/digital-editions/download.html)

Features

Adobe Digital Editions software is a recent offering from Adobe to support the explosion of ebooks in the publishing industry and the subsequent increase in ebook readership. Designed exclusively to enable users to manage ebooks and other digital collections, this tool allows readers to download, view, and read ebooks (purchased or borrowed from local libraries) both on and offline. Other features include the ability to transfer copyrighted ebooks from a personal computer to other devices (including USB connected ereaders), sort and organize ebook collections, change page layout, orientation, and font size, access an online dictionary, print pages, annotate text, and integrate voice reading software. Adobe Digital Editions supports industry standard ebook formats PDF/A and EPUB.

Adobe Flash Player—free software
(www.adobe.com/products/flashplayer.html) and Adobe AIR (www.adobe.com/products/air.html)

Features

➤   Adobe Flash Player is a multiplatform client runtime that web users must download and install in order to view and interact with SWF content, Adobe's Flash proprietary file format used for displaying animated vector graphics on the web. Commonly referred to as Flash, this piece of software is widely considered the standard for delivering high-impact rich web content and an engaging end-user experience. To support users in the growing multilingual web community, the Mobile and Tablet Development Center (www.adobe .com/devnet/devices.edu.html) provides resources in multiple languages for building new applications and content for mobile devices.

➤ Adobe AIR is a cross-platform runtime that provides users with access to familiar tools within the Adobe suite (Dreamweaver, Flash Builder, Flash Catalyst, and Flash Professional) or any other text editor to build and deploy applications (apps), games, and videos for desktops and mobile devices. The Adobe AIR Developer Center (www .adobe.com/devnet/air.edu.html) provides user support to developers through online tutorials covering core skills, free access to manuals and other reference documents, regularly updated blog postings on new features, and an online gallery for showcasing new games built with Flash technology.

Adobe Creative Cloud—free 30-day trial
(www.adobe.com/downloads.html)

Features

➤ All of the desktop applications in the Adobe Creative Cloud suite are eligible for a free 30-day trial (https://creative .adobe.com/join/starter). The Creative Cloud trial includes 2 gigabytes (GB) of cloud storage and limited access to services. After completion of these free trials, clients are offered access to the full suite including more cloud storage at discounted subscription rates. Trials are available for individuals, businesses, and educators.

➤ Creative Cloud provides one-stop access to the Adobe suite of tools and services for working with digital photography, creating audio and video, gaming, designing graphics,

In addition to its consumer products, Adobe offers free productivity
tools for download and use in the office environment.

developing apps, and publishing on the web. The flexibility of cloud computing enables users to download and install new applications, receive alerts when new features and updates are available, seamlessly share files, collaborate online, save user settings, and sync files across multiple devices.

Adobe Connect—free 30-day trial
(www.adobe.com/products/adobeconnect/ buying-guide.html)

Features

Connect is Adobe's enterprise web conferencing platform for hosting online meetings, elearning, webinars, and virtual conferences. Features include integrated audio and video conferencing functions, unlimited webcam streams, real-time collaboration tools, customized URLs, company branding, and pod creation. Connection is enabled virtually for mobile devices (iOS, Android, and BlackBerry) and on desktops. The trial version is available for organizing events with a maximum number of 25 attendees.

Acrobat XI Pro—free 30-day trial
(www.adobe.com/products/acrobatpro .html?promoid=KATIV)

Features

Described by Adobe as the complete PDF solution for working "in the office or on the go," Adobe Acrobat XI Pro is a PDF converter packed with tools to increase productivity. Pro users can create, edit, delete, and combine PDF files, create online forms, and convert PDF files to Microsoft Office formats. The trial version is fully functional, offering all features of the subscription product.

How Cybrarians Can Use This Resource

Promote Access to a Suite of Online Productivity and Creativity Tools

Faced with budget cuts in an economically frugal climate, many library administrators are tasked with reassessing existing services and collections and are becoming more adept at deploying scarce resources. When considering new software to support creative and productive staff efforts, administrators can take advantage of Adobe's free trial versions to evaluate products before purchase. This strategy guarantees that the product is tested and compared with similar proprietary software currently available and ensures that budget allocations are wisely spent on products best suited to the communities served.

Offering Library Workshops on Using Adobe Products

Adobe Digital Editions, Adobe Reader, Adobe Flash Player, and Adobe AIR are indispensable software for the office and home environments and can be promoted as free productivity tools to patrons during library workshops. Teaching patrons how to use Adobe Digital Editions (Adobe's free ereading application) to download econtent (ebooks and audiobooks) from the library's online catalog or vendor-supported platforms such as 3M Cloud Library or OverDrive to their desktops, laptops, and mobile devices is necessary if administrators wish to support continued budgetary allocations for purchasing costly ecollections. Cybrarians can model and adopt the strategies and best practices of the following libraries to introduce this ereading application to library patrons and promote its use.

➤ The Yolo County Library system in California regularly hosts programs to promote new services to surrounding communities. For example, the Mary L. Stephens Branch (Davis, California) organized workshops on digital media downloading to market the library's collection of OverDrive ebooks and audiobooks to patrons with mobile devices.[1]

➤ The Bedford Free Public Library (Bedford, Massachusetts) developed a comprehensive guide for patrons on "Using Library ebooks with Adobe Digital Editions" (www .bedfordlibrary.net/pdf_files/ade.pdf).

➤ For libraries using OverDrive as an ebook vendor, OverDrive's Help Center (http://help.overdrive.com/customer/portal/ topics/632802-adobe-digital-editions/articles) provides valuable tips on installing, navigating, and troubleshooting within Adobe Digital Editions.

FYI

Adobe Labs (www.labs.adobe.com) are incubators for innovators and developers to experiment with and evaluate Adobe's prerelease software, emerging technologies, and code samples, as well as to assist in preparing technical documentation and tutorials.

Note

1. "Digital Media Download Workshops at Library," *The Davis Enterprise*, January 7, 2014, accessed January 24, 2014, www.davisenterprise.com/local-news/digital-media-download-workshops-at-library.

2

Amazon CreateSpace
Self-Publishing Platform
https://www.createspace.com

Overview

Described as an on-demand self-publishing platform, Amazon CreateSpace provides innovative tools and professional services that enable independent authors to publish and distribute their works on their own terms. Within CreateSpace, authors, publishers, film studios, and music labels can create, market, distribute, and sell books, CDs, and DVDs through Amazon.com (including its European subsidiaries), online retailers, bookstores, libraries, academic institutions, and personal websites linked to CreateSpace's eStore.

With mounting competition from other self-publishing and distribution services such as Lulu (https://www.lulu.com), Project Gutenberg Self-Publishing Press (Chapter 38), Scribd (Chapter 42), and Smashwords (Chapter 43), Amazon strives to keep ahead of the game by offering incentives and bonus add-ons: allowing authors to select list prices and sales channels, waiving set-up fees, and providing free ISBNs, inventory freedom (books are printed on demand), the latest digital tools, fee-based professional publishing services, competitive royalties, conversion to Kindle ebooks, and a recognizable branded digital marketplace in Amazon.com.

The rapid growth of self-publishing services such as CreateSpace, driven by innovative tools and services that help authors complete their work and reach "millions of potential readers," [1] reflects the phenomenal growth in print-on-demand services, the increasing readership for ebooks and other digital collections, and a push by independent authors to bypass mainstream publishing houses and opt for nontraditional publishing outlets that market and sell user-generated econtent.

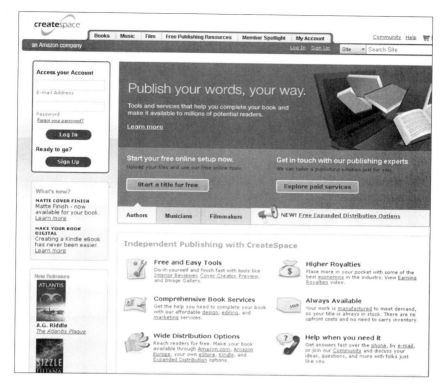

Amazon CreateSpace provides tools and professional services for independent authors to self-publish and distribute their works.

Established in 2007, CreateSpace is the result of the acquisition and subsequent merger by Amazon of two independent companies, CustomFlix Labs and BookSurge.

Features

CreateSpace offers authors, musicians, and filmmakers fast, easy, and economical ways to publish and distribute their content through Amazon.com and other distribution channels. Users must first create an account (https://www.createspace.com/Signup.jsp) and sign off on a member agreement in order to access CreateSpace's dashboard and take advantage of the following features:

➤ Choice of using either a free, self-guided or a paid, professionally-rendered workflow

➤ Control in setting list prices and selecting standard sales and distribution channels, such as Amazon.com, Amazon's European websites, CreateSpace's eStore, and Amazon's Kindle store

➤ Access to publishing on Amazon.com, to take advantage of Amazon's advanced features such as "Look Inside" and its discounted shipping offers

➤ Access to free CreateSpace-assigned ISBNs

➤ Assignment of Library of Congress Control Number (must be purchased)

➤ Print-on-demand options to limit upfront inventory costs

➤ Online access to three online publishing tools:

  • Interior Reviewer—previews uploaded files (.doc, docx, .rtf and PDF) as fully-formatted, virtual versions

  • Preview Tool—shares content with colleagues, friends, and the Amazon community of authors before publication

  • Cover Creator—provides access to an online gallery of designs, themes, and color templates to create cover artwork for books, CDs, and DVDs

➤ Fee-based professional services to assist with layout and design, editing, marketing, and Kindle ebook conversions

➤ Access to CreateSpace's Royalty Calculator and link to its "Earning Royalties" video (https://www.createspace.com/Products/Book)

➤ Professional trade paperback binding for a library-quality product

➤ Technical support in the form of help pages, live support, and access to an online community of knowledgeable authors (CreateSpace Central; https://www.createspace.com/en/community/community/createspaceoverview)

How Cybrarians Can Use This Resource
Professional Publishing

The self-publishing industry is rapidly evolving as many authors are foregoing traditional publishing arrangements in pursuit of what they deem the "fastest, most profitable and easiest way to get their written thoughts out there."[2] Concerns about the ability to promote, distribute, and sell self-published works have declined with the emergence of social networks and large etailers willing to work with virtually any author. These are channels through which friends, fans, and followers can share their recommendations and help put unknown authors on the map.

CreateSpace can be marketed by librarians as a self-publishing platform to the following group of authors: practicing professionals wishing to generate new revenue streams based on their expertise; published authors wishing to discover new approaches to publishing, to advance as well as retool their careers; and emerging authors wishing to increase readership using online distribution channels.

FYI

The Amazon Breakthrough Novel Award is an international contest co-sponsored by Amazon, Penguin Group, and CreateSpace. The grand prize winner receives a cash prize and full publishing contract with Amazon. Genres accepted include general fiction, romance, mystery, thriller, science fiction, fantasy, horror, and young adult fiction.

Notes

1. "CreateSpace: About CreateSpace," CreateSpace, accessed February 7, 2015, https://createspace.com/AboutUs.jsp.
2. Yuli Ziv, "How to: Self Publish Your Book with Amazon's CreateSpace," Mashable (blog), July 19, 2011, www.mashable.com/2011/07/19/self-publish-amazon-createspace.

3

Aurasma
Augmented Reality Service
www.aurasma.com

Overview

Facebook's purchase of the augmented reality headset developed by Oculus Rift for $2 billion in March 2014, and Google's sale of its wearable computer with optical head-mounted display, Google Glass, to early adopters for $1500 per headset in April 2014 have gained the media buzz that many marketing campaigns hope for in their attempt to profit from and promote the concepts of augmented reality and wearable technology to tech-savvy consumers. Augmented reality (AR)—the interaction of superimposed graphics, audio, and other sense enhancements over a real-world environment that's displayed in real time—is already well established in some sectors, including science, military, industry, medicine, commerce, gaming, sports, and entertainment.[1]

In the field of science, for example, NASA has created Spacecraft 3D, an AR app available for free on smartphones and tablets that allows explorers to learn about and interact with a variety of the agency's spacecraft used to explore the solar system. In the world of entertainment, the Rolling Stones incorporated AR technology in the promotion of their album *GRRR!* using virtual 3D gorillas in the album artwork. *Esquire* used AR as an inventive means of publicizing its December 2009 "living, breathing, moving, talking" interactive cover, and the magazine has also been at the helm of AR innovation by creating its own in-house AR app.[2]

Established communities in education, publishing, and information services are also exploring ways to incorporate AR into curricula, book publishing, and client services respectively. Using the built-in cameras in mobile devices, along with developers' apps such as Aurasma, Layar, and Wikitude, teachers, book editors, and librarians can, in real time, turn static, inanimate images and objects into interactive, lively experiences that enable end users to launch a website, watch a video, listen to an audio recording, play a game, and add animation or 3D modeling to a drawing.

Since its launch in 2011, Aurasma, a subsidiary of Hewlett Packard, has been regarded as one of the leading AR platforms in the world, with more than 80,000 customers in 100 countries. Popular Aurasma user-generated content (referred to as Auras) include adding 3D dinosaurs to street locations, sending video messages on greeting cards, leaving hidden clues in treasure hunts, adding instructional information to machines, and augmenting textbooks and classroom projects. These types of innovations reflect the company's stated vision, "to enable an augmented world, where every image, object, and place has its own Aura."[3]

AR content on Aurasma-branded consumer products can be identified by locating the signature Aurasma logo (as shown in the screenshot) and by following Aurasma channels within the downloaded app. The company has offices in the U.S. and the U.K.

Readers can discover augmented reality content on Aurasma products by locating the branded Aurasma signature icon.

Features

➤   The Aurasma app is available in both the Apple and Google Play stores. In order for users to have the best AR experience and benefit from Aurasma's image recognition technology, mobile devices such as tablets and smartphones must have the following system requirements:

- High-powered ARM x86 processor

- Rear-facing camera (preferably with autofocus)

- iOS or Android operating system

➤   When the Aurasma app is downloaded to smartphones and tablets, users point the device's built-in camera viewfinder to trigger images and immediately unlock rich content or Auras (audio and video files, graphics, and 3D animations). An online cheat sheet (www.aurasma.com/aura/#) provides simple tips on using the Aurasma App to quickly view Auras.

➤   Aurasma Studio (https://studio.aurasma.com/register) is a free online tool within the Aurasma app for creating and publishing augmented content. After registering to use the tool online, new users have immediate access to a tutorial that outlines the step-by-step process for creating Auras:

1.   Upload a trigger image

2.   Upload an overlay image or video

3.   Create a channel for Auras

4.   Add finished Auras to dedicated channel

➤   Aurasma's graphically-enhanced website (www.aurasma.com) is regularly updated with information on the latest advertising campaigns launched by businesses and organizations partnering with Aurasma to integrate AR into their products. Notable brands include GQ, Vanity Fair, Marvel, DreamWorks, Universal, Office Depot, and Best Western. Designated campaigns on the website are arranged by broad categories (entertainment, publishing, retail, fashion, sport, technology, food and drink, motoring, the arts, travel, finance, and health and wellness).

➤ Customer and technical support is available in several forums:

- The Aurasma Community Network (https://aurasma
  .zendesk.com/home) is an online knowledge base offering
  tips and tricks, links to FAQs and online resources, and
  information for technical developers.
- Aurasma's online manual (www-cdn.aurasma.com/
  wp-content/uploads/Customer-Guidelines.pdf) provides
  information on how to use the Aurasma Studio, create
  Aurasma-powered apps, work with Trigger images, and
  access channels and other advanced features.
- The Aurasma Webinar series is hosted on a dedicated
  YouTube channel (on YouTube search for *Aurasma
  Tutorials and Webinars*) and provides access to recorded
  discussions and demonstrations of the product.
- Viewers can access a short Aurasma Demo YouTube video
  (youtu.be/GBKy-hSedg8) describing how to use Aurasma
  on smartphones to view interactive experiences.

How Cybrarians Can Use This Resource

Integrating Augmented Reality into Library Services

Augmented reality capabilities, when successfully integrated into existing services, are affording various communities the opportunity to creatively merge the digital and physical worlds. Digital content overlaid onto physical objects supports learning activities in classrooms and provides promotional and teaching opportunities for libraries.

Organizations can partner with Aurasma (via commercial accounts) to create and publish innovative AR campaigns in several ways:

➤ Create Auras using the cloud-based Aurasma Studio and view
these through the Aurasma App (available from the Apple
App Store and Google Play)

➤ Request a version of Aurasma skinned with an institution's
branding

➤ Embed the Aurasma Software Development Kit (SDK) into apps

➤ Embed Aurasma into hardware

At the W.I. Dykes Library (University of Houston-Downtown, Texas), librarians are experimenting with AR by developing a dedicated library channel on Aurasma to support the following tasks:

➤ Orient students to library resources and services

➤ Increase student retention of material

➤ Reach out to students beyond traditional library instruction sessions

➤ Increase librarians' "approachability" as perceived by students[4]

As shown in this library example, librarians are on board as advocates of this new technology and are willing to explore new approaches in using AR to extend and enhance learning programs and library services.

FYI

The term "augmented reality" was coined in 1990 by Tom Caudell, an employee of Boeing, to describe a digital display used by aircraft electricians that blended virtual graphics with a physical reality.

Notes

1. Dena Cassella, "What is Augmented Reality (AR): Augmented Reality Defined, iPhone Augmented Reality Apps and Games and More," Digital Trends, November 3, 2009, accessed February 7, 2015, www.digitaltrends.com/mobile/what-is-augmented-reality-iphone-apps-games-flash-yelp-android-ar-software-and-more.
2. Sanhita SinhaRoy, "Augmented Reality in the (Real) Library: Exploring Ways to Capitalize on Emerging Technology," American Libraries, June 29, 2013, accessed March 27, 2014, www.americanlibrariesmagazine.org/blog/augmented-reality-real-library.
3. "Aurasma: About Us," Aurasma, accessed February 6, 2015, www.aurasma.com/about-us.
4. "Library Orientation: Augmented Reality in the Library," accessed March 27, 2014, www.ala13.ala.org/files/ala13/UHDLibrARyOrientation_final_0.pdf.

4

BrandYourself
Online Reputation Management Service
https://brandyourself.com

Overview

In a digital environment where privacy increasingly appears to be a thing of the past, online reputation management—the ability to track our personal information on the web and ensure that it accurately reflects who we are—is a timely concept. Regularly Googling one's name is a common practice, but far more sophisticated, dedicated techniques and services are now available.

A good example is BrandYourself, a free service that offers do-it-yourself (DIY) tools for managing one's online reputation. The service relies heavily on tailoring the Search Engine Optimization (SEO) process to simplify the often complex tasks of online reputation management and improving search results. Once enrolled, users can effectively control the URL links in social media and company profiles that show up as top search results on Google, and—via online alerts and analyzed search scores—are able to monitor how and when others are searching for them.

The New York-based company purposely developed the platform to educate and empower searchers to "improve search results, pushing positive links higher in search engines and burying unwanted links" and is adamant about providing this service "without any price barrier."[1] The basic service provides free web management tools, and a fee-based concierge program assigns experts to assist clients with developing advanced strategies for improving search results. Since its launch in 2010, BrandYourself has registered more than 500,000 users.[2]

Features

➤ New users can create a BrandYourself profile and access the suite of free DIY web tools offered for reputation management by first visiting the site's homepage (www .brandyourself.com) and entering the required information (email address and password) to register with the service.

➤ When registered with the service, users are guided through the intricate steps necessary to publish a hub—an optimized profile populated with relevant information (biography, professional experience, education background) to manage and maintain an online reputation.

➤ Registered BrandYourself members complete the following tasks:

  • Submit and boost profiles/links for searchers to find when the registered user name is entered in a Google search. The site easily integrates existing profiles on social media sites such as Facebook, Twitter, Google Plus, and LinkedIn, along with online profiles on organizational or personal websites.

  • Improve Search Engine Optimization (SEO) and rankings in a Google search.

  • Track search scores periodically in a system-generated online report card to effectively monitor positive/negative results appearing on the first page in a Google search. Users receive instant alerts via email when there are changes in scores and ranking.

  • Receive online alerts when potential employers and clients search online for information.

➤ The BrandYourself Press Page (https://brandyourself.com/ info/about/press) and blog (blog.brandyourself.com) provides readers with current information on media reviews, awards received, case studies, tips and tricks, and enhanced features.

(*Continued*)

BrandYourself offers a unique service for users wishing
to take control of their online reputation.

How Cybrarians Can Use This Resource

Online Reputation Manager

This online service is useful for managing one's reputation online. It simplifies the process of seamlessly creating the personal or professional brand required in an online environment. During library-sponsored workshops, the service can be promoted as a DIY product that provides the tools needed to boost the ranking of professional profiles on search engines such as Google.

As part of the process of advocating best practices to protect individual privacy and security online, librarians should advance other key strategies for managing reputations online. Such practices entail proactively creating content reflective of the user's personal brand, developing a custom domain, establishing a uniform, well-articulated presence when registering with multiple social networking sites, optimizing the use of privacy settings when registering on social networking sites, and consistently monitoring the web for negative content by utilizing services like BrandYourself.[3]

FYI

More than a billion names are Googled every day and 75 percent of human resources departments are required to Google prospective applicants.[4]

Notes

1. "BrandYourself: About," BrandYourself, accessed February 3, 2015, https://brandyourself.com/info/about.
2. Ibid.
3. Susan Adams, "6 Steps to Managing Your Online Reputation," Forbes, March 14, 2013, accessed January 23, 2014, www.forbes.com/sites/susanadams/2013/03/14/6-steps-to-managing-your-online-reputation.
4. "Why Your Google Results Matter," BrandYourself, accessed January 23, 2014, https://brandyourself.com/info/about/whyCare.

5

Camtasia
Screen Recording and Video Editing Software
www.techsmith.com/camtasia.html

Overview

Developed by TechSmith, the company whose portfolio includes the free visual communication products Jing and Screencast.com, Camtasia is a suite of productivity tools designed to perform the dual functions of screen recording and video editing. TechSmith has received high praise for Camtasia, mainly from clients working in educational institutions, for integrating screen capture technology with editing tools that assist both skilled and nonskilled videographers in creating professional-quality videos.

Available on two distinct platforms, Camtasia Studio for Windows and Camtasia for Mac, the suite offers two basic tools to assist users in recording, editing, and producing screencasts: Camtasia Recorder, the component used for capturing screen audio and video; and Camtasia Studio Editor, the component used to modify audio and video by adding themes, animated backgrounds, and callouts. The suite also includes post-processing tools required to share presentations online.

Launched in 1987 primarily as a technology company, Michigan-based TechSmith currently serves more than 10 million customers with a variety of products used across multiple devices and designed to improve productivity. Despite TechSmith's popularity in the education marketplace (97 of the top 100 universities in the U.S. use TechSmith products)[1], many of its customers have questioned the need to pay the high licensing fees associated with products, especially when there are open source alternatives. Within the library community, payment of these fees is often considered cost effective and justifiable as other

22

competing screencast software and services like Screenr and Jing can only be utilized in developing short, patron-driven online tutorials. Camtasia's advanced features offer the immediate advantage of producing professional-quality screencasts of longer duration.

TechSmith provides a free trial (www.techsmith.com/download/camtasia) for prospective users wishing to evaluate the product, along with special pricing and discounts for educational institutions, government agencies, and nonprofit organizations.

Camtasia Studio offers screen recording and video editing software for new and skilled videographers to produce videos of near-professional quality.

Features

Main features of Camtasia Recorder

➤ This component of the suite supports the capture of high-quality video and audio using Camtasia's advanced screen recording technology tools and includes a Microsoft PowerPoint plug-in that integrates screen capture and audio recording within PowerPoint. Camtasia Recorder also supports recording audio while screen capturing is in progress, thus enabling the user to capture live narrations during a demonstration or presentation.

➤ Camtasia Recorder supports the import of various types of multimedia video and audio files, including MP4, MP3, WMV, WMA, AVI, WAV and other formats into Camtasia's proprietary CAMREC format. Final video presentations can be exported to common video formats MPEG-2, MPEG-4, WMV, AVI, and Adobe Flash.

Main features of Camtasia Studio Editor

This component of the suite is essential for modifying audio and video captured with the Camtasia Recorder. Presenters can arrange video, audio, images, callouts, and animated content on multiple tracks, then use the drag-and-drop feature to add preinstalled music tracks, callouts, buttons, banners, and animated backgrounds from Camtasia's Media Asset Library. Users of Camtasia Studio also have the ability to enhance presentations by embedding visual and sound effects.

Main features of post-processing tools that enable video sharing across multiple devices

Videos developed using the suite can be shared on YouTube or Screencast.com, Camtasia's free hosting site. Camtasia Studio automatically generates a hyperlink and embed code to allow sharing videos via emails, tweets, or blog posts. The suite's expansive platform-sharing capabilities also allow viewers to watch captured content anywhere, anytime, on nearly any device.

TechSmith's online support

➤ TechSmith provides access to an online library of free training resources to support all of its products. Within this library, Camtasia Studio customers can view tutorials, read user manuals, and request online technical support (www.techsmith.com/tutorial.html).

➤ TechSmith's Camtasia case study page highlights innovative examples of the tool's multifunctional capabilities in the areas of teaching, training, and marketing (www.techsmith.com/camtasia-uses.html).

How Cybrarians Can Use This Resource

Within the library environment, Camtasia is arguably one of the most widely used productivity tools for recording, editing, and producing advanced screencast-based tutorials. WebJunction, the library learning online community, reviews the advanced features of the product that support the creation of lengthy, professional-quality screencasts and presents a convincing case for undertaking what may be viewed by some as a costly investment.[2]

Developing Screencast Tutorials and Other Presentations at Libraries

➤ The University of Aberdeen Library, Special Collections and Museums (Aberdeen, Scotland) developed Camtasia recordings as PowerPoint presentations with audio commentary.[3] These instructional videos cover a variety of essential skills for patrons wishing to search, find, and manage academic resources:

  • Quick Fix! Series

  • Essential Skills

  • Searching Databases

  • Managing References

  • Subject Specific Recordings

  • Postgraduate Refresher Sessions

➤ To support the use of Camtasia in developing instructional videos, the University Libraries at Texas A & M University (College Station, Texas) published detailed instructions and guidelines on best practices in creating two videos, "Let-It-V" (streaming video) and "How to Use Get It for Me" (Flash video)[4].

➤ The University Library at the University of Illinois at Urbana-Champaign (Champaign, Illinois) illustrated how Camtasia can be used to create tutorials, online demonstrations, and website tours for library patrons and library staff.[5]

FYI

TechSmith averages close to 900,000 Camtasia downloads per month.[6]

Notes

1. "Press Kit," TechSmith, accessed February 6, 2015, www.techsmith.com/techsmith-press-kit.pdf.
2. Dawne Tortorella, "Camtasia Examples—Beyond Simple Screencasts," OCLC WebJunction, last modified 21 March, 2012, https://www.webjunction.org/documents/webjunction/Camtasia_Examples_045_Beyond_Simple_Screencasts.html.
3. "The University of Aberdeen Library, Special Collections and Museums," The University of Aberdeen, accessed March 13, 2014, www.abdn.ac.uk/library/myzone/camtasiarecordings.
4. "Recording with Camtasia Studio Recorder," Texas A & M University, University Libraries, accessed March 13, 2014, www.library.tamu.edu/services/media-reserves/handouts/recording-with-camtasia-studio-recorder.html.
5. "Camtasia," University Library, University of Illinois at Urbana-Champaign, accessed March 13, 2014, www.library.illinois.edu/it/helpdesk/quicklinks/camtasia.html.
6. "Press Kit," TechSmith.

6

Codecademy
Online Education Platform
(Programming)
www.codecademy.com

Overview

Within an increasingly mobile environment, the job market for information technology (IT) professionals continues to be lucrative. In 2014, close to one-third (32 percent) of U.S. companies were expected to "increase head count in IT jobs," and this figure compares favorably to similar figures (33 percent) recorded in 2013. This survey data also indicates that the top IT skill in demand is programming, specifically app development, and the most sought-after technology worker is the software developer.[1]

Codecademy attempts to fill this need by offering an online platform where developers can learn to code interactively for free. Established in 2011 by co-founders Ryan Bubinski and Zach Sims, this innovative startup is "committed to building the best learning experience ... and create the online learning experience of the future." To bolster this effort, the company, which has its headquarters in New York City, developed what they describe as the first "truly net native education" platform, taking "cues from Facebook and Zynga in creating an engaging educational experience" for coders.[2]

This engaging and interactive educational experience is evident in Codecademy's online infrastructure and the services offered to apprentice coders. Developers can utilize the platform as a knowledge tool to build interactive websites, games, and apps as they learn the art of coding. Within a collaborative forum, users register with groups and code with members of an online community who share similar interests. Coders also strengthen their online presence and personal brand by building online profiles and highlighting their expertise in specific programming areas. This communal approach to the learning process has enjoyed marked success as the Codecademy community collectively submitted "more than a billion lines of code," and the company has recorded positive reviews published by mainstream and technology-focused news outlets, including *The New York Times*, Bloomberg, *USA Today*, CNBC, and TechCrunch.[3]

The push to teach individuals to program for free is both a philan-thropic effort and a stopgap measure to fill a void, as reports indicate that

Codecademy helps users interactively learn how to code content for the web.

despite high demand there is "a looming shortage of computer programmers and the current public education system isn't teaching the skill set that will be in high demand in the future." By 2020, it is expected that there will be "one million more computer science jobs than there are graduates."[4]

Features

➤ Codecademy learners register on the product homepage (www.codecademy.com) either with an existing social media account or with their email address. All registered Codecademy learners must create an online profile including their name, brief biography, photo/headshot, goals, and Codecademy groups of interest.

➤ Members of Codecademy have access to two online portals *Learn* and *Teach*.

- Learners (www.codecademy.com/learn) have immediate access to the resources—interactive courses and tutorials—that teach web fundamentals and multiple programming languages such as JavaScript, jQuery, HTML/CSS, PHP, Python, and Ruby. They also learn to code while simultaneously building projects. Learners are motivated to complete courses with rewards in the form of points and badges along with the assignment of scores based on a "total day streak." They can also monitor daily goals as they progress and obtain feedback from mentors.

- Teachers (Course Curators) have access to a dedicated portal (www.codecademy.com/teach) designed for preparing interactive, quick-fire, detailed lessons for programmers. Course curators can create courses (individually or as a collaborative project) on any programming topic, use the online course creator with predefined templates to create new courses, learn best practices, share their knowledge on any of the computer programs offered, and build an online reputation as experts in their specific fields.

➤ Codecademy Schools (www.codecademy.com/schools) is an initiative that provides teachers with the resources required to develop curricula for computer science.

➤   Codecademy Stories (www.codecademy.com/stories) provide user testimonials.

➤   Codecademy Lab (http://labs.codecademy.com) is an online sandbox to experiment with programming codes such as Ruby, Python, and JavaScript.

➤   Codecademy Code Year Learning Program (www.codecademy .com/en/tracks/code-year) offers aspiring programmers the opportunity to commit to the task of learning code for one specific year. Enrollment in the program requires completion of an online form and each applicant receives a free customized learning plan.

How Cybrarians Can Use This Resource

Promote an Online Education Service for Programmers

Codecademy is both a philanthropic and a pragmatic service. The resource not only teaches the average person how to program for free, but also fills a void in a field where there is a high demand for computer programmers, serving as a catalyst for the economy by "building the basic steps of competency to help people start their own companies ... and learn the skills to help them find jobs."[5] Librarians can promote Codecademy as a free interactive online education service that provides programming courses for learners and a platform for sharing knowledge for expert programmers.

FYI

Codecademy has won several awards, including being named to *Time* magazine's 50 Best Websites of 2012 and the New York City Venture Fellows program in 2013.

Notes

1. Mary Brandel, "8 Hot IT Skills for 2014," *ComputerWorld*, September 23, 2013, accessed March 29, 2014, www.computerworld.com/s/article/9242548/8_hot_IT_skills_for_2014.
2. "Codecademy : Our Mission," Codecademy, accessed March 29, 2014, www.codecademy.com/about.
3. Ibid.
4. Cadie Thompson, "Codecademy: Teach People to Code, Boost the Economy," *USA Today*, April 23, 2013, accessed March 29, 2014, www.usatoday.com/story/tech/2013/04/23/coding-economy-codecademy/2106707.
5. Ibid.

7

Coursera
Massive Open Online Courses (MOOCs) Platform
https://www.coursera.org

Overview

The ultimate goal of the educational institutions offering Massive Open Online Courses (MOOCs), free courses aimed at unlimited participation and designed to facilitate online interaction via the internet, is similar to the goals of other "open" movements—open data, open source, open content and open access. Coursera, a for-profit educational technology company, is one company dedicated to helping academic institutions achieve this goal, as it willingly partners with universities, including Ivy League universities Princeton University, the University of Pennsylvania, and Yale University, to offer free online courses. In its role as facilitator between lecturer and student, the company envisions a "future where everyone has access to a world-class education... that will improve their lives, the lives of their families, and the communities they live in."[1]

Since the launch of the first MOOC in 2008, the MOOC movement has steadily grown in momentum, culminating in 2012 being declared as the "Year of the MOOC" by *The New York Times*.[2] The popularity of these open online courses can be attributed to the inherent advantages for elearners: the price of courses (free or at minimal cost), broad topic range, instant global accessibility, and adherence to the "free information" ethos. Despite these obvious benefits, critics have been quick to weigh in on analogous disadvantages: absence (in some instances) of credible assessment methods and the underlying difficulty in tracking students' progress, lack of formal accreditation, and increasing student isolation.[3]

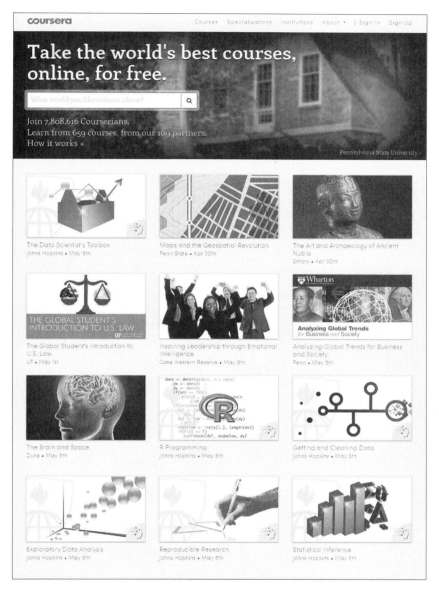

Coursera is an education platform that partners with top universities and organizations worldwide to offer free online courses for any user.

Comparable to other MOOC providers (Udacity and edX), the Coursera platform provides open access to traditional course materials in the form of lectures, videos, and quizzes within a peer-assessed interactive online learning community. Courses offered online include those in traditional subjects (physics, engineering, humanities, medicine, biology, social sciences, mathematics, business, and computer science) and specialized topics (Mobile Cloud Computing with Android, Challenges in Global Affairs, Modern Musician, the Virtual Teacher Program, and Foundations of Teaching for Learning).

Launched in April 2012 by Stanford University (California) computer science professors Andrew Ng and Daphne Koller, Coursera offers more than 900 courses and has partnered with more than 100 institutions around the globe. The growing list of participants includes the University of Florida, University of California (San Diego), University of Michigan, University of Washington, University of Chicago, University of British Columbia, Tel Aviv University, University of Edinburgh, University of Amsterdam, and the University of Melbourne.

Features

➤   Prospective students must first create an account on the Coursera website (https://accounts.coursera.org/signup). Required information includes full name, email address, and password.

➤   Registered students have access to a database of current course offerings from U.S.-based higher education institutions and Coursera global partners. Within this database, searches can be refined by course subject area, time period (when the course starts), courses eligible for certificates (specialization and verified certificate courses), and language of instruction.

➤   Each course has a dedicated webpage with *Course at a Glance* information: course format, duration, description, syllabus, instructor biodata, course requirements, prerequisites, learning outcomes, suggested readings, and FAQs. When students successfully register for a course, they receive verification in the form of an onscreen message, such as: "*Congratulations. You're signed up for Introduction to*

Computational Arts: Visual Arts. The course will start on March 3rd 2015, and we will notify you just before then to remind you when class will begin."

➤ The MOOC environment is designed to foster interaction, communication, and connection between classmates and teachers. Students learn at their own pace and on their own schedule by viewing short video lectures, taking interactive quizzes, and completing assignments and projects graded by a computer or assessed by peers.

➤ Students typically receive a Statement of Accomplishment signed by the instructor upon completion of the course. Verified certificates can be purchased for a minimal fee. Fees are also attached to some specialized courses, particularly groups of related courses designed to develop expertise in specific subjects.

➤ Coursera has developed mobile apps for both iOS and Android users wishing to learn offline and on the go. These apps allow users to track course progress, stream lectures online, or download lectures for offline viewing. The apps are currently available in the Apple iTunes and Google Play stores.

How Cybrarians Can Use This Resource
Promote the Free Online Learning Experience
Online learning plays a significant role in lifelong education. In fact, a recent report by the U.S. Department of Education posted to the Coursera website notes that "classes with online learning (whether taught completely online or blended) on average produce stronger student learning outcomes than do classes with solely face-to-face instruction." Coursera offers a model of how free online education can be organized into a centralized platform.[4]

Coursera, as one of several education delivery platforms within the larger MOOC movement, offers opportunities for a variety of stakeholders. For lifelong learners, there is the reward of personal enrichment and educational access. Coursera's growing collection of innovative courses should be of interest to practicing professionals and job seekers as well. Librarians in academic and public libraries are afforded new opportunities to engage their communities, embed new services, foster new alliances, and promote information literacy and the lifelong learning experience by connecting end users with quality education resources. Librarians can also assist faculty and other educators in preparing MOOC materials and point to the Coursera repository as a useful resource for faculty to study the teaching methods of other MOOC instructors.

Libraries as MOOC Developers

There are real-world examples of librarians offering successful MOOCs. At Wake Forest University's Z. Smith Reynolds Library (Winston-Salem, North Carolina), eLearning librarian Kyle Denlinger created ZSRx: The Cure for the Common Web, a MOOC-like course that is free and open to anyone in the Wake Forest University community, and designed to foster interaction in a collaborative learning environment during the process of learning web literacy skills. Launched in March 2013, the course curated third-party web content (readings, videos, and websites), established a discussion forum and community blog, and built a simple website using free tools available on the web. Although ZSRx was modeled on MOOC principles, Denlinger admits that "it was certainly not massive;" but by all accounts it can be categorized as a successful "lightweight, informal" MOOC model, attracting more than 700 students from 23 states and 10 countries.[5]

FYI

The phrase MOOC was first coined in 2008 by Dave Cormier of the University of Prince Edward Island (Canada) and Senior Research Fellow Bryan Alexander of the National Institute for Technology in Liberal Education in response to a course called Connectivism and Connective Knowledge that was offered to a hybrid class of tuition and nonpaying tuition students.[6]

Notes

1. "Coursera: Our Mission," Coursera, accessed March 17, 2014, https://www.coursera .org/about.
2. Laura Pappano, "The Year of the MOOC," *The New York Times*, November 2, 2012, accessed March 17, 2014, www.nytimes.com/2012/11/04/education/edlife/massive-open-online-courses-are-multiplying-at-a-rapid-pace.html?smid=pl-share.
3. Brandi Scardilli, "MOOCs: Classes for the Masses," *Information Today* 30 (2013): 32.
4. "Coursera: Our Mission."
5. Kyle Denlinger, "ZSRx: The MOOC that Wasn't a MOOC," *Library Gazette* (blog), May 10, 2013, cloud.lib.wfu.edu/blog/gazette/2013/05/10/zsrx-library-mooc.
6. Wikipedia, s.v. "Massive Open Online Course," accessed March 17, 2014, www.en .wikipedia.org/wiki/Massive_open_online_course.

8

Digital Public Library of America
Digital Library
www.dp.la

Overview

The Digital Public Library of America (DPLA) "brings together the riches of America's libraries, archives, and museums, and makes them freely available to the world"[1] from a centralized digital platform. Launched in April 2013, DPLA is the culmination of the collaborative efforts of leaders from varied sectors of society—libraries, foundations, academia, and technology circles—to develop a portal that provides access to online resources spanning the "full breath of human expression from the written word, to works of art and culture, to records of America's heritage to the efforts and data of science."[2]

DPLA is valuable to disparate target audiences. For students, teachers, scholars, and the public, DPLA serves as a search engine and portal to explore unique collections of millions of items in a multitude of formats. For software developers and researchers, DLPA's role is that of incubator, providing application programming interfaces (APIs) and open data to create tools for content discovery and interactive apps. For public libraries, DPLA serves as an ally, augmenting and enhancing existing digital collections in these libraries and advocating for continued community support for all public libraries.

With the development of the innovative Digital Hubs Program and the support of more than 40 state and regional libraries, the DPLA is working to establish a national network of Service Hubs, which will aggregate data on behalf of a given state or region, and larger Content Hubs, defined as advanced digital libraries, museums, archives, and repositories with at least 200,000 metadata records and digital objects. The ultimate goal of the Hubs Program is to serve as a curator, "bringing together digitized content from across the U.S. into a single access point for end users and an open platform for developers."[3] To date, the program has garnered more than 1,300 partners, and the

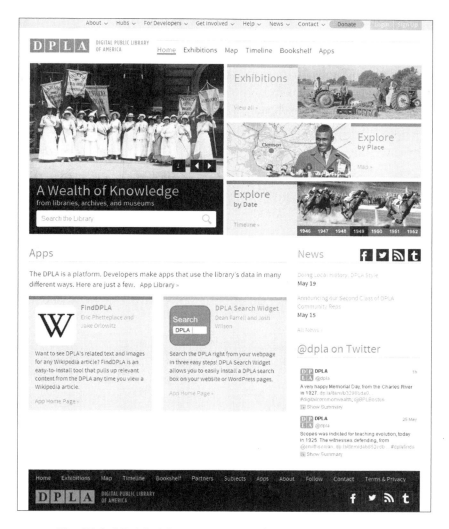

The Digital Public Library of America (DPLA) brings together the riches of America's libraries, archives, and museums, making them freely available to internet users.

DPLA database has amassed millions of items, many of which are in the public domain.[4] Access to DPLA is provided free of charge to all users.

Features

➤   DPLA's centralized portal offers single-point access to metadata records and associated thumbnails (not the physical items) for millions of materials in varied formats— photographs, manuscripts, books, audio, and moving images—curated from libraries, archives, and museums in the United States. Each record links to the original object on the content provider's website.

➤   Within the DPLA portal, users can perform the following tasks:

- Search and browse DPLA's collections utilizing search strategies refined by facets such as format, contributing institution, partner, date, language, location, and subject
- View items retrieved on a map, on a timeline or bookshelf
- Save items to customized lists and share these lists via Facebook, Twitter, and Google Plus
- Explore digital exhibitions curated by the DPLA's content partners

➤   The DPLA Bookshelf is a unique way of searching DPLA's collection of books, serials, and journals. Search results are displayed as a stacked virtual bookshelf, with a darker shade of blue on the spine indicating the degree of relevance in the results. Users can click on a book spine for metadata details and related images. Book thickness on stacks indicates the page count, and the horizontal length reflects the book's actual height.

➤   For developers, there is immediate access to open API and content-rich open metadata to create apps, tools, and other digital resources. Tools built using the DPLA API are added to an expanding App Library (www.dp.la/apps). Current offerings include:

- FindDPLA (finds relevant DPLA content within Wikipedia articles)

- DPLA Search Widget (installs a DPLA search box on a website or WordPress pages)

- DPLA by County and State (view how well DPLA is represented in individual counties and states)

- Culture Collage (allows users to search DPLA image archive and view results as a collage of images)

- EBSCO Discovery Service and DPLA Highlights (enables libraries to include content from the DPLA in their EBSCO search and discovery profile in the form of a widget)

- Historical Cats (randomly sends tweets on Twitter about items hosted in DPLA)

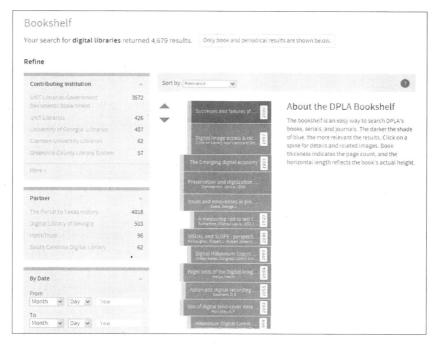

The DPLA bookshelf is a unique way of searching DPLA's collection of books, serials, and journals. Search results are displayed as a virtual bookshelf, where the darker shade indicates the relevancy of results.

How Cybrarians Can Use This Resource

Participation in the DPLA Hubs Program

There is the opportunity for libraries, museums, and archives to participate and partner in the DPLA Hubs Pilot Project, working collectively to bring disparate digitized collections into a centralized platform and provide a single access point for end users. Large content providers can apply to serve as Content Hubs. Libraries and organizations currently participating as Content Hubs include Harvard Library, HathiTrust Digital Library, the Internet Archive, and the New York Public Library. Libraries wishing to contribute as Content Hubs must meet the following criteria:

➤ Hold at least 200,000 unique metadata records that resolve to digital objects and comply with a national standard (DC, QDC, MODS)

➤ Be willing to share metadata records and associated content previews (thumbnails, clips, etc.) with DPLA in accordance with a Data Exchange Agreement, which describes how hubs provide data to the DPLA and how the DPLA uses this data

➤ Agree to work with DPLA staff to edit records as needed for global metadata quality

Smaller institutions with fewer resources can apply to serve as Service Hubs with a commitment to undertake the following:

➤ Have community support to represent the institution as the metadata aggregation point for the DPLA

➤ Actively address the issue of metadata quality

➤ Provide outreach to their metadata providers, including working in partnership with the DPLA to educate partner institutions on open data, data quality, data consistency, data standards, rights, and other relevant subjects

➤ Maintain technologies (such as OAI-PMH, API, and Resource Sync) that allow for metadata to be shared with the DPLA

➤ Actively engage with the broader community of data creators, providers, and users

An updated list of Service Hubs (www.dp.la/info/hubs) is maintained on the DPLA website, and current partners include the Digital Library of Georgia, Empire State Digital Network (New York), Kentucky Digital

Library, Minnesota Digital Library, and the North Carolina Digital Heritage Center.

Expanding and Enhancing Existing Digital Collections

Within a digital environment where libraries are actively seeking new strategies and utilizing existing models to expand, enhance, and promote digital collections to end users, the DPLA offers a unique opportunity for libraries to supplement existing collections by providing online access to this multifaceted, expanding digital repository.

FYI

Notable statistics as DPLA celebrated its first anniversary on April 18, 2014:[5]

➤ Tripled the size of its collection from 2.4 million to 7 million

➤ Curated materials from more than 1,300 organizations, up from 500 organizations recorded at project launch

➤ Attracted more than 1 million visitors to its website

➤ Recorded more than 9 million hits to its API

➤ Received more than $2 million in grant funding from U.S.-based foundations and donors

Notes

1. "About DPLA," DPLA, accessed March 17, 2014, www. dp.la/info.
2. Ibid.
3. "DPLA: Hubs," DPLA, accessed March 17, 2014, www.dp.la/info/hubs.
4. "Digital Public Library of America Celebrates its First Birthday with the Arrival of Six New Partners, Over 7 Million Items, and a Growing Community," *DPLA* (blog), April 17, 2014 www.dp.la/info/2014/04/17/dpla-1st-birthday-announcement.
5. Ibid.

9

Diigo
Social Bookmarking Service
https://www.diigo.com

Overview

Diigo (pronounced "DEE-go") is widely regarded as one of the top social bookmarking resources on the web, particularly for its web annotation and collaborative research services. Available on multiple platforms, this intuitive, cloud-based personal information management (PIM) system enables users to collect, access, highlight and share information available on the web. Launched in 2005 primarily as a social bookmarking service, the Nevada-based company has since offered several groundbreaking updates.

This commitment to steadily improve its product to satisfy an expanding group of users (more than 7 million as of this writing) with a penchant for collecting and consuming vast amount of digital information is motivated by consumer demand. As stated on the Diigo website, "much of our information consumption and research has shifted online. We are now spending a big part of our day working with online information … yet the workflow with information (browsing, reading, researching, annotating, storing, organizing, remembering, collaborating, sharing) is still largely ad-hoc and inefficient. Diigo is here to streamline [this] information workflow and dramatically improve productivity."[1]

For information consumers who may be overwhelmed and overloaded with data, Diigo provides quick access to browser-based tools (bookmarklets and toolbars) that enable end users to bookmark, highlight, annotate, and post notes to webpages, all the while saving this data to personal libraries (My Library) in the cloud. Additional features include screen shot capture, creation of reading lists for offline reading, and the ability to share saved data on blogs and popular social

44

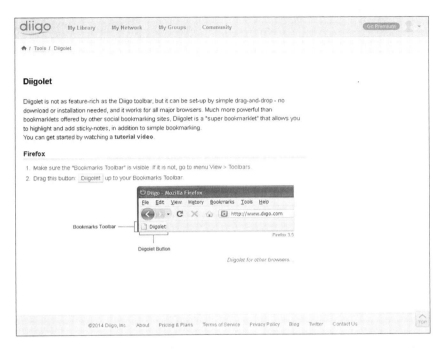

To quickly access and utilize Diigo's bookmarking, annotation, and collaborative services, users must first download and install a bookmarklet (Diigolet) or the Diigo toolbar.

networks. Diigo users can download and install toolbars for Chrome and Firefox web browsers, and app versions of Diigo are available for iOS and Android devices.

Features

> Online registration and account verification from the homepage (https://www.diigo.com) is required to use the service, and a four-tiered package (free, social, standard, and professional) is offered to registered users. Subscribers to the social, standard, and professional plans have access to advanced features, priority technical support, and ad-free viewing.

➤ To quickly access and utilize Diigo's bookmarking, annotation, and collaborative services, users must first download and install a bookmarklet (Diigolet) or the Diigo toolbar. The latter is available as a Firefox toolbar or Chrome extension. Diigolet is a basic bookmarklet, supported on all web browsers, but with limited features. The feature-rich Diigo toolbar provides access to all the features and functions available within the free, basic, and premium plans.

➤ Users have immediate access to My Library, a personal virtual storage place in the cloud (Diigo's servers) to collect, view, organize, and access all their materials captured on the web.

➤ Subscribers to Diigo's free service (including a plan designed for educators) have access to the following features:

- Bookmarks (unlimited)—saves links to bookmarked webpages in My Library allowing users to quickly access resources when needed

- Highlights (up to 500)—selects and highlights text and saves this highlighted text to My Library

- Graphics (up to 100)—saves visible images on webpages

- Screenshots (up to 100)—allows users to select an area of the webpage for capture and annotation

- Sticky Notes—records comments on webpages

- Share this Page—shares links to the annotated versions of captured webpages with social networks, blogs, or email providers

- Tagging and Listing—organizes bookmarked resources by adding tags or adding items to customized lists

- Read Later—saves the page to My Library as unread to be retrieved later for offline viewing

- Meta info Search—searches title, tags, highlights, and descriptions

- Displayed Ads—includes ads captured on webpages

How Cybrarians Can Use This Resource

Social Media Tool for Teaching and Sharing Information

Diigo is much more than a simple social bookmarking or web annotation service. Diigo can be characterized as an online productivity, personal research, and collaborative tool that simplifies the task of information management, enabling users to quickly organize, access, and share information. One example of the tool's effectiveness in collating and providing quick access to data is ALA Library's Public Lists (https://www.diigo.com/list/alalibrary), created on Diigo by ALA to keep members actively informed on trending issues. Using Diigo's bookmarking and annotating features, curated data in the form of articles, news reports, and blog postings from popular news sources are harvested regularly to provide timely information on topics such as self-publishing, marketing books to libraries, and resources for aspiring authors.

Diigo can also be utilized by librarians in their role as instructors and should be viewed as an effective social media tool for teaching and engagement during collaborative projects in libraries and other learning environments. Librarians and other educators can apply for a free Diigo Educator upgrade (unlimited highlights; PDF annotations, screenshots, and images; and access to a Teacher Console or online dashboard) available on the Diigo website (https://www.diigo.com/education).

FYI

Diigo is an abbreviation for "Digest of Internet Information, Groups, and Other Stuff."

Note

1. "About Diigo," Diigo, accessed April 27, 2014, https://www.diigo.com/about.

10

Dropbox
Cloud Storage/File Hosting/ Sharing Service
www.dropbox.com

Overview

Dropbox is a file hosting service offering cloud storage, file synchronization, and subscription-based client services. Among a tech-savvy user community that has steadily gravitated towards storing content on the cloud, Dropbox has gained a reputation as a valuable resource for accessing content on the go. Users can store a myriad of content (documents, photos, and videos) in Dropbox and easily access and share this content from their computers, smartphones, or tablets.

Competition in the file hosting/cloud storage arena is steadily increasing, as new players are launching services on a regular basis and are offering premium deals to eager consumers. Consumers, despite being sensitive and alert to issues of security and privacy in the cloud, are willing to research and utilize the best options for storing their accumulated data for office and personal use.

Similar services attempting to gain the lion's share of the market include Microsoft OneDrive, (formerly SkyDrive), Google Drive, Apple iCloud, Amazon Cloud Drive, and Box. In this highly competitive sphere, Dropbox is perceived as a top contender, as the service regularly introduces new features in its bid to stay ahead of competitors. These features include availability, accessibility, and synchronization across multiple devices, increased free storage space (mainly by referrals), automatic upload of photos and videos captured with mobile devices, a new photo sharing app (Carousel), and integration with social network giant Facebook.

Launched in 2008, the service now has more than 300 million users in 200 countries and is offered in 19 different languages.[1] In 2011, Dropbox was named the world's fifth most valuable startup after Facebook, Twitter, Zynga, and Groupon. It is operated by Dropbox Inc., headquartered in San Diego, California.

(*Continued*)

New Dropbox users can both access and download
the software from the homepage.

Features

➣   New users can download and install Dropbox for free on their
    computers (supports Windows, Mac, and Linux) and mobile
    devices from the service's homepage (www.dropbox.com).
    During installation, a unique Dropbox folder is created on
    the computer. Any files added to this folder will automatically
    save and sync to the user's other personal computers,
    smartphones, tablets, and the Dropbox website. Other users
    can be invited to view and share individual Dropbox folders
    to allow online collaboration.

➤ All new Dropbox users are guaranteed 2 GB of free space. Monthly or annual subscriptions to a Dropbox Pro (500 GB) or Dropbox for Business account (1 terabyte for 5 users) are offered for users wishing to upgrade for additional storage space, increased security, and administrative control.

➤ The Dropbox app is available for iOS, BlackBerry, and Android devices. When files are uploaded to these devices, they are automatically synced with the desktop version. To ensure the sync process is successful, users should assign the same Dropbox login credentials to all of their devices.

➤ A referral service allows users to earn extra storage space by inviting friends to review and use Dropbox. Free accounts created in this way immediately yield 500 MB of free space to both accounts (current users and invited friends). Referrals can earn users up to 16 GB in bonus space.

➤ An active Dropbox Developer community (300,000 active apps have been built on the Dropbox platform) supports the development of third-party apps including Docs to Go, CloudOn, GoodReader, and 1Password.

➤ Dropbox provides a backup service (one month history of work stored) for easy restoration of lost files along with encryption for secured transmission of files.

How Cybrarians Can Use This Resource
File Hosting and Cloud Storage Service

Dropbox's online file hosting and cloud storage services have a strong following of established users who utilize the service to manage their digital lives by storing personal documents, videos, and digital photographs. Cybrarians can easily promote this tool as a free service for performing the following tasks:

➤ Storing and accessing content in multiple formats (documents, audio and video files, images) on multiple devices (desktops, laptops, smartphones, tablets)

➤   Sharing folders (information and subject guides, fact sheets)
     in a networked environment and allowing multiple users to
     access, review, edit, and delete these files

➤   Sharing data for group collaborative projects

➤   Sharing photographs in digital galleries with Dropbox's photo
     browsing and sharing app Carousel

FYI

It's estimated that Dropbox users save one billion files
to Dropbox every 24 hours.[2]

Notes

1. "Dropbox—Company Info," Dropbox, accessed February 7, 2015, https://www
   .dropbox.com/news/company-info.
2. Ibid.

11

Ebooks
Ebook Collections and Services
https://en.wikipedia.org/wiki/Ebooks

Overview

This chapter on ebooks was written in an attempt to document the not-so-discreet societal shift—borne out by numerous statistics—from the printed book to its digital surrogate, and the importance to libraries of leveraging opportunities afforded in this new environment. As early as 2010, online bookseller Amazon reported that sales of ebooks for its proprietary Kindle outnumbered sales of hardcover books for the first time.[1] In May 2011, Amazon made another dramatic announcement: that ebook sales on its U.S. site now exceeded all of its printed book sales.[2] Exposing a similar trend, the Bookstats Project (jointly produced by the Association of American Publishers and the Book Industry Study Group) reported that U.S. publishers collected about $3 billion in trade ebook sales in 2013, and noted that sales appear to be leveling off, as this figure is virtually unchanged from 2012.[3]

With the rising demand for ebooks, there is concomitant interest in and demand for ebook reading devices (tablets and dedicated ebook readers). A 2014 report from the Pew Research Center concluded that "three in ten adults [have] read an ebook and that half own a tablet or ereader."[4] Given the trends suggested by these statistics, one can safely conclude that ebooks will be the preferred, if not dominant, format for esavvy readers in the future.

This increasing consumer demand for ebooks is visible in all market segments, including public, academic, and special libraries. As noted in the study aptly titled "Libraries: At the Epicenter of the Digital Disruption" sponsored by *Library Resource Guide*, digital content continues to be a priority for the majority of the libraries surveyed and print continues to lose ground: "three-fourths of libraries [surveyed]

(74 percent) continue to see rising demand for electronic resources, while more move away from print… nine out of the 10 public community libraries say they are seeing demand for ebooks which leads the way in purchasing intentions." This move has occurred even as budgets for library acquisitions started to improve after the economic recession of the last decade.[5]

These statistics point to increases in ebook usage across all communities and signal the arrival of the required tipping point in how libraries examine all the issues related to ebooks. Any review of current literature on ebooks in libraries and allied communities will readily identify topics that reflect the growing impact of these resources on library collections, services, budgets, and end users. The impact is broad, and it includes factors such as ebook collections (free and subscription), ebook readers and associated apps, ebook platforms and software, ebook services, ebook business models, licensing terms, statistics, standards and formats, Digital Rights Management (DRM) issues, workflows, ebook circulation and lending policies, preservation and archiving strategies, and cooperative projects with ebook vendors and publishers.

The dual issue of cooperation and compensation between ebook publishers and libraries has long been considered a contentious topic, centering largely around legal wrangling to allow greater library access to ebooks while appropriately compensating publishers. In 2013, the library community collectively breathed a sigh of relief as after "years of conflict, ebook publishers and libraries made peace… with the year ending with the majority of the Big Six publishers (Macmillan, Simon & Schuster, Penguin Book Group, U.S.A., and Hachette Book Group) participating [at some level] in the library ebook market"[6] and agreeing to make ebook collections available to libraries. Although important challenges such as availability and pricing remain, this decision marks an important milestone for libraries seeking to provide ebook collections to satisfy increasing consumer demand.

Features

The explosion of interest in ebooks and ereaders across all sectors brings with it obvious advantages for libraries wishing to purchase ebook collections: 24/7 access to content; no additional physical space required for storage; no weeding of virtual shelves; and no potential physical damage or loss of materials incurred. However, there are some basic questions regarding features and related factors that libraries should address before embarking on acquiring ebooks and other types of econtent.[7] The following is a sample listing of these questions:

➤ Needs of the Library Community Served—Is this type of content of interest to communities being served? If yes, then what type of content do they need: fiction, nonfiction, children's books, reference materials, or classic literature? What are their preferred types of ereading devices—Amazon Kindles, Barnes & Noble Nooks, Apple iPads, Android tablets, smartphones, laptops, or personal computers?

➤ Type of Ebook Content (Fee vs. Free)—There are a number of services offering free access to ebooks that are out of copyright and in the public domain. Project Gutenberg, HathiTrust, Internet Archive, and Google Books are popular free ebook collections. When purchasing fee-based econtent, it is critical, especially for libraries with limited budgets, to evaluate all vendors and consider the following:

   · Purchasing factors such as the number of titles available

   · Robustness of the vendor ebook platform

   · Lending and download options

   · Ereader and ebook formats supported

   · Availability of other econtent

   · Business models and costs, including maintenance and hosting fees

   · Licensing terms

   · Availability of consortial partnerships

   · Statistics and other modes of reporting

   · Customer support and training

➤ Leading vendors for ebook content include Baker & Taylor (B&T), Freading, OverDrive, and 3M Cloud Library. The leading ebook aggregators and distributors in the U.S. include

Books24x7, ebooks on EBSCOhost, ProQuest-owned Ebook Library (EBL), Follett ebooks, Ingram's MyiLibrary, Knovel, and Safari Books Online. Reference material distributors include Credo Reference and Gale Virtual Reference Library (GVRL).

➤ Technical Support and Training Sessions for Staff—While it benefits library patrons to have access to technology and digital content, one of the challenges for libraries offering ebooks as a service is the issue of having staff who are knowledgeable about and have an affinity for working with emerging technologies. It is critical, therefore, that libraries plan for providing the required assistance and support for all patron types, ranging from those with basic knowledge to those who are savvy with digital technologies, and train staff for these services. Just-in-time and advanced training is required for working with multiple ebook devices on the current market (dedicated ereaders and tablets such as the Nook, Kobo, iPad, and Kindle), identifying different file formats (PDF, EPUB, and AZW), and developing and implementing new circulation policies and download procedures. Librarians have been proactive in obtaining the hands-on training required through workshops, technology zoos, and vendor demonstrations.

How Cybrarians Can Use This Resource

Ebooks in Libraries: A Proactive Response

Some libraries have been more adept than others at overcoming the challenges—the so-called grey areas—often encountered in the early adoption phase of providing ebook services and have successfully moved on to the next phase of implementing, managing, and promoting their ebook collections. There is substantial library literature on the potential for ebook success in *all* libraries, including case studies outlining successful and transformative ebook initiatives that have guaranteed improved services and unique end-user experiences. Initiatives include using ebooks as tools for improving literacy, adding innovative approaches such as Patron Driven Acquisition (PDA) to the collection development process, and implementing marketing strategies to guarantee acceptance by patrons of the service.

Identifying best practices and innovative experiments of early adopters can ensure that libraries are prepared to deliver effective ebook services. An example of one such initiative is the bold move made at Douglas County (Colorado) Libraries (DCL), where Library Director James LaRue and his staff have taken steps to develop a new model for library ownership of ebooks. In adopting this new model, the DC staff successfully boosted the role of libraries as publishers, simplified the complex contractual agreements with ebook vendors, engaged in dialogue and the purchase of ebooks directly from established and independent publishers, and hosted multiple ebook collections on DCL's local server.[8,9]

Provide Access to Free Ebook Collections

The following is a list of free ebook collections available for libraries:

> Project Gutenberg (www.gutenberg.org/wiki/Main_Page)—With more than 46,000 downloadable ebook titles (including audio ebooks), Project Gutenberg supplements any library's ebook collection. Supported formats include EPUB, HTML, Kindle, PDF, and plain text. The Library of Congress is currently promoting the project by including it as a resource in its online catalog (eresources.loc.gov).

> Internet Archive (https://archive.org/index.php)—The Internet Archive is a nonprofit digital library offering free universal access to books, movies, and music. This digital repository also provides access to more than 400 billion archived webpages via its Way Back Machine (https://archive.org/web).

> Google Books (www.books.google.com)—Previously known as Google Book Search and Google Print, this service from Google searches the full text of books and magazines that Google has scanned and stored in its digital library. Books out of copyright and in the public domain are freely available for downloading and printing as PDF files.

Free ebooks - Project Gutenberg

From Project Gutenberg, the first producer of free ebooks.

Book search · Book categories · Browse catalog · Mobile site · Report errors · Terms of use

search book catalog

- Search Catalog
- Book Categories

search website

- Main Page
- Categories
- News
- Contact Info

donate
Project Gutenberg needs your donation!

Donate

- More Info

in other languages

- Português
- Deutsch
- Français

hosted by ibiblio

Some of Our Latest Books

Welcome

Project Gutenberg offers over 45,000 free ebooks: choose among free epub books, free kindle books, download them or read them online.

We carry high quality ebooks: All our ebooks were previously published by *bona fide* publishers. We digitized and diligently proofread them with the help of thousands of volunteers.

No fee or registration is required, but if you find Project Gutenberg useful, we kindly ask you to donate a small amount so we can buy and digitize more books. Other ways to help include digitizing more books, recording audio books, or reporting errors.

Over 100,000 free ebooks are available through our Partners, Affiliates and Resources.

Project Gutenberg
Mobile Site

News

Self-Publishing Portal

Visit self.gutenberg.org to see how Project Gutenberg is facilitating online publishing by contemporary authors. This new service is bringing the Project Gutenberg moniker to authors in virtually any genre or subject. The portal is open at self.gutenberg.org and invites all readers and publishers. All items are free to download and share. There is also an RSS feed, at http://self.gutenberg.org/rss/authors.aspx.

Loss of Project Gutenberg's founder, Michael S. Hart (1947-2011)

Michael's 67th birthday would have been March 8, 2014. Here are some thoughts and remembrances from Jim Berger, along with a photo from one of his presentations. Project Gutenberg's founder, Michael Hart, passed away September 6. Here is our brief obituary and related documents.

Terms of Use

Our ebooks are free in the United States because their copyright has expired. They may not be free of copyright in other countries. Readers outside of the United States must check the copyright laws of their countries before downloading or redistributing our ebooks. We also have a number of copyrighted titles, for which the copyright holder has given permission for unlimited non-commercial worldwide use.

The Project Gutenberg website is for human users only. Any real or perceived use of automated tools to access our site will result in a block of your IP address.

For more details see our Terms of Use page.

Site Map

The Online Book Catalog

- Book Search: Search for books.
- Recent Books: The latest books.
- Most Downloaded Books: The most popular books.

Special areas

- Offline Catalogs: handy ebook Listings to consult offline.
- Old Online Catalog: more ways to browse the book catalog.
- New Books Feeds: ways to keep you updated on new publications.
- Top 100 Books and Authors: the most downloaded books and authors.
- Report errors, bugs, typos (or, see detailed information about errata reporting)
- Audio Books, both human-read and computer-generated.
- CD and DVD Project: Download entire CDs or DVDs, or have a free disc sent to you
- Digitized Sheet Music (dormant)
- Free Kindle Books: about free kindle books at Project Gutenberg
- Mobile Reader Devices How-To: about kindle, nook, cell phone, and other mobile devices

Project Gutenberg's extensive collection of downloadable ebook titles supplements any library's collection.

➤ Open Library (https://openlibrary.org)—This project, developed by the Internet Archive (IA), is an open, editable library catalog with the lofty goal of publishing a webpage for every book published. To date, there are more than a million free ebook titles available in this online database. In a collaborative In-Library Lending program, IA allows participating libraries to select digitized books from their collections and circulate these titles to library patrons free of charge. Books in this program are available for download in PDF, EPUB, and Daisy (for the print disabled) formats and viewable in BookReader, a free Open Library ereader that allows reading within a web browser.

➤ Adobe Digital Editions Sample Ebook Library (www.adobe .com/products/digital-editions/ebook.html)—This online library provides free downloads of a few select titles and previews chapters from leading publishers. In order to download and read the titles offered, readers must first install the Adobe Digital Editions software.

➤ Baen Ebooks (www.baenebooks.com/c-1-free-library. aspx)—Selected DRM-free ebook titles are available in the Baen Ebook store for free download. Supported formats for ereaders include MOBI (Amazon Kindle and Palm devices), EPUB (for devices like the Nook, Kobo, and iPad/iPhone), HTML (web browsers) and RTF (word processing programs).

➤ EPub Bud (www.epubbud.com)—A database of free children's ebooks available for download as EPUB files.

➤ Amazon free ebooks (http://www.amazon.com/ b?node=2245146011)—In addition to its extensive collection of "for purchase" titles, the Amazon Kindle store offers free access to popular classics and older out-of-copyright, pre-1923 ebooks. Titles selected are delivered wirelessly to Kindles, computers, and supported mobile devices.

➤ Audiobooksforfree (www.Audiobooksforfree.com)—This U.K.-based audiobook retailer offers a selection of books in multiple genres and claims that "every audiobook is produced and recorded by professional actors/narrators and experienced directors and that no computerised text-to-voice conversions have been used." Free titles (the quality of which is not standardized as with for-purchase files) are available for download as MP3 files and can be played on computers, smartphones, and portable MP3 players.

➤   LibriVox (https://librivox.org)—This project, powered by volunteers, produces audiobooks of works in the public domain. Reading texts are selected from Project Gutenberg, and the Internet Archive hosts and provides access to all recorded audio files in MP3 format.

FYI

The late Michael S. Hart, Founder of Project Gutenberg, is sometimes credited as the inventor of the ebook. He created his first electronic document by typing the U.S. Declaration of Independence on a mainframe computer.[10]

Notes

1. Claire Cain Miller, "Ebooks Top Hardcovers at Amazon," *The New York Times*, July 19, 2010, accessed January 27, 2014, www.nytimes.com/2010/07/20/technology/20kindle.html?_r=0.

2. Lisa Rapaport, "Amazon.com Says Kindle Ebook Sales Surpass Printed Books for First Time," Bloomberg, May 19, 2011, accessed January 27, 2014, www.bloomberg.com/news/2011-05-19/amazon-com-says-kindle-electronic-book-sales-surpass-printed-format.html.

3. Aaron Pressman, "Slowing ebook sales may embolden publishers in Amazon spat," June 26, 2014, Yahoo! Finance, accessed February 7, 2015, www.finance.yahoo.com/blogs/breakout/slowing-ebook-sales-could-hurt-amazon-in-battle-with-publishers-174752232.html.

4. Pew Research Center, "E-Reading Rises as Device Ownership Jumps," January 16, 2014," accessed February 8, 2015, www.pewinternet.org/Reports/2014/E-Reading-Update.aspx.

5. Joseph McKendrick, "Libraries: At the Epicenter of the Digital Disruption: The Library Resource Guide Benchmark Study on 2013/14 Library Spending Plans," accessed January 21, 2014, www.comminfo.rutgers.edu/~tefko/Courses/

e553/Readings/Libraries-At-the-Epicenter-of-the-Digital-DisruptionThe-Library-Resource-Guide-Benchmark-Study-on-2013-2014-Library-Spending-Plans.pdf.

6. "State of America's Libraries Report 2014: Executive Summary," ALA, accessed January 27, 2014, www.ala.org/news/state-americas-libraries-report-2014/executive-summary.

7. Sue Polanka, "A Primer on Ebooks for Libraries Just Starting with Downloadable Media," The Digital Shift, April 18, 2012, accessed January 27, 2014, www.thedigitalshift.com/2012/04/ebooks/an-ebook-primer-many-small-libraries-are-still-just-getting-started-with-ebooks-heres-a-helpful-guide-on-those-first-steps/

8. Rochelle Logan, "Working Directly with Publishers: Lessons Learned," *American Libraries E-Content Supplement,* June 2013, 8–11.

9. LaRue, James, "Wanna Write a Good One? Library as Publisher," *American Libraries E-Content Supplement,* June 2013, 18–21.

10. "Michael S. Hart," Project Gutenberg, accessed January 27, 2014, https://www.gutenberg.org/wiki/Michael_S._Hart

12

Ebook Readers
Ebook Reading Devices
www.en.wikipedia.org/wiki/E-reader

Overview

As the demand for ebooks exploded, so did the development of a new generation of dedicated ereading devices. Early innovations on the market included the Amazon Kindle, Barnes & Noble Nook, Kobo, and Sony Reader. As the market became increasingly lucrative, there was immediate competition from other vendors offering similar yet more multifunctional ereading options. In 2010, Apple released its tablet computer, the iPad, with a built-in app for ebooks called iBooks, and the iBookstore. This successful product launch was quickly followed by the release of several Android-based tablets with similar capabilities.

From studies such as "Libraries: At the Epicenter of the Digital Disruption," it is becoming increasingly apparent that dedicated ebook readers such as the Amazon Kindle, and Barnes and Noble Nook, "which were hot just a couple of years ago are showing signs of being disrupted by smartphones and tablet computers."[1] The popularity and marketability of smartphones and tablets with built-in reading capabilities, as opposed to dedicated ereaders, lies in their added functionality, the utilization of LCD displays (usually touch screens), and the tendency of these devices to be more agnostic to formats offered by ebook vendors. This kind of quickfire change in technology often presents challenges for library administrators, who are faced with the dilemma of making "the right judgment calls and selecting the appropriate technology that will be adopted by patrons."[2]

Current statistics show that "ebooks are the dominant technology in demand across libraries," and this demand is equally evident in the three primary library segments: public, academic, and special libraries. This trend has naturally led to patron demands for accompanying viewing and reading devices, and the decision by libraries to include ebook readers as a major purchase in their budget plans: "Thirty-one percent of libraries are now circulating ebook readers—this figure represents a significant increase from what was recorded two years ago (14 percent)."[3]

The continuing popularity of ebooks has also led a group of third-party developers to offer free ereader applications for both desktops and mobile devices. These free apps enable the reading of ebooks and other econtent and compare favorably to their trademarked rivals, thus providing users with the tools to access and read digital content from a wide range of sources instantly and seamlessly.

Features

The task of choosing the right ebook reader to facilitate a flawless on-the-go reading experience can be challenging, particularly given the wealth of choices available from vendors supplying ebook readers, smartphones, tablets, and free ereader apps. The following list identifies features to compare in determining the appropriate ereader for personal or professional use:

- Readability (nonreflective e-ink screens vs. LCD screens, built-in front light, screen resolution, touchscreen display, display size, and portrait or landscape display modes)

- Portability (weight, casing material, dimensions, durability, battery life, Wi-Fi and cellular connectivity, and expandable memory)

- Ebook download factors (cost of ebooks, convenience of immediately downloading ebooks to device, availability of integrated ebook store with direct access to titles, access to other formats such as magazines, newspapers and audiobooks, ability to borrow titles from local library, storage space, and multilanguage support)

- Supporting/supplementary features (product warranty, automatic syncing of ebooks across multiple devices, adjustable fonts, built-in dictionary, ability to add bookmarks and annotations, and use of actual page numbers)

How Cybrarians Can Use This Resource

Promoting Ebook Readers in Libraries

➤ Circulation of Ebook Readers to Patrons—Most libraries can apply for and obtain a grant to engage in this type of service. A number of cheat sheets are available to assist with this innovative service. For example, the WebJunction website offers a list of ereader policies and procedures in select libraries (www.webjunction.org/documents/webjunction/E_045_reader_Policies_and_Procedures_045_Samples_from_Libraries.html).

➤ Develop Technology/Gadget Petting Zoos—As ereaders become more affordable, there has been a notable increase in the demand for assistance with these devices from patrons. In response, many libraries proactively host technology training in the form of petting or gadget zoos, where patrons evaluate the features of devices side-by-side for an optimum ereading experience. Some libraries partner with local vendors or book stores to host similar technology workshops. The Williamson County Public Library in Tennessee (www.tinyurl.com/kek4d23) offers tips on hosting such events.

➤ Promote Free Ebook Readers—The following is a list of free ereaders to promote to patrons:

- Adobe Digital Editions (www.adobe.com/products/digital-editions.html)—This multifunctional software allows users to download, read, (on- and offline), and manage ebooks and other digital publications. This software is widely used to transfer copyright-protected ebooks from personal computers to USB-connected reader devices. It also provides options for organizing ebooks into custom libraries, annotating pages, and switching to full screen mode. Digital Editions supports most industry-standard ebook formats, including PDF/A and EPUB. It is designed to work with Windows and Mac operating systems, and with assistive software such as JAWS and NVDA.

- Aldiko Book Reader (www.aldiko.com)—This software allows readers to browse and download books to

Android-based smartphones or tablets. It supports EPUB and PDF ebook formats.

- Blio https://www.blio.com/web1/screens/homepage.jsp— Blio is a full-featured ereader available on Windows, Android, and iOS platforms, purposely designed to give readers a colorful, authentic reading experience. The Blio ebook store provides online access to fiction, nonfiction, and children's selections.

- Ebook reader app from Ebooks.com (http://ebookreader .ebooks.com/#)—Readers who download this free app have immediate access to more than 100,000 titles available in the ebook.com store. The app can be downloaded to iPhones, iPads, Kindle Fire tablets, and all Android smartphones and tablets.

Amazon's free Kindle reading app is available for most devices.

- FBReader (www.fbreader.org)—FBReader is a customizable ebook reader for devices running on the following platforms: Android, Linux, Windows, BlackBerry, and Mac OS X. Support is available for EPUB, FB2, MOBI, and HTML ebook formats and plain text. Online access is provided to free U.S.-based and international ebook collections.

- Amazon Kindle App (http://tinyurl.com/kbvx66x)— "Buy Once, Read Everywhere" is Amazon's tag line to promote its free Kindle reading app that affords readers the flexibility of buying a Kindle book and reading it on any device with the Kindle app installed. This app is available on multiple platforms. The Kindle Cloud Reader, also offered by Amazon, is a web-based ereader allowing instant online access and offering the capability to read ebooks in a web browser.

Notes

1. "Joseph McKendrick, "Libraries: At the Epicenter of the Digital Disruption: The Library Resource Guide Benchmark Study on 2013/14 Library Spending Plans," accessed January 21, 2014, www.comminfo.rutgers.edu/~tefko/Courses/e553/Readings/Libraries-At-the-Epicenter-of-the-Digital-DisruptionThe-Library-Resource-Guide-Benchmark-Study-on-2013-2014-Library-Spending-Plans.pdf.
2. Ibid.
3. Ibid.

13

Evernote
Note-taking Software
https://evernote.com

Overview

The Evernote suite of productivity tools was designed specifically for users on the go who wish to find, capture, organize, and archive information across multiple platforms. The company's tagline, "capture anything, remember everything," is reflective of the product's functionality, enabling users to take notes (including handwritten notes), clip webpages, upload images, create to-do lists, schedule reminders and deadlines, and record voice memos. This saved data, along with other user data stored in the cloud, can be backed up and synchronized on Evernote's web-based version or across multiple devices (computers, smartphones, and tablets).

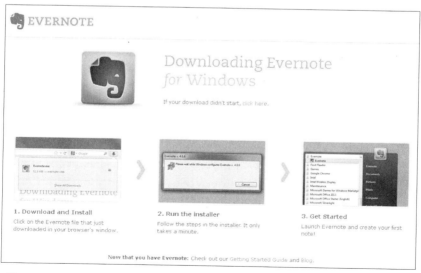

Evernote can be downloaded and installed from the service's homepage.

In an environment dotted with similar and highly competitive note-taking and archiving software, including Simplenote, Google Keep, Microsoft OneNote and Fetchnotes, Evernote stands out for its user-friendly editing and browsing interface packed with features to assist the average user in taking notes, staying organized, and increasing productivity.

Evernote was launched into open beta service in June 2008. Since its launch, it has benefitted from more than $250 million in venture funding, and supports millions of users.[1] The service's U.S.-based operations are located in California and Texas.

Features

➤ Registration is required to use the service. The application can be freely downloaded and installed from Evernote's homepage (https://evernote.com) and is supported on multiple systems and platforms.

➤ Evernote users can utilize the service for their home and business productivity needs. The monthly account quota is tied to the type of service subscription. Each service tier (free, premium, and business) offers unlimited storage but restricts the amount of data uploaded into personal notebooks each month. Users with free accounts can upload up to 60 MB of data each month, create 100,000 notes and tags, and upload file attachments up to 25 MB. Premium and business accounts have access to upgraded features, including increased data uploads, access to offline notes, advanced searching, passcode locks, and collaboration tools.

➤ The service supports quick access to a "What You See Is What You Get" (WYSIWYG) interface designed for note-taking and archiving. Users can add notes in multiple formats, including formatted text, a handwritten "ink" note, a webpage, digital photograph, or voice memo. Notes can be edited and deleted, organized into folders, organized by location, tagged with keywords, annotated with comments, uploaded as attachments, and shared with other users via email, Facebook, Twitter, or LinkedIn.

➤ The Evernote Web Clipper (https://evernote.com/webclipper) is a plug-in or extension that can be installed within a web browser allowing users to immediately save, mark up, and share items found via their Evernote account when browsing the web. When installed, the Web Clipper provides a toolbar button and context menu providing options to add a full webpage, selected text, or permanent URL.

➤ Evernote's Tumblr blog (www.evernote.tumblr.com) provides online access to tutorials, demos, new features, and tips and tricks.

➤ The App Center (https://appcenter.evernote.com) provides an updated listing of third-party tools that integrate with Evernote.

How Cybrarians Can Use This Resource

Developing Library Workshops on Evernote

Evernote, like Delicious, is a social bookmarking tool, which can be promoted via workshops to library patrons interested in taking notes, saving ideas, and bookmarking resources in multiple formats to support their online research. There are several learning resources that have been developed to provide support for using Evernote in libraries:

➤ Workshops sponsored by the library network Lyrasis have been developed to "identify strategies for using Evernote as a tool for teaching information literacy, library instruction and professional productivity."[2]

➤ In a post on the blog Learning 2.0 Module Archive: A Compendium of Learning 2.0 Modules (www .thehyperlinkedlibrary.org/learning20/tag/evernote), students in the School of Library and Information Science (SLIS) at San Jose State University highlight Evernote's usefulness as a social media bookmarking tool. The students promote the tool's multifunctional features for recording notes from multiple sources, information management, collection development, and library instruction.

FYI

Evernote's productivity tools (www.evernote.com/products) were developed to help users "remember everything, communicate effectively and get things done." Additional tools developed to support these tasks include Skitch (sketches, annotations, and shapes) and Food (food directory).

Notes

1. Ingrid Lunden, "After Pledging A "Better Evernote", Evernote Updates Data Sync, Now 4X Faster," TechCrunch, January 28, 2014, accessed February 7, 2015, www.techcrunch.com/2014/01/28/evernote-sync.
2. Buffy J. Hamilton, "Evernote for Libraries and Librarians," Lyrasis, July 2010, accessed March 15, 2014, www.buffyhamilton-lyrasis.wikispaces.com/Evernote+for+Libraries+and+Librarians.

14

Flipboard
Social News Aggregator
https://flipboard.com

Overview

Since the demise of Google's popular newsfeed aggregator Google Reader in July 2013, news enthusiasts have been scouring the web for an alternate platform for serving up and collating news from their favorite resources. Flipboard, a social network and news aggregator, is often promoted as a worthy substitute to fill this void.

As the name suggests, Flipboard curates content from social media networks, blogs, and other websites, and it blends and formats this content into a personalized magazine that enables users to flip through and read their news feeds. In designing a social news service in this format, Flipboard developers by their own admission are "on a quest to transform how people discover, view and share content by combining the beauty and ease of print with the power of social media."[1]

Using feeds from their popular social networks Twitter, Facebook, Instagram, and Tumblr and favorite curated media channels, Flipboarders are discovering unique ways to create, share, and promote subject-specific digital magazines with eclectic titles such as Travel Buzz, Dream Homes, International News, DIY Health, Mysterious Universe, Women's Rights, Big Data Daily, Marketing and Social Media, and Digital Resume.

Developed initially and exclusively for iPads and recognized by Apple as the iPad App of the Year in 2010, Flipboard has since expanded to other mobile platforms including the iPhone, Android, Kindle Fire, and Barnes and Noble Nook.[2] The company has its headquarters in Palo Alto, California.

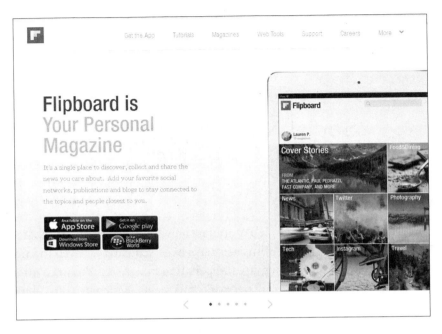

Several options for downloading Flipboard
are available from the homepage.

Features

➤ New users must complete the following steps to use the
service:

- From the homepage, download a free version of Flipboard
  from one of the following sources: App Store, Google Play,
  and Windows Phone Store.

- Register for the service by completing the online
  application form (user name, password, and email
  address) and signing the Terms of Use and Privacy
  Policy.

- Start building a Flipboard or personal magazine by
  subscribing to content within specific categories (News,
  Technology, Design, Photography, Business, Sports, Style,
  Travel, Politics, Food, Music, Film, Gaming, Auto, and
  Science). There is also the option to connect feeds from
  social networks (Twitter, Facebook, Flickr, Google Plus,

LinkedIn, Instagram, and Tumblr) directly to Flipboard accounts to quickly browse newsfeeds and share content with others.

- Click "Build Your Flipboard" to complete the process.

➤ The front page of each Flipboard magazine is characterized by a graphically-enhanced, user-friendly interface that also serves as an aggregated Table of Contents, providing quick access to the following features:

- Cover stories that allow users to quickly browse all content currently subscribed to or content being shared via social networks

- Curated channels categorized by subject

- A search box to discover new content using keywords

- A main content guide that provides recommendations including editorial staff picks for news sources in all formats from major publications and blogs

➤ All content curated on Flipboard can be easily shared via social networks, SMS, and email.

➤ The Flipboard Editor (https://editor.flipboard.com) allows users to manage and personalize magazines (rearrange and delete items, set covers, and share content) from a central dashboard.

➤ "Flip it" bookmarklets (https://editor.flipboard.com/ bookmarklet), available as add-ons for web browsers, iPhones, and iPads, permit seamless integration of various types of content (articles, blog posts, videos, images, music files, and webpages) from the web. Profile buttons, badges, and widgets can be embedded into personal websites to promote magazines created using the service.

How Cybrarians Can Use This Resource

Promote Library Services and Collections

Flipboard as a social news aggregator service can be used to create library theme-based magazines to promote collections, new services, library exhibits, outreach programs, and library events. The following is a select listing of magazines created on Flipboard on specific library topics:

- Library 2.013
- Education Technology and Libraries
- Ebooks, Ereaders and Libraries
- Libraries and Archives
- Not an Ebook
- Long Interesting Library Reads

FYI

In February 2014, Facebook released Paper (https://www.facebook.com/paper), a resource comparable in purpose and design to Flipboard. Using Paper's full-screen interface filled with immersive designs and distraction-free layouts, Facebook fans can explore, curate, and share personal stories with "friends and the world." The app, initially released for iOS, can be downloaded from the App Store.

Notes

1. "Flipboard: About Us," Flipboard, accessed March 17, 2014, https://flipboard.com/about.
2. Jay Yarow, "Apple Calls Flipboard iPad App of The Year," *Business Insider*, December 9, 2010, accessed March 25, 2014, www.businessinsider.com/apple-calls-flipboard-ipad-app-of-the-year-2010-12.

15

Google Drive
Cloud Storage/File Hosting/ Sharing Service
https://drive.google.com

Overview

Touted as a redesign of an old concept, Google Drive provides users with cloud space to store and retrieve files from multiple devices. Google introduced the cloud storage service in a bid to accomplish two pressing service goals: as a practical option to bundle all of its productivity applications into one platform, and to compete on an even keel with similar cloud storage providers Microsoft OneDrive (formerly SkyDrive), Apple iCloud, Amazon Cloud Drive, and Box.

In addition to providing 15 GB of cloud space for storing files and data, Google Drive is a useful tool for collaboration, allowing shared creation and general sharing of documents in real time, using Google's productivity suite of tools available within the Google Drive interface. Productivity tools currently available include Google Docs (Google's long-established standalone word processing app), Spreadsheets, Forms, Drawings, and Presentations.

Promoted as an "access from anywhere, on the go" application, Google Drive is available on the web and can be installed on desktops and mobile devices. Disparate files stored on multiple devices are automatically synced and updated simultaneously. The software was released on April 24, 2012.

Features

➤ New users can register an account on the product website (https://drive.google.com) or use their existing Google account. Once the user is signed in, the software can be downloaded and installed on a computer, laptop, or mobile device.

➤ The 15 GB of free storage space is shared across the following Google services: Google Drive, Gmail, and Google Plus Photos. Users wishing for more storage space (extra storage ranges from 100 GB to 16 TB) must pay monthly subscription costs.

➤ Offline access is available when using Google Chrome (browser) or a Chrome OS device (such as Google Chromebook). If using Google Chrome, users must install the Drive Chrome app to enable offline access; this feature is automatically enabled in Google Chromebooks.

➤ Google Drive's customizable web interface offers several ways to filter, view, and search files, folders, documents,

Google Drive provides users with online file storage, often referred to as cloud space, to store and retrieve files from any internet-enabled device.

spreadsheets, and presentations stored in the cloud. Search and sort filters include My Drive, Shared with Me, Starred, Recent Activity, and All Items.

➤ The Google Drive desktop application installs a folder on a personal computer when downloaded. Within this folder, users can save, move, rename, edit, and delete files. All changes made within files and documents stored in this folder are mirrored (automatically synced) in the web version.

➤ The Google Drive app is available for Android (Google Play Store) and iOS (Apple's App Store) devices. The app version provides seamless, on-the-go access to Google Drive and has similar features to the web and PC version.

How Cybrarians Can Use This Resource
Collaborating and Sharing in the Cloud

Google Drive's popularity and widespread usage within libraries and other work environments can be attributed in part to its productivity applications (managing, viewing, editing, and sharing files created using Google office suite) and its competitive free cloud storage options.

Leah Kulikowski, director of the Wamego Public Library (Kansas), in her article, "Using Google Drive for Library Communication and Collaboration," recommends having at least one administrator account (accessible to all library staff), and offers a list of immediate benefits for cybrarians wishing to use the service:

➤ Reducing the use of post-it notes and the number of lost messages

➤ Improving staff communication

➤ Accessing files from anywhere

➤ Eliminating the task of emailing files for a workshop or conference presentation to a personal email account

She also provides step-by-step instructions in the form of cheat sheets for creative ways to use Google Drive in libraries:

➤ Creating communication notebooks

➤ Summer reading and other program registrations

➤   Staff work schedules

➤   Staff time sheets

➤   Shopping lists

➤   Items to order (patron requests, recommendations, replacements, etc.)

➤   Surveys

Kulikowski concludes this informative article by providing tips on how to share documents, create folders to organize documents, and access tutorials using Google Forms.[1]

FYI

In April 2014, Google uncoupled standalone versions of Google Docs and Google Sheets productivity apps from Google Drive and released Slides, an app for creating and editing presentations. These apps (also offered within the central Google Drive service) are currently available exclusively for download to Android and iOS devices.

Note

1. Leah Kulikowski, "*Going Google: Using Google Drive for Library Communication and Collaboration*," accessed July 24, 2014, www.arsl.info/wp-content/uploads/2012/09/Cheat-Sheet-Getting-Started-with-Google-Drive.pdf.

16

Google Glass
Augmented Reality/Wearable Technology
www.google.com/glass/start

Overview

Wearable technology has been identified by industry insiders as one of the notable trends of the decade, and Google Glass—Google's patented wearable computer with an optical-mounted display—is credited for taking the lead in responding to mass-market consumer demand for this innovative technology. Using a clever marketing ploy, Google expanded its inaugural Glass Explorer program (developed in June 2012 and offered exclusively to developers) to include a diverse group of 8,000 beta testers, sometimes referred to as "Glassholes," through its invitation-only Explorer Program (#ifihadglass campaign). The strategy was so successful that when, in April 2014, Google officially offered the product online to the general public as an expansion of the Explorer program for the pricey sum of $1500, all units were sold out in a matter of hours.[1]

Google Glass wearers communicate via the headset in a hands-free format using natural language (similarly to users of Apple's intelligent personal assistant service SIRI) to convey commands, such as "Glass: record a video," "Glass: take a picture," "Glass: hang out on Google Plus," and "Glass: send a message to John Smith." Users can also request responses to specific reference queries like "Glass: what year was the U.S. Declaration of Independence written?" or "Glass: give me directions to the Library of Congress," or "Glass: translate 'Good Morning' into French." Glass purportedly looks like standard eyeglasses, is lighter than an average pair of sunglasses (weighing a little over 40 grams), stores 16 GB of data, is more streamlined than competing head-mounted displays and has a superior design, provides the wearer with a choice

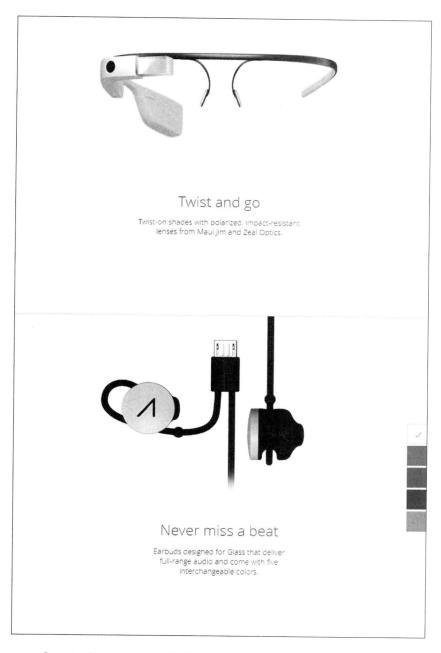

Twist and go

Twist-on shades with polarized, impact-resistant lenses from Maui Jim and Zeal Optics.

Never miss a beat

Earbuds designed for Glass that deliver full-range audio and come with five interchangeable colors.

Google Glass purportedly looks like standard eyeglasses, stores 16 GB of data, and provides prescription frame choices.

of four prescription frame choices, and, when activated, resembles a 25-inch color TV floating about 8 feet in front of the wearer.

Notwithstanding Google's vision for developing Glass "to put users back in control of technology" by giving them a simple, elegantly designed, hands-free device that makes "exploring and sharing the world ... faster and easier," the Explorer Program was controversial from the start, with fears voiced in several sectors regarding privacy, security, and safety issues. Of particular concern has been the etiquette and ethics of using the device in public, including the ability of Glass wearers to record people on video without their knowledge or permission.[2]

Among its attempts to proactively address questions and concerns about the device, Google added a FAQ page (https://sites.google.com/site/glasscomms/faqs) to its website. However, the company's initial efforts to reassure Glass users, privacy advocates, and the general public were not successful. In January 2015, Google halted the development of Glass and discontinued sales of the product through the Explorer Program.

As of this writing, Glass owners are able to continue using their devices but will not receive further software updates from Google. As reported by the firm, prototype testing—wherein the product was given to early adopters in order to use their feedback "to iterate and improve the design"—was the goal of the Explorer Program. Developers at Google stated that "early Glass efforts have broken ground and allowed us to learn what's important to consumers and enterprises alike," adding that they will continue "to work together to integrate those learnings into future products."[3]

Features

➤ Integration of Google Search—Google Glass responds instantaneously to user-issued commands such as translating a phrase into another language, solving complex math problems, finding recipes, verifying historical and political facts, issuing weather updates and flight information, and providing word definitions. The YouTube video "20 Searches through Google Glass" provides an overview of the extensive search capabilities of Google Glass (https://www.youtube.com/watch?v=r7MRdBHz-cg).

➤ Navigation—Glass's navigational feature is comparable to Google Maps as it provides detailed, real-time directions to various locations.

➤ Integration of Gmail and Google Calendar—Glass allows users to manage multiple Gmail accounts.

➤ Integration of Google Now—Glass provides regular updates on traffic, flights, and weather through Google Now.

➤ Phone Calls and SMS—By connecting via Bluetooth to smartphones, Glass users can quickly place phone calls or send text messages to their contacts through speech-to-text transcription.

➤ Built-In Camera—Glass users can take photos, video record events (720p HD video, LED illuminated display), and place video calls. The touchpad built into the side of Glass allows users to control the device.

➤ Glassware—Free Google Glass applications built by third-party developers called Glassware are available. Many of these apps created by Google Glassware partners offer more complex functionality.

➤ My Glass—The availability of Android and iOS apps, referred to as MyGlass, allows users to configure and manage the device.

How Cybrarians Can Use This Resource

Delivering Library Services with Google Glass

Google Glass, or simply Glass, has offered a fascinating lesson in the potential uses of wearable, head-mounted consumer technology. Reviews of the product, however, have been decidedly mixed, with some praising its application in, for instance, the health care sector (eg, for video streaming during live surgical procedures) and—as we have already discussed—many others expressing serious concerns about personal privacy, security, and safety issues.

Librarians have long been cast in the role of early adopters, seeking out new technologies that enhance and improve library services, programs, and collections, and Glass has been viewed with great interest by libraries and educational institutions. But the technology has also been hotly debated within the library community. As one critic noted, "Since its release in early 2013, Glass has come to represent far more than a technical innovation: it has sparked controversies related

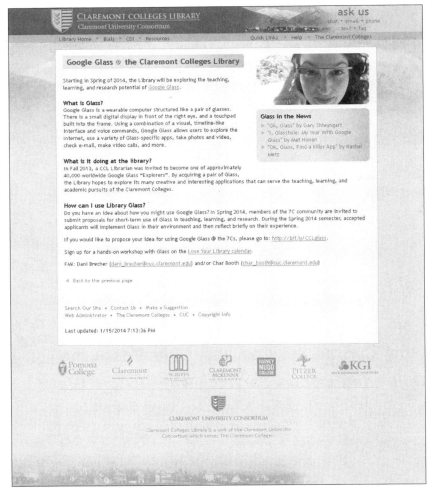

Google Glass is in use at the Claremont Colleges Library (California).

to privacy, awkward social interactions with 'Glassholes,' the legality of wearable technology, and technoelitism along gender, racial, and class privilege lines… early library adopters have begun to grapple with Glass within this context, confronting everything from the usual program design challenges to the unusual implications of appearing to 'endorse' a socially fraught Google product."[4]

While it might seem that Glass detractors have won the day, with the development of the product halted by Google in its current iteration, there is little doubt that wearable technology in the form of smart glasses and similar devices will enjoy widespread use in the near future. With that in mind, we will briefly consider here the experiences of librarians who have tested Google's pioneering product.

Jen Waller, interdisciplinary librarian at the King Library at Miami University (Oxford, Ohio) was privileged to be chosen as one of 8,000 Google Glass Explorers during the open beta phase of the program and charged with wearing, testing, and providing feedback about Glass. Waller's winning tweet, which led to her selection, contained the following text: "MT @glennplatt: #ifihadglass my students and I would show that learning is everywhere. We'd help lead our university redefine higher ed."

Waller welcomed the chance to experiment and evaluate the new technology, believing that "Google should be working with librarians on Glass because it is an information delivery tool" and librarians should "begin thinking about providing future services with Glass in mind." Waller shares the Google Glass with students and uses it as a teaching tool in the classroom, "I'm really interested in privacy and sharing and I like using this device to teach about it."[5,6]

The Claremont Colleges Library (CCL) in Claremont, California developed a Glass project with goals similar to Waller's: "[G]et Glass on as many faces as possible, and create a forum for critical conversations about the issues surrounding it and other wearable technologies." Despite initial skepticism at the start of the project, the CCL community reactions to Glass have been "nothing short of amazing," with comparable "interest from STEM, media studies, psychology students and faculty, and IT staff." This response further underscores the potential uses of Glass in academic libraries in areas such as "pedagogy, research, community lending and application development."[7]

FYI

An extensive library of videos highlighting Glass features and functionality can be viewed on the Google Videos webpage (https://sites.google.com/site/glasscomms/videos).

Notes

1. Colleen Curry, "Google Glass 1-Day 'Explorer' Offer a Sell Out," ABC News, April 16, 2014, accessed May 17, 2014, www.abcnews.go.com/blogs/technology/2014/04/google-glass-1-day-explorer-offer-a-sell-out.
2. "GLASS FAQ," GLASS, accessed May 17, 2014, https://sites.google.com/site/glasscomms/faqs.
3. Nick Bilton, "Why Google Glass Broke," *New York Times*, February 4, 2015, accessed February 7, 2015, www.nytimes.com/2015/02/05/style/why-google-glass-broke.html?_r=0
4. Char Booth and Dani Brecher, "Ok, Library Implications and Opportunities for Google Glass," *College and Research Library News* 75 (2014): 234–239, accessed May 24, 2014, www.crln.acrl.org/content/75/5/234.full.
5. "Miami U. Students Get to Try Google Glass," Fox 19, October 4, 2013, accessed May 24, 2014, www.fox19.com/story/23611483/miami-university-students-get-to-try-google-glass.
6. Don Hawkins, "Library Services and Google Glass," *LibConf.com* (blog), April 9, 2014, www.libconf.com/2014/04/09/library-services-google-glass.
7. Char Booth and Dani Brecher, "Ok, Library Implications and Opportunities for Google Glass."

17

Google Hangouts
Video Conferencing Service
www.google.com/hangouts

Overview

Google Hangouts is a combined instant messaging and video chat service enabling Google subscribers to send and receive instant messages, photos, videos, and emoji (animated GIFs) as well as initiate free video calls (individual or group). Launched in May 2013, this service is an amalgamation of two defunct Google products (Google Talk and Google Plus Messenger) and evidence of Google's attempt to unify and simplify its instant messaging services in response to increased competition from similar services (Facebook Messenger, WhatsApp, Apple's iMessage, and Skype).

Within Hangouts, users can post individual or group conversations (SMS/MMS), host a group video chat (up to 10 users at a time), send GPS location to contacts, share content in different formats (emoji, text, photographs, videos) and make free telephone calls (within the U.S. and Canada). A unique service offered within Hangouts is the ability to stream live local or global events such as conferences and webinars using the Hangouts On Air service. Streamed events are recorded, archived, and publicly available on Google Plus or a dedicated YouTube channel.

The service is accessible to anyone with a current Google Account and is available as a free download on multiple platforms and mobile devices.

Features

➤ Users with existing Google accounts have access to the Google Hangouts service. Once signed in to the service, users initiate Hangouts sessions with other Google Plus account subscribers. Within these sessions, they can do the following:

- Send and receive text messages via individual or group conversations

- Convert conversations into video calls by videoconferencing up to ten contacts in Google Plus circles

- Share, photos, emoji, animated GIFs, videos, and full screen views

Within Google Hangouts, broadcasters can stream live local or global events using Hangouts On Air service.

- Add special effects (sounds, backgrounds, props)

- Share information on current geographic location

- Archive conversations

- Initiate telephone calls (free calls to U.S. and Canada only)

- Sync Hangouts to start and continue conversations across multiple devices

➤ Google users can opt to broadcast live events by starting a Hangouts on Air session. These sessions can be streamed live or scheduled for a later date, and they can be viewed by multiple viewers in different locations around the globe. Hangouts on Air can be initiated by following these steps:

1. Sign in to a Google Plus account. From the menu options on the left navigation bar, select "Hangouts."

2. Select "Start a Hangouts On Air."

3. Provide a name and description for the Hangouts.

4. Select a specific date, time, and duration for the Hangouts.

5. Invite specific contacts (Google Plus circles or public viewers) to join the broadcast.

6. Link a YouTube channel by following the onscreen instructions (Hangouts On Air are broadcasted publicly on YouTube).

7. Click "Start Broadcast" to go live. After a short countdown, the Hangouts On Air session will start broadcasting on one of several available platforms: Google Plus profile homepage, a dedicated YouTube channel, or any website where the URL has been embedded.

How Cybrarians Can Use This Resource

Hosting Online Events

Phil Bradley, an information specialist and internet consultant who is known in some circles as the "U.K. search guru," maintains that Google Hangouts is a valuable resource that can provide benefits for a library or information service. On his blog, Phil Bradley's Weblog,[1] he provides a step-by-step guide to using the service (including screen-shots) and identifies how the Google Hangouts concept can be utilized to host the following types of events:

➤ Small training sessions

➤ Quick reference interviews

➤ Webinars and conferences

➤ Live author readings and book club discussions

Promoting Google Hangouts on Air Archived Collections

In addition to live streams, users have access to archived events. The Hangouts on Air website can be monitored and searched for past events relevant to libraries, and is increasingly being recommended by tech-savvy librarians as a source of innovative ideas for library services and programs. As of this writing, there were several sessions of note for libraries and information centers available on the site, including:

➤ "How to Make Your Website Faster" (categorized under Technology and hosted on May 3, 2014)

➤ "NASA & Made in Space: 3D Printing in Space" (categorized under Science & Nature and hosted on May 9, 2014)

➤ "Richard Branson Debates the State of Innovation" (categorized under Business and Finance and hosted on May 9, 2014)

FYI

Emoji are pictographs or smileys originally used in Japanese electronic messages and webpages. Similar in function to emoticons, they have become very popular and are now seamlessly integrated in smartphones and other mobile devices.

Note

1. Phil Bradley, "Google+ Hangouts For Libraries," Phil Bradley's Weblog (blog), May 4, 2012 www.philbradley.typepad.com/phil_bradleys_weblog/2012/05/google-hangouts-for-libraries.html.

18

GoToMeeting
Video Conferencing Service
www.gotomeeting.com

Overview

GoToMeeting from Citrix Systems is bundled web conferencing software with desktop sharing and video conferencing capabilities that facilitates online meetings between a host and group of attendees in real time. The marketing and sale of bundled web conferencing software like GoToMeeting, WebEx, and Adobe Connect is currently viewed as a profitable enterprise, as these products support the contemporary work environment where employers are constantly looking for new ways to reduce costs, save time, and boost productivity by eliminating unnecessary work-related travel.

For libraries, nonprofits, and business enterprises, GoToMeeting holds a significant lead in this fairly competitive arena by offering several built-in features that enable seamless online collaboration with onsite and offsite participants. Inherent advantages include usability (one-click meeting set up and start capability), intuitive user interface, minimal technical assistance to register for a meeting (attendees can join a meeting by clicking a URL link or typing in the meeting ID), integrated HD videoconferencing, audio and VOIP options, and application sharing (shared screens and webcams). GoToMeeting's availability on multiple platforms affords hosts and attendees the flexibility and convenience of participating in meetings via desktops, smartphones, and tablets.

GoToMeeting currently hosts about 30 million secured meetings every year.[1] The parent company, Citrix, has multiple locations, with its strategic headquarters located in Santa Clara, California and its operational headquarters in Fort Lauderdale, Florida.

(*Continued*)

GoToMeeting is bundled web conferencing software with desktop sharing and video conferencing capabilities.

Features

Individuals or organizations register online for the 30-day free trial by completing an online application on the product homepage (www .gotomeeting.com/online/start online) and signing off on the terms of service. Competitive subscription plans (GoToMeeting Essentials, Pro, and Pro+) offer unlimited usage for flat fees ranging from $7 per month (Essentials, hosting a maximum of 5 participants) to $31 per month (Pro+, hosting a maximum of 100). GoToWebinar, ideal for hosting marketing presentations and company events, and GoToTraining, an online solution for employee education, are two similar online meeting products offered by the company, complete with advanced features (toll-free numbers and self-service webcasts) and the scalability to host as many as 5,000 attendees.

GoToMeeting features offer seamless online collaboration:

➤   Start instant ad-hoc meetings or schedule future meetings

➤   One-click meetings with easy set up:

- Choose device

- Launch GoToMeeting

- Send invitations via phone, email, or instant message

- Attendees join the meeting for free by clicking a URL link or entering a meeting ID

➤   Option to record meetings and email an archived copy to attendees to replay at a later date

➤   Start scheduled meetings from Microsoft Outlook, IBM Lotus Notes, and other instant messaging services

➤   Availability of high-definition video conferencing services

➤   Desktop or application sharing with hosts or attendees, capable of sharing whole screens, programs, or files

➤   Shared keyboard and mouse control to facilitate collaborative file editing during online sessions

➤   Flexibility of switching out and instantly changing presenters during a collaborative presentation.

➤ Drawing and annotation tools to highlight and point to items of interest on screen

➤ Built-in audio capabilities allowing attendees to call in to the meeting or conference via phone or VOIP utilizing the computer's microphone and speakers

➤ Speaker identification to view current speaker, and ability to mute the speaker

➤ Text chat availability to allow public conversations with all attendees or private talks with specific participants

➤ Online administration center to allocate seats, monitor usage, enable or disable features according to security requirements, and track accountability with attendance reports

➤ Ability to integrate organization's logo on screen to brand meetings

How Cybrarians Can Use This Resource

Host Online Web Conferences, Webinars and Workshops

GoToMeeting offers an immediate solution for organizations where hosting web conferences, webinars, and workshops to facilitate online collaboration and training are essential goals. On the GoToMeeting website (www.gotomeeting.com/online/meeting/business-web-conferencing-solutions), the company provides case studies profiling innovative ways in which customers are using the service.

University Libraries at the Roger Williams University (Bristol, Rhode Island) use GoToMeeting as a web conferencing tool to support live (synchronous) web classes and meetings.[2] This web conferencing option is viewed as a valuable learning tool offering the following benefits to faculty, staff, and students:

➤ Connect via the internet from remote locations in a single meeting space

➤ Collaborate online using audio, video, and chat functions

➤   Conduct instant polls

➤   View and annotate PowerPoint presentations

➤   Share desktop applications

➤   Record and archive sessions as streaming videos for later review

FYI

GoToMeeting offers access to a library of online training videos (support.citrixonline.com/en_US/Meeting/videos) regularly updated with new content.

Notes

1. "GoToMeeting," GoToMeeting, accessed February 7, 2015, www.citrix.com/products/gotomeeting/overview.html.
2. "Roger Williams University, University Libraries: GoToMeeting," Roger Williams University Libraries, accessed March 17, 2014, www.library.rwu.edu/lib/learning-commons/id/tutorials/go-to-training-go-to-meeting.

19

Hootsuite
Social Media Management Service
https://hootsuite.com

Overview

Social networking sites are pervasive. It is not unusual for bloggers and other social media followers, as part of their daily regimen, to log in, read, and post content on networking sites such as Facebook, LinkedIn, Twitter, Google Plus, Foursquare, and Tumblr. The task of logging in to multiple accounts on different social platforms is time consuming and requires dedication, organization, and time management. Within organizations where social networks are perceived as highly effective marketing and promotional tools, invaluable to maintaining connections and communications with online clients, management of multiple social networks to showcase the organization's brand is often mandated as priority and requires assignment of dedicated personnel to perform social media tasks.

Hootsuite is a service that assists organizations in managing multiple social media accounts. Popular social networks are effectively launched and controlled from a secure, web-based, centralized dashboard. Advanced functionality includes tools for audience engagement, team collaboration, account security, and social analytics.

Highly regarded as a multifaceted social relationship platform for business enterprises and nonprofit organizations spanning a broad range of industries, Hootsuite has garnered a user base of millions of dedicated users. Included in this growing list of clients are brand-name heavyweights Virgin, Sony Music, CBS Interactive, Chrysler, the Red Cross, Tiffany & Company, H&M, and IBM. Hootsuite is located in Vancouver, Canada.

Features

➤ The basic Hootsuite plan is free for individuals and offers a host of features ranging from creating social profiles to accessing analytic reports and managing RSS feeds. Upgrading to the Pro or Enterprise versions provides immediate access to advanced features including geo-targeting, message archiving, URL customization, and enhanced technical support.

➤ Hootsuite's user-friendly dashboard has integrated functionality allowing users to easily create accounts, log in to the Hootsuite platform, and immediately start the process of monitoring, analyzing, and posting messages to multiple social networks.

➤ Hootsuite integrates with popular social network sites like Facebook, Twitter, LinkedIn, Google Plus, Foursquare, and WordPress. Hootsuite seamlessly incorporates the following functions into these networks:

- Facebook account integration functionality allows users to post updates, add images, and monitor feeds.

- Twitter users can send and schedule Tweets as well as monitor Mentions, Direct Messages, Tweets Sent, Favorited Tweets, and other content in dedicated streams.

- LinkedIn users can connect with clients, broadcast news, enhance recruitment efforts, and monitor industry conversations.

- Google Plus integration permits account management and publishing targeted messaging to circles.

- WordPress integrated management tools assist with scheduling and cross-posting content to multiple accounts.

- Hootsuite combines with Foursquare to enhance location-based social marketing and gaming functionality, permitting Foursquarers to check in at their location, alert friends, share tips, and participate in games and other events.

➤   Hootsuite provides a robust suite of social analytics applications that allow organizations to monitor and manage social campaigns, create customizable reports, and effectively measure their participation within social spaces.

➤   The Hootsuite app is available for iOS and Android devices and offers similar features to the web-based version.

➤   The Hootsuite App Directory (https://hootsuite.com/app-directory) is an additional resource for users, hosting a collection of extensions and applications (free and premium) built and maintained by third-party developers. Users can integrate these apps into their dashboard to create a customized experience. Free apps include Blogger, Evernote, Instagram, Flickr, SlideShare, Tumblr, and YouTube.

➤   Hootlet is a free bookmarklet (www.hootlet.com) for the Google Chrome browser that allows users to schedule posts and quickly and easily share content with social networks while browsing the web.

Hootsuite's user-friendly dashboard enables users to easily connect with multiple social networks.

How Cybrarians Can Use This Resource
Social Network Management

Hootsuite provides daily updates to its Case Studies page in order to demonstrate the versatility and popularity of its product.[1] The New York Public Library (NYPL) publicized its use of Hootsuite as a centralized platform to "coordinate a decentralized team of contributors and help manage over 100 social media profiles." Hootsuite's social media management services enabled NYPL to develop a brand awareness campaign and assisted in its efforts to streamline workflow, expand and maintain the library's social media presence, drive website visits, maintain a consistent voice and volume of messaging, and promote @NYPL as a discovery tool for library resources. Utilizing the service to achieve these goals has paid dividends, as the NYPL presently maintains a position as one of the leading public libraries on Facebook and Twitter, with traffic on the site increased by more than 350 percent in one year.[2,3]

FYI

Hootsuite University (learn.hootsuite.com), established in 2011, provides on-demand social media training and certification for thousands of students, educators, and working professionals.

Notes

1. "Hootsuite: Case Studies," Hootsuite, accessed January 20, 2014, https://hootsuite .com/resources/case-study.
2. Andy Au, "Empowering a Team with Scheduling and Assignment Tools—Case Study with the New York Public Library," Hootsuite Blog, February 8, 2011, blog.hootsuite .com/nypl-case.
3. Meghan Peters, "How To: Use Hootsuite as a Marketing Tool," Mashable (blog), May 11, 2011, www.mashable.com/2011/05/11/hootsuite-marketing-guide.

20

Infogr.am
Infographics Creator
https://infogr.am

Overview

Interactive infographics have trended quickly as individuals (bloggers, website creators, marketers, and researchers) and organizations (including libraries) increasingly use data visualization methods to narrate a great story, explain a complex problem, or portray compelling statistics. The mass appeal and extensive use of interactive infographics can be attributed to the tool's inherent features (portability and visibility) and its function (to simplify the process of presenting voluminous data to end users).

Infogr.am is a free online resource that offers users a dual service: creating and sharing infographics online, and searching for and discovering user-generated content (infographics and illustrative charts) within an online library. Creating and sharing infographics on the service can be achieved in four easy steps: picking a template; adding and customizing data (text, charts, videos, maps); embedding the infograph in a blog post or website; and sending the URL link to colleagues or friends.

Launched in February 2012, the service has facilitated the creation of more than "two million infographics and averages approximately 15,000 new sign-ups a week."[1]Infogr.am's headquarters are located in Riga, Latvia.

Features

➢ Users register for the service by creating a new account or signing in with an existing Facebook or Twitter account.

➤ Infogr.am's dashboard enables quick and easy creation of infographics with minimal technical skill required. Access to predesigned templates with various themes and a built-in spreadsheet ensure easy data editing and the flexibility of adding videos, maps, pictures, and text.

➤ Infogr.am supports the creation of multiple (more than 30) chart types including bar and line graphs, bubble and pie charts, tables, word clouds, and tree maps.

➤ Infographics created on the fly in Infogr.am can be previewed before saving to an online library or instantly published on the web for public viewing.

➤ Infogr.am supports the import of different file types including XLS, XLSX, and CSV.

➤ Infographics created on the service can be shared via email, embedded in a presentation, published on a personal website or blog post, or shared with followers through popular social networks Facebook, Twitter, and Pinterest.

➤ Upgrading to the PRO version allows users to download infographics as PDF or PNG files, share infographics privately with nonpublic URLs, protect infographics with passwords, and access additional design themes.

Infogr.am enables easy creation of infographics
and requires minimal technical skill.

How Cybrarians Can Use This Resource

Visually Market Library Services

Infogr.am provides cybrarians with the resources required to utilize data visualization in the marketing of library services. With the use of infographics, voluminous statistical data can be presented as interactive visually appealing graphics, simplifying complex stories that could become lost in translation. Inept presentation of complex data can (and often will) jeopardize an argument for the implementation of new products or services. Many libraries have shown the effectiveness of this tool by publishing library infographics on the social pinboard Pinterest (www.pinterest.com/yeoldefort/library-infographics).

FYI

Three additional infographics services currently compete with Infogr.am for top billing:

➤ Easel.ly (www.easel.ly)

➤ Creately (www.creately.com)

➤ Piktochart (www.piktochart.com)

Note

1. "Press Info," The Infogram Blog, accessed April 24, 2014, blog.infogr.am/press.

21

Instagram
Photo and Video Sharing Service
www.instagram.com

Overview

Instagram is a dual-function online photo and video sharing service that enables its users to take pictures and record videos, apply transformational digital filters, and share the finished product on a variety of social networking services, such as Facebook, Twitter, Tumblr, and Flickr. The service has gained notoriety, and a boost to what was already characterized as an expansive user base (300 million users), since its acquisition by Facebook in 2012 for the unprecedented sum of $1 billion. Technology insiders surmised that Facebook's efforts to acquire this mobile photo sharing service were not wholly based on profit margins and a push to gain leverage in the explosive mobile market, but were in fact an attempt to squash a threat to its dominance in photo sharing and social networking.[1,2]

Instagram co-founders Kevin Systrom and Mike Krieger, both harboring interests in photography and social media products, developed the service to solve what they perceived as three simple problems—they aimed to eliminate the mediocrity long associated with mobile photos by applying filters guaranteed to transform amateurish attempts into professional-looking snapshots; increase users' capability to take pictures and share instantly on multiple services; and optimize the sometimes tedious task of uploading photos, making the process fast and efficient.[3] Based on user response and industry insider analysis, this relatively new service has achieved its goal and is widely regarded as superior in a highly competitive field populated by similar services Flickr, Pheed, and Vine.

The Instagram mobile app is distributed through the Apple App Store, Google Play, and Windows Phone Store. Third-party Instagram apps are also available for BlackBerry 10 and Nokia-Symbian Devices. In October 2013, Facebook announced its intention to sell advertising on Instagram in a bid to push the photo service's earning and marketing potential. (Users, however, have the option of hiding promotions they do not like, and are encouraged to offer feedback about the advertising.)[4] This new revenue-earning strategy replaced an earlier move by Facebook, in late 2012, to change Instagram's existing Terms of Service and allow the app to sell images to advertisers without any compensation to those who had posted them. In the face of widespread negative feedback, Facebook retracted the policy before it ever went into effect.[5]

Notwithstanding the controversies over its advertising policies, Instagram continues to be popular and has an extensive user base comprising celebrities, entertainers, and politicians. The service was named App of the Year by Apple in 2011[6] and listed among *Time* magazine's 50 Best Android Applications for 2013.[7]

Instagram is a photo and video sharing app that allows users to take pictures, record videos, apply transformational digital filters, and share on social networks.

Features

➤ New users to this mobile photo and video sharing app must first install it on their devices using the following steps:

- Download the Instagram app from the device's online app store.

- Once the app is installed, tap the Instagram icon to open it.

- Tap "Register" to sign on to the service with an email or Facebook account.

- Create a username and password and complete the user profile.

- Tap "Done."

- Take a picture or video.

- Choose a filter (if desired) to transform its look and feel.

- Post the digital image or video directly on Instagram or share to social networks Facebook, Twitter, Tumblr, or Flickr.

➤ The intuitive interface with built-in tabs allows users to perform the following functions:

- The "Profile" tab is the hub for all captured photos, recorded videos, and lists of people followed by the user along with the user's followers. Within this tab, Instagram users can edit their online profiles and adjust account settings.

- The "Camera" tab allows users to snap, add a caption, and share photos with the Instagram camera or from the mobile device photo gallery. There is a wide selection of special effects or filters to digitally transform images (with names such as Slumber, Crema, Ludwig, Aden, and Perpetua).

- The "Explore" tab is useful for finding new people to follow, searching for other Instagramers, and exploring hashtags with keywords.

- The "Home" tab shows updated feeds of posted photos. These feeds are interactive, allowing users to like and add comments to them.

- The "News" tab displays all recent activity on posts, for example listing all the likes and comments on recent photo or video postings.

- The Photo Map allows users to showcase geographic locations where photos have been taken. This feature is enabled only when a photo is taken while connected to Wi-Fi or a cellular network, and the device has the capability of logging the coordinates where the photo was taken. To protect user privacy, adding location or adding to the Photo Map is turned off by default for all photos uploaded to Instagram.

➤ Instagram's Weekend Hashtag Project (www.tinyurl .com/jvuvqqv) is a series featuring weekly challenges with designated themes and hashtags. Followers who follow @jayzombie receive the weekend's project every Friday, and these projects encourage participants to post creative photographs or videos according to the designated theme by the end of the weekend.

➤ In December 2013, Instagram added Instagram Direct (blog.instagram.com/post/69789416311/instagram-direct), which allows users to send photos and videos to a specific user or group of users. This feature was added in direct response to the growing popularity of competing services like Snapchat (see Chapter 44), a photo messaging app that also permits sharing within a dedicated group.

➤ Third-party application developers can register on the Instagram Developer Site (www.instagram.com/developer) for full access to the Instagram API.

How Cybrarians Can Use This Resource

Marketing Library Services

The acquisition of Instagram by Facebook was widely viewed as a marketing strategy aimed at securing Facebook's longevity in the mobile market and increasing its already extensive client base. Libraries are riding the wave of this growing popularity and adopting innovative ways to use the mobile photo and video sharing app. Ellyssa Kroski shares "9 Interesting Ways to Use Instagram in Your Library":[8]

1. Show off your books

2. Show off your events and services

3. Go behind the scenes for a renovation project

4. Provide sneak peeks of upcoming events such as exhibits and author visits

5. Share photos of the office, showing librarians in their natural habitat

6. Take patrons along virtually by sharing photos from annual conferences

7. Introduce the library staff by sharing photos of new and experienced staff

8. Show off library spaces such as an Information Commons or Teen Room

9. Turn print marketing materials into digital surrogates

The University Libraries at the University of Maryland (College Park) created a blog post on how academic libraries are creatively using Instagram photo sharing capabilities to promote services, collections, and programs (https://storify.com/UMDLibraries/libraries-on-instagram).

FYI

Instagram was named by combining the words "instant camera" and "telegram."

Notes

1. "300 million: Sharing Real Moments," Instagram Blog, December 2014, blog.instagram .com/post/104847837897/141210-300million.

2. Josh Constine and Kim-Mai Cutler, "Facebook Buys Instagram For $1 Billion, Turns Budding Rival Into Its Standalone Photo App," TechCrunch, April 9, 2012, accessed March 24, 2014, www.techcrunch.com/2012/04/09/facebook-to-acquire-instagram-for-1-billion.

3. "Instagram: FAQ," Instagram, accessed March 24, 2014, www.instagram.com/about/faq.

4. Emil Protalinski, "Zuckerberg: Facebook Will Generate 'A Lot of Profit' from Instagram, Expect Ads 'When the Right Time Comes," TNW (blog), July 24, 2013, accessed March 24, 2014, www.thenextweb.com/facebook/2013/07/24/zuckerberg-facebook-will-generate-a-lot-of-profit-from-instagram-ads-will-come-when-the-time-is-right.

5. Julianne Pepitone, "Instagram Can Now Sell Your Photos for Ads," CNN Money, December 8, 2012, accessed March 24, 2014, www.money.cnn.com/2012/12/18/technology/social/instagram-sell-photos/index.html?iid=s_mpm#comments.

6. Hayley Tsukayama, "Apple Names Instagram Top App of the Year," The Washington Post, December 9, 2011, accessed March 24, 2014, www.washingtonpost.com/business/technology/apple-names-instagram-top-app-of-the-year/2011/12/09/gIQAg1VuhO_story.html.

7. "50 Best Android Apps for 2013," Time, accessed March 24, 2014, www.techland .time.com/2013/07/01/50-best-android-apps-for-2013/slide/all.

8. Ellyssa Kroski, "9 Interesting Ways to Use Instagram in Your Library," OEDb Open Education Database, October 4, 2012, accessed March 24, 2014, www.oedb.org/ilibrarian/10-interesting-ways-to-use-instagram-for-your-library.

22

Issuu
Digital Publishing Service
www.issuu.com

Overview

Hosting a banner "Publish like a Pro," a growing database of 85 million monthly active readers, and a digital newsstand of 21 million new publications, Issuu is one of the leading free digital publishing platforms available for authors to publish their works online. The service's steady advances in providing innovative technology that "preserves the experience of reading a print publication" has guaranteed a user base that ranges from established publishers in the fields of fashion, lifestyle, art, culture, sports, and global affairs to an emerging population of independent publishers who utilize the free tools on the platform to create magazines, catalogs, newspapers, newsletters, and reports.[1]

Issuu is optimized for popular search engines and supported on mobile platforms. Visitors to the publishing network can also search for content and customize their reading choices into online stacks categorized under subject areas such as art and design, business, fashion, food and cooking, photography, and science.

Established in 2006, Issuu is managed by a transatlantic team with offices in Copenhagen and California.

Features

➤ In order to have quick access to and immediate use of all the features required to start self-publishing, users must first create an account as a *reader* or *publisher* by selecting either role within a three-tiered service (basic, plus, or

111

premium service). Paid subscriptions (plus and premium) are available as 14-day free trials.

➤ Online publishing utilizing the service is accomplished in five easy steps:

- Signing in as a publisher
- Uploading a file in any popular document format from a desktop or mobile device

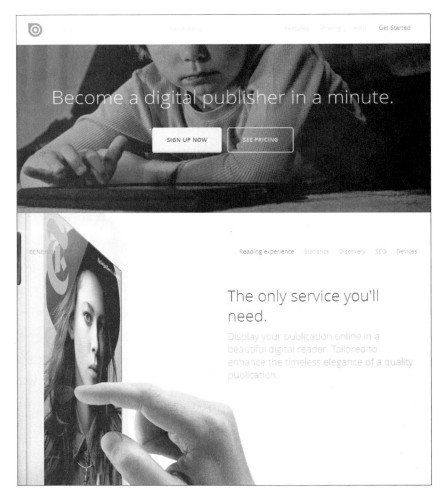

Issuu provides users with the tools to immediately self-publish their work.

- Providing a title, short description, and publication embargo date of the work (if applicable)

- Selecting the option to allow readers to download or preview the work

- Clicking the "Publish Now" button

➤ Built-in user customization within Issuu digital reader allows the selection of page numbers, page layout (e.g. autoflip pages), background colors, download options (the free version allows a maximum of 25 downloads), and user options such as integrating an audio URL and adding buttons or icons pointing to URLs.

➤ All publications developed using the Issuu platform can be shared and promoted instantly on social media networks, distributed via email, or embedded on blogs and personal webpages. Widgets are available to generate a URL and embed code pointing directly to the online publication.

➤ Detailed web analytics measure the performance of all publications, including the number of active readers, number of impressions, average time viewed, number of downloads, type of platform used to access the publication, and an infograph of readership.

How Cybrarians Can Use This Resource

Promote Access to a Free Online Digital Publishing Platform

Cybrarians can promote Issuu to library administrators, colleagues, students and faculty members at their institutions, as well as independent authors within their communities, as a free online digital publishing platform to produce self-published works. Immediate benefits include the following:

➤ Providing the library community with the tools to produce quality publications that promote new collections, services, and events to library patrons

➤ Enhancing the publishing efforts within the library community by providing the tools required to experiment, create, and host digital content in a shared virtual environment

➤ Sharing and distributing digital content with peer institutions and lifelong learners, allowing more audiences to benefit from an institution's virtual archive of knowledge and information

➤ Extending the libraries' social reach to users within popular social spaces

Libraries on Issuu

➤ University of Maryland Libraries (College Park, Maryland) used Issuu to publish its annual report and strategic plan (www.issuu.com/umdlibraries/docs/2013annualreport).

➤ Tipperary Libraries (Tipperary, Ireland) created a monthly newsletter using Issuu (www.issuu.com/tipperarylibraries/docs/tipperary_libraries_newsletter_augu).

➤ Christiana Care Health System (Wilmington, Delaware) developed pathfinders using Issuu for its consumer health libraries, to guide patrons to health information resources (www.issuu.com/christianacare/stacks/903463e6a2114251bb924f9da2fba892).

➤ Guides developed with Issuu promote rare books, manuscripts and special collections in fourteen Rhode Island research libraries (www.issuu.com/rwu_archives/docs/binder).

FYI

The Issuu blog provides regular updates on new features added to the platform (www.blog.issuu.com).

Note

1. "About Issuu," Issuu, accessed January 27, 2015, www.issuu.com/about.

23

Jumpshare
Cloud Storage/File Hosting/ Sharing Service
https://jumpshare.com

Overview

Like Dropbox (Chapter 10), Google Drive (Chapter 15), and Microsoft OneDrive (Chapter 33), Jumpshare is a real-time file sharing service that permits users to upload, store, and share files online. The current iteration supports more than 200 file formats, different content types (photos, videos, documents, presentations, spreadsheets, codes, fonts, and audio files), and multiple platforms and devices.

Jumpshare offers new users a free account with 2 GB of cloud storage space with a 100 MB limit for file uploads. Subscription-based accounts offering additional storage and features are also available. Uploaded files can be shared instantly via a URL link or sent via email.

Jumpshare was launched in September 2012 with a goal of setting itself apart from similar file sharing services—including Dropbox, OneDrive, and Google Drive—through its innovative approaches to some notable limitations of the competition. In February 2013, Jumpshare embarked on a radical site redesign with the goal of making the site more user friendly by affording users several new options for organizing files.

Features

> New users register on the product homepage (https:// jumpshare.com) to obtain a free account. New accounts are guaranteed 2 GB of free storage space.

> Jumpshare enables file sharing in real time via email, Facebook, Twitter, and a "Copy URL" feature.

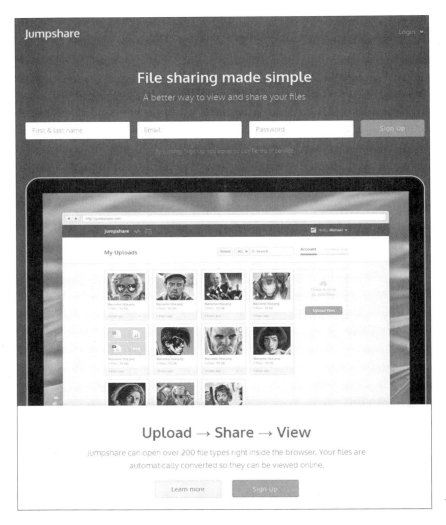

Jumpshare's redesigned homepage provides new options for managing, organizing, and storing digital files.

➤ Jumpshare's enhanced functionality allows users to view files immediately on desktops, tablets, and smartphones irrespective of platform, thus eliminating the need for third-party apps.

➤ The service maintains a dedicated webpage with a list of more than 200 supported file formats. The current list includes the following formats:

- Images (JPEG, Bitmap, GIF, PNG, TIFF, GIMP)

- Audio (MP3, Windows Media Audio, Ogg Vorbis, Real Audio File, MIDI file)

- Video (MP4, Apple QuickTime Movie, iTunes Video File, MPEG Movie, Windows Media, Flash)

- Font Types (True Type, OpenType)

- Documents (Apple Pages, Microsoft Word, Rich Text Format, Open Document, WordPerfect, PDF)

- Ebooks (Amazon Kindle AZW, EPUB, Mobipocket)

- Presentations (Open Document, PowerPoint)

- Codes (XML files, Cascading Style sheets, JavaScript, Hypertext Markup Language)

➤ Jumpshare's drag-and-drop functionality allows users to upload files into folders created and named automatically based on the number and types of files uploaded. Within the My Uploads page, users have ready access to editing functions that allow merging, renaming, copying, moving, and deleting files and folders. All files can be downloaded to a PC. Saved files are encrypted with AES-256 to protect against unauthorized access.

How Cybrarians Can Use This Resource
Productivity, Cloud Storage, and File Sharing

Given its real-time file sharing capabilities and support for multiple file formats, Jumpshare has been widely implemented in client communities for sharing codes (programmers), sharing video albums (photographers), and sharing large spreadsheets (data miners). A similar adoption seems likely within the library community as this free online service is ideally suited for the following tasks:

➤ Sharing documents with colleagues and library patrons

➤ Storing and accessing presentations for library conferences or workshops, library instruction sessions, or online tutorials

➤   Collaborating on shared projects

➤   Creation of online multimedia galleries to store content (video and audio) designated for sharing on social networks

FYI

Founder Ghaus Iftikhar developed Jumpshare out of frustration with file sharing services that lacked ease-of-use and had limited drag-and-drop capabilities (https://jumpshare.com/about).

24

Kaywa
QR Code Scanner and Generator
www.reader.kaywa.com/en

Overview

The Kaywa Reader is a two-dimensional (2D) barcode reader easily installed on mobile phones running on the iOS or Android platform. This popular app, available as a free download from Apple and Google Play, scans Quick Response (QR) codes and quickly resolves content leading to URLs, SMS messages, contacts, and text, audio, or video files. Kaywa also offers a free generator for creating QR codes.

The release of Kaywa and similar, if not competitive, barcode readers has proven to be a profitable enterprise for developers due to the widespread acceptance and popularity of QR codes in industries such as manufacturing, communication, and sales. Developed by Denso Wave in 1994, QR codes have achieved extensive marketing reach due to their inherent advantages when compared with one dimensional linear barcodes (EAN, UPC, ITF, and Code39). QR codes hold large amounts of data (numbers or letters) in any language, their reproduction or printout size can be reduced, and they can be read at high speeds from any side (omnidirectional or 360° scan).

QR codes have become so pervasive in many countries around the globe (Japan maintains the lead) that it is almost impossible for the average consumer to be unfamiliar with their existence and use in advertisements, marketing campaigns, store fronts, maps, magazines, books, newspapers, and even clothing. Kaywa's two corporate offices are located in Zurich, Switzerland and San Francisco, California.

The Kaywa Reader is a two-dimensional (2D) barcode reader designed to scan and create Quick Response (QR) codes.

Features

➤ The Kaywa Reader is marketed as lightning fast and easy to use. Unlike other readers, it does not require logging in to an account, and scanning with the Kaywa Reader does not require using the device's camera or pressing a scan button.

➤ Kaywa can be downloaded to mobile phones (www.reader .kaywa.com/getit) via direct download, or by downloading the installation files to a computer and transferring the files to a phone via Bluetooth or USB.

➤ Supported platforms for mobile phones include iOS and Android, Motorola, Samsung, and Sony Ericsson.

➤ The following steps can be utilized when using Kaywa to scan QR codes:

• Download and launch the application on a mobile device (smartphone or tablet).

• Point or hover the device over the selected QR code.

• Kaywa automatically detects the code and immediately guides users to content. For example, if the code encodes a web address (URL), the user is redirected to the website. If the code encodes contact information (vCard), the reader displays contact information and adds it to the user's address book. If the code encodes a text message, the user can view the message and share it.

➤ Kaywa supports the scanning of all types of codes and geolocations, provides support for multiple languages, and offers a free QR code generator (www.qrcode.kaywa.com).

How Cybrarians Can Use This Resource

Connecting Print and Digital Collections

In a hybrid environment where print and digital collections coexist, libraries are often challenged to make a connection between these two disparate collections and provide a single point of access for library patrons. Meredith Farkas, in her article "E-Discovery with QR Codes," presents a case for using QR codes as online discovery tools "connecting the physical library to digital holdings."[1] She identifies case studies where libraries are actively embedding QR codes in print collections to provide leads to their digital surrogates:

➤ Libraries at George Fox University in Portland, Oregon (www.georgefox.edu/offices/murdock) and the University of Huddersfield in West Yorkshire, U.K. (www.hud.ac.uk/library) place QR codes at the end of print journals or next to current issues to lead patrons to the online versions.

➤ At the Half Hollow Hills Community Library serving Dix Hills and Melville, New York (www.hhhlibrary.org/main.php), posters with QR codes that link to subject-specific pathfinders are placed in the stacks near books on relevant subjects. Farkas identifies this use of QR codes as an innovative way to promote patron use of pathfinders and other research guides.

FYI

Kaywa Reader has been identified by Google and Nokia as the QR code reader of choice.

Note

1. Meredith Farkas, "E-Discovery with QR Codes: Connecting Physical and Digital Content," *American Libraries,* February 27, 2013, accessed May 24, 2014, www .americanlibrariesmagazine.org/article/e-discovery-qr-codes.

25

Kickstarter
Crowdfunding Platform
https://www.kickstarter.com

Overview

With platforms in the U.S., U.K., Canada, Australia, and New Zealand, Kickstarter is arguably the world's largest online funding source for entrepreneurial projects. This crowdfunding platform is one of many such grassroots services (others include Indiegogo, GoFundMe, YouCaring, Causes, Giveforward, FundRazr, and Fundly) developed to harvest public funding for projects wishing to circumvent traditional sources of financing. Since its launch on April 28, 2009, the service has garnered more than $2 billion in pledges by more than 7 million people around the world, and these donations have been used to fund more than 78,000 creative projects in art, comics, dance, design, fashion, film, food, games, music, photography, publishing, technology, and theater arts.[1]

The platform's philanthropic model is designed to allow for a high level of public accountability and transparency. Following strictly enforced project guidelines, creators spend the time required to complete all aspects of project proposals, set funding goals and deadlines, build project pages, shoot promotional videos, brainstorm rewards to potential backers, and launch and share final projects with the Kickstarter community.

The major drawback for creators who devote the time and effort in developing projects is Kickstarter's all-or-nothing funding policy. If the project succeeds in reaching its funding goal by the allotted deadline, all pledges by donors are collected using Amazon Payments. If the project falls short, zero funds are collected.

As of February 2015, 40 percent of Kickstarter projects had reached their funding goals, with dance, theater, comics, and art projects ranked among the most successful.[2] Examples of Kickstarter-funded projects

Kickstarter is a crowdfunding platform developed to harvest public funding for projects wishing to circumvent traditional sources of financing.

include a Reading Rainbow project (2014); Rob Thomas's *Veronica Mars* movie (2013); Pebble, a smartwatch compatible with iPhones and Android devices (2012); the video game console Ouya (2012); and the virtual reality headset Oculus Rift (2012).

The Kickstarter mobile app is currently available for Apple's iPhone, iPad, and iPod Touch. Kickstarter is based in Brooklyn, New York.

Features

As a collaborative platform, Kickstarter enables creators and project backers to work together to fund creative projects.

Features for Creators

➤ To initiate the process of soliciting funding on the platform, creators first click the "Start" button on the "Create your project" landing page (https://www.kickstarter.com/start) and complete the online registration form, agreeing to the terms of use and privacy policy. Tips for structuring and running projects are available on the Kickstarter Rules page (https://www.kickstarter.com/rules) and Kickstarter Creator Handbook page (https://www.kickstarter.com/help/handbook).

➤ Creators assume independent control and responsibility for their projects. Kickstarter functions as a platform only, providing the resources required to promote and host the projects, and it is not involved in the development of the projects. Creators retain 100 percent ownership of their works.

➤ As an open platform, Kickstarter can be used by anyone to launch a project, with the caveat that the project must meet the criteria set forth in the guidelines (https://www.kickstarter.com/rules):

  • Creators must create projects which are honest, clearly presented, and easily shared with the world.

  • Projects must fit within one of the platform's creative categories.

  • Creators must abide by Kickstarter's list of prohibited uses, which includes projects represented as "charitable," or that offer financial incentives to their Kickstarter backers.

➤ Creators determine the funding goal and deadline for their projects.

➤ Creators can thank backers for their support in ways that do not involve financial equity or payouts. For example, funded authors and inventors may offer a copy of their finished work to backers, and funded artists may create a wall installation and distribute pieces of artwork to supporters when the exhibit ends.

➤ Prospective creators can discover new ideas by searching existing projects curated and profiled by the Kickstarter team. Categories include Staff Picks, Popular, Recently Launched, Ending Soon, and Most Funded. Searches can be limited by hash tag (e.g., #Library), city, or genre.

Features for Backers

➤ Backers are required to register with a Kickstarter account. To pledge to a project, backers must click the green "Back This Project" button on any project page, enter a pledge amount, and select a reward tier. Monetary pledges are collected only for projects that meet their funding deadlines. Project creators see the backer's registered Kickstarter name, pledge amount, and the reward selected.

➤ In most cases, initial support for projects is provided by fans, friends, family, and colleagues inspired by an innovative idea or motivated to pledge by the project's rewards. Backers are encouraged to look for creators who share a clear plan for how their project will be completed and have demonstrable experience working on similar projects.

➤ If a project is successfully funded, Kickstarter applies a 5 percent fee to the funds collected. For U.S.-based projects, pledges are processed by Amazon Payments.

➤ There are several ways to discover projects seeking pledges:

- The Kickstarter Newsletter (https://www.kickstarter. com/newsletters/weekly) is distributed every week and highlights potential projects.

- The Staff Picks (https://www.kickstarter.com/discover/ recommended) section on the homepage profiles projects selected by the Kickstarter team.

- Limiting to "Popular" searches when conducting a keyword search on the website is another option for discovering projects that are trending and approved by backers.

How Cybrarians Can Use This Resource

Soliciting Funding for Library Projects

Kickstarter's innovative and transformative approach to funding projects has found appeal within the library community, and there are libraries that have developed successful Kickstarter projects or are actively seeking funding on the site.

Library Projects on Kickstarter

A number of library projects have been successfully funded on Kickstarter (you can replicate this search for library projects using the strategy #Library on Kickstarter's main webpage https://www .kickstarter.com), including:

➤ The Nyack Library's (Nyack, New York) 2012 project to digitize back issues of *Rockland County Journal* (held on microfilm) was successfully funded with pledges totaling $3,530 (https:// www.kickstarter.com/projects/nyacklibrary/rockland-county-journal-digital-the-edward-hopper?ref=dropdown).

➤ The Little Free Library (Washington, DC) 2014 project to create a place where members of the community could "take a book and return a book" was successfully funded, with a goal of just $375 and pledges totaling $513. Similar successes have been achieved for other Little Free Library projects in Portland, Oregon; Saskatchewan, Canada; Baton Rouge, Louisiana; Winston Salem, North Carolina; Boulder County, Colorado; Lawrenceville, Georgia; Lakeville, Minnesota; Bargersville, Indiana; and Schuylkill Haven, Pennsylvania (https://www.kickstarter.com/projects/903652966/little-free-library-project-col-heights-washington?ref=discovery).

➤ Circulating Ideas: The Librarian Interview Podcast, a 2013 project by librarian Steve Thomas to expand an existing podcast stream to include in-person interviews at conferences and improve overall sound quality, was successful, with pledges totaling $2,930 (https://www.kickstarter.com/projects/201101936/circulating-ideas-the-librarian-interview-podcast?ref=dropdown).

➤   "Librii: New Model Library in Africa," a 2013 project from
        Architecture for Humanity DC to develop a digitally-
        enhanced, community-based, revenue-generating library
        on the frontiers of broadband connectivity was successful
        with pledges totaling $52,350 (https://www.kickstarter
        .com/projects/248645035/librii-new-model-library-in-
        africa?ref=dropdown).

FYI

The Kickstarter blog (https://www.kickstarter.com/blog)
provides updates on new projects around the globe
and offers tips for creators and backers.

Notes

1. "Seven Things to Know about Kickstarter," Kickstarter, accessed February 5, 2015,
   https://www.kickstarter.com/hello?ref=footer.
2. "Kickstarter Stats," Kickstarter, accessed February 5, 2015, https://www.kickstarter
   .com/help/stats.

26

Learnist
Digital Learning Board
https://learni.st

Overview

The "World's Knowledge at Your Fingertips," "Bookstore of the Future," and "Pinterest for Learning" are common phrases associated with Learnist, a crowdsourced collection of digital works. Taking a page from the playbook of popular social network Pinterest, Learnist contributors create digital learning boards by curating content from the internet on a wide range of topics. Web searchers are afforded the opportunity to browse a library of crowdsourced learning materials, discovering content that matches their areas of interest. This symbiotic relationship between experts and learners furthers Learnist co-founder Farbood Nivi's long-term goal for the platform to become a "smart RSS feed for learning, allowing anyone and everyone to share pieces of content and discover topics and lessons that are relevant to them."[1]

Learnboards offer learning opportunities for everyone, covering topics that range from niche areas in academia to broad interests such as business, technology, food and drink, health and fitness, sports, and entertainment. As learners browse through categories and featured content, they can add their favorite Learnboards to personal reading lists and share these lists with friends and colleagues. Reading lists are automatically synced across a user's web browser and mobile devices.

Premium content by notable experts—director Gus Van Sant, actress and activist Olivia Wilde, *Mythbusters* TV host Kari Byron, and author Brad Meltzer—is also available as an in-app purchase for $0.99 per board on iOS devices. This offering of premium for-pay content was planned as a first step toward "bringing in revenue;" however, there is assurance from the developers that the "vast majority of Learnist content will remain free."[2]

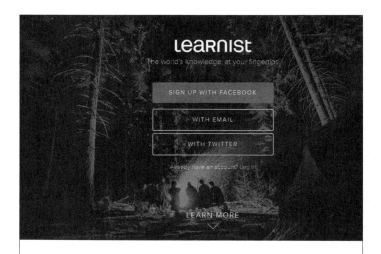

THE BOOKSTORE OF THE FUTURE

LEARNIST IS A CROWDSOURCED COLLECTION OF THE WORLD'S KNOWLEDGE

Basic Textile Embellishment Techniques

KATE MORRISSEY

Affordable Ways to Revamp Your Wardrobe

MARY B

A Brief History of the Origins of the Internet

CARLOS RODELA

Factors, Multiples, and the Distributive Property

ANN VASELIADES

Weird but Awesome Furniture

CARLOS RODELA

10 Scams to Protect Your Parents From

DAVID CHRISTOPHER MARINO

What Is Social Entrepreneurship?

NATHAN AYERS

Higgs Boson Theorists Win Physics Nobel Prize

LEARNIST

Learnist contributors create digital learning boards
by curating content from the internet.

Learnist was initially developed in 2012 for K–12 teachers and students but has expanded in scope and coverage across mobile platforms in an effort to attract, in much the same vein as Coursera (Chapter 7), a network of lifelong formal and casual learners. This knowledge-sharing portal presently supports the learning needs of millions of users and is available on multiple platforms and mobile devices.[3]

Features

Signing up to add or browse content on the service is free. New users register on the product homepage (https://learni.st) using their email, Facebook, or Twitter account to immediately create an online profile that includes an avatar, biodata, and cover photo.

Learnist for Learners

➤ Learners can discover content by using various search strategies, typing in keywords, or browsing Learnboards in curated categories such as What's New, Learnist Essentials, Recommended Boards, and a wide range of topics.

➤ Learners have the option to follow and add Learnboards to personal reading lists and access this content at a later date. Reading lists are automatically saved and synced across multiple web browsers and mobile devices. There is also the option to follow other Learners.

➤ Learnboards can be bookmarked and shared on Facebook and Twitter.

Learnist for Contributors

➤ Experts as well as casual contributors can create multiple Learnboards through a web browser. All potential contributors must first set up an account and user profile. After logging in, click the "+" (plus sign) and follow the on-screen instructions to add an image, board title, description, and category to embed content in multiple formats.

➤ Boards can be restricted to collaborators only or set to be viewed publicly.

➤   Boards created can be immediately shared on Facebook and Twitter if these social networks are linked to the user's Learnist account during the initial profile setup.

➤   The Learnist homepage features Learnboards selected by the Learnist staff. Contributors wishing to have their boards evaluated for posting as curated content can email a version to the Learnist team (submissions@learnist.com).

How Cybrarians Can Use This Resource

Providing Online Access to a Portal for Lifelong Learning

Learnist can be promoted to library patrons as a resource to discover expertly-curated content, collaborate with like-minded learners, and connect and share content across social networks. Librarians in specialized fields can create Learnboards in their area of expertise and share this content with a global audience. Libraries can also create boards to promote innovative services, current exhibits, and niche collections. The following is a sampling of Learnboards on library-related topics:

➤   Great Books for Food Lovers (https://learni.st/users/laurenatkinsbudde/boards/24278-great-books-for-food-lovers)

➤   The Best Writing Spots in New Orleans (https://learni.st/users/maggiemessitt/boards/74507-the-best-writing-spots-in-new-orleans)

➤   Successfully Sell Books on Amazon (https://learni.st/users/ElliottCNathan/boards/2337-successfully-sell-books-on-amazon)

➤   The Best Free Web Tools For Education (https://learni.st/users/gwen.duralek/boards/11101-best-free-web-tools-for-education)

➤   Staying Safe with Social Networking (https://learni.st/users/dave.stancliff.9/boards/64639-staying-safe-with-social-networking)

➤   The Importance of Makerspaces (https://learni.st/users/
dawncasey/boards/33414-the-importance-of-makerspaces)

FYI

The Learnist Digital Bookstore offers content from
bestselling novelist and comics writer Brad Meltzer,
who said about the service, "[W]ith the help of Learnist,
I get to reach my audience via smartphones, offer
them brand new content, and most of all, give them
something that's optimized for actual learning."[4]

Notes

1. Rip Empson, "With 1M Users Now On Board, Learnist Brings Its 'Pinterest For Learning' To Android," TechCrunch, September 18, 2013, accessed March 25, 2014, www.techcrunch.com/2013/09/18/with-1m-users-now-on-board-learnist-brings-its-pinterest-for-learning-to-android-as-it-looks-to-go-big-abroad.
2. Calvin Reid, "Learnist Releases App, Debuts Digital Bookstore," *Publishers Weekly*, February 27, 2014, accessed March 25, 2014, www.publishersweekly.com/pw/by-topic/digital/content-and-ebooks/article/61217-learnist-releases-app-debuts-digital-bookstore.html.
3. Ibid.
4. Ibid.

27

LiveBinders
Social Bookmarking Service
www.livebinders.com

Overview

Physical three-ring binders with color-coded subject tabs remain a staple in the workplace and classroom for organizing and providing quick access to documents and other printed resources. In an increasingly virtual environment where the majority of resources are available online, however, web users and researchers are looking for tools to access and quickly organize saved digital resources. LiveBinders, virtual three-ring binders, not only replace their physical counterparts in curating and organizing information, but also offer new opportunities to collaborate and share this information online.

Marketed as a social bookmarking service ideally suited for educational institutions and business enterprises, LiveBinders provides users with a free tool that can curate content on any subject; save this content in varied formats; quickly organize it using tabs, sub-tabs, and virtual shelves; display it in an aesthetically pleasing, creative, virtual three-ring binder; and (if desired) limit public access.

The LiveBinders app is available for iPads, iPhones, and Android devices. This on-the-go version provides ready access to all of the binders in the user's LiveBinders account and supports quick installation of the LiveBinder It bookmarklet to seamlessly add content while browsing the web. The developer of this service, LiveBinders Inc., is located in San Francisco, California.

Features

➤ New users can register for a free basic LiveBinders account on the product homepage (www.livebinders.com/login).

The LiveBinders app provides access to binders created
and stored on a LiveBinders web account.

This freemium account allows access to 10 binders. Storage size, however, is restricted to 100 MB, and file size is limited to 5 MB. Upgrades are available to premium plans (Basic and Pro) that provide unlimited binders, additional storage, increased file size, private and collaborator uploads, and access to the "email binder" icon.

➤   A library of featured binders (www.livebinders.com/shelf/featured#) provides ready access to binders developed within the community of LiveBinders users. Registered users can utilize these publicly available binders by adding them to their own virtual shelves, making mirror copies, presenting them as a slideshow within a web browser, and can share them by posting to Twitter or Facebook or embedding in a blog or website.

➤   Searchers can discover public binders by conducting keyword searches or browsing subject categories such as Art, Business, Craft/Hobbies, Education, Food/Recipes, Health, News/Politics, and Tech/Science.

➤   An intuitive dashboard provides the tools required to create, edit, organize, and customize online shelves and binders, add tabs and subtabs, upload content from multiple sources (web, computer, Flickr, YouTube, Dropbox, Delicious, and QR codes), access binder statistics (number of online views and downloads), and review comments.

➤   The LiveBinders Toolkit (http://www.livebinders.com/welcome/tools) is a veritable treasure trove of apps and third-party plug-ins (bookmarklets, "LiveBinder It" button) to embed LiveBinders in a blog or website. The Toolkit also provides online access to links for users wishing to download apps to their mobile devices.

➤   The LiveBinders Chrome App provides easy access to LiveBinders within Google's Chrome web browser.

➤   Tutorials, videos, and the LiveBinders blog are learning tools accessible from the product's main page.

How Cybrarians Can Use This Resource

Curate and Organize Online Resources in a Centralized Portal

Given the current explosion of content on the web, LiveBinders offer a cost-effective solution for librarians, educators, and business managers wishing to filter, curate, organize, and share online content. On the LiveBinders website, there are numerous testimonials and case studies that support the use of this product in creative ways:[1]

➤ ePortfolios—Promote LiveBinders to students as a tool to create eportfolios and showcase their work.

➤ Teaching Tool—Use LiveBinders to integrate a variety of online learning resources in a centralized location to provide end users with direct access to content in multiple formats (videos, text, images, web resources, PowerPoint, SlideShare, and Prezi slideshows/presentations, and spreadsheets).

➤ Administration—For new employees, curate links to create an online handbook or employee manual with information on the organization's best practices, policies, and resources.

➤ Professional Development—Curate resources on professional development (conferences, workshops, webinars, and eresources) and embed LiveBinders of these resources in blogs and websites to share with colleagues.

FYI

The LiveBinders Top 10 is an annual award presented to innovative and creative LiveBinders (www.livebinders.com/welcome/top_10?showsubtab=top_10).

Note

1. "LiveBinders: Education," LiveBinders, accessed March 17, 2014, www.livebinders.com/welcome/education?showsubtab=education.

28

Makerspaces
DIY Collaborative Workspaces
www.en.wikipedia.org/wiki/Maker_culture

Overview

New and emerging technologies have paved the way for libraries to be perceived as much more than brick and mortar (or even virtual) places for content consumers. Many libraries are now well established in the role of content creators or are actively acquiring the resources to partner with others to enhance content creation. Makerspaces are tangible evidence of this sweeping change, eroding the notion of the traditional role of the library as a passive provider that merely reacts to changing community needs. Many libraries are actively on board with the do-it-yourself (DIY) movement, offering a variety of tools that allow patrons to produce their own works within dedicated shared community spaces.

At the simplest level, Makerspaces—also referred to within the library community as creation labs, hackerspaces, TechShops, and FabLabs—are DIY spaces where innovators and entrepreneurs gather to create, invent, and learn. Within these fertile spaces, library patrons learn through hands-on experience, engaging in activities ranging from high-tech projects such as building robots and drones; creating digital music, movies, and games; 3D printing; and self-publishing with Espresso Book Machines; to more mundane activities such as writing workshops, jewelry and costume making, knitting, and gardening.

There are inherent advantages in incorporating Makerspaces into library services. These spaces can have a life-altering impact on community members who, long regarded as mere patrons, now have the "tools, access, training, and permission to make, hack, tinker and remake their world."[1] Just as libraries are reflections of their patrons,

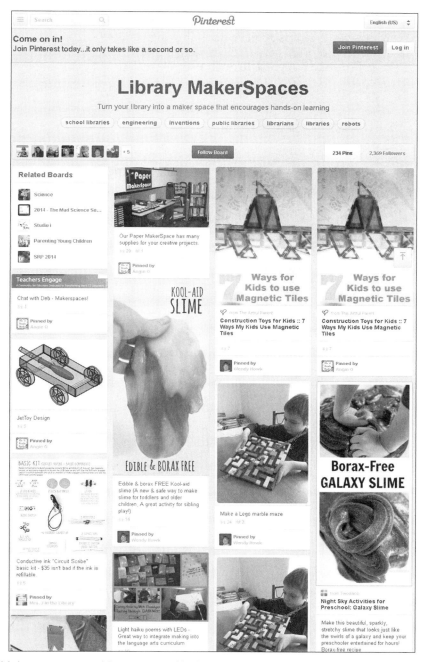

Makerspaces provide patrons with the tools, access, training, and permission to make, hack, tinker, and remake their digital worlds.

Makerspaces can reflect the needs and desires of their communities. Typically, Makerspaces achieve the following results:

➤ Promote learning through play

➤ Cultivate an interest in Science, Technology, Engineering, and Math (STEM) education and design

➤ Foster play and exploration

➤ Facilitate informal learning opportunities

➤ Nurture peer-to-peer learning and training

➤ Develop a culture of creating as opposed to consuming

➤ Provide libraries with an opportunity to reimagine and reinvent how they engage with community members, thus retaining and reinforcing their role as community hubs

➤ Encourage collaboration in a team-based library environment through engagement in a culture of making and innovating

➤ Promote working with community members as true partners, not as users or patrons

➤ Acknowledge environmental concerns by reconnecting consumers to the labor involved in producing what they use

Features

The following is a list of key features of Makerspaces established in library spaces:

➤ Promoted as incubators where patrons and experts come together to learn new techniques and train others in a skill.

➤ Developed with funding acquired through existing library budgets, grants, or by entering into cost-effective partnerships with corporate, government, or nonprofit organizations.

➤ Characterized by the provision of cutting-edge, technologically advanced spaces, equipped with hardware, software, and fabrication equipment that helps patrons transform their ideas into reality.

➤ Equipped with an eclectic mix of tools, running the gamut from the traditional (computer hardware, software, and digital media) to the practical (needle, threads, soldering irons, pliers, and hand tools) to the high tech (3D printers, Espresso print-on-demand machines, and licensed proprietary toolkits such as the SparkFun Inventor's Kit for Arduino, K'NEX kits, and littleBits.

➤   3D Printing is a staple resource of library-developed Makerspaces. This innovative technology allows users to create three dimensional objects (3D models) using plastic 'ink' and special software.

➤   Unique opportunities for the library to combine traditional art and craft programs (writing workshops, jewelry and costume making, knitting, quilting, and gardening) with high-tech experiences such as robot assembly, circuit bending, holography, welding, vinyl and laser fabrication, 3D printing, self-publishing, audio and video production, and digital music, movie, and game creation.

➤   Community sponsorship to assist the library in hosting a Maker-in-Residence (expert in a specialized field) and for developing MakerLabs. Both programs offer beneficial learning opportunities for patrons and library staff.

How Cybrarians Can Use This Resource

Proactively Developing Library Makerspaces: Providing a Space to Create, Build, and Innovate

In a successful and thriving Makerspace environment, "[K]ids gather to make LEGO robots; teens create digital music, movies, and games with computers and mixers, students engineer new projects, while adults create prototypes for small business products with laser cutters and 3D printers. For public libraries, they are places to promote community engagement. For academic libraries, they are places where students and faculty feel welcome to do classwork and research."[2]

The following is a sampling of libraries that have successfully developed Makerspaces as places to create, build, and innovate:

➤   Allen County Public Library in Fort Wayne, Indiana (www .acpl.lib.in.us) entered into a partnership with the Indiana-based nonprofit corporation TekVenture to create the

TekVenture Maker Station (www.tekventure.org/maker-station), a 50-foot mobile classroom equipped with digitally-controlled rapid prototyping and fabrication tools and assembly areas for makers. Tools in this Makerspace include a CNC router, milling machines, 3D printers, a metal lathe, small-injection molder, and a vacuum-forming prototype. Since opening in March 2012, TekVenture has offered more than 100 demonstrations and hands-on workshops to library patrons and other community makers interested in using digital design and prototyping tools. The library benefits from the ability to promote the Maker Station programs, and the company benefits by securing a permanent facility to deliver its innovative workshops. Library staff also benefit from the cooperative venture by receiving hands-on practical experience in building and creating in the lab.

➤ In July 2012, The Cleveland Public Library (www.cpl.org) opened what is considered Ohio's first makerspace in a public library. Located in the Louis Stokes Wing, the new space called TechCentral (www.cpl.org/TheLibrary/TechCentral.aspx) is marketed as an innovative technology and learning center designed for visitors to "create, collaborate and make cool stuff." Patrons can access one of nearly 90 computers, MyCloud's personalized desktop service, and TechCentral's MakerSpace lab, a cutting-edge space equipped with industry-standard technology and fabrication equipment along with the hardware and software required for innovative designs. Innovative TechCentral programs include 3D printing and scanning, vinyl and laser fabrication, and audio and video production.

➤ The Free Library in Fayetteville, New York (www.fflib.org) provides access to three unique Makerspaces: the Creation Lab (digital creation), the Fab Lab (fabrication of tangible objects), and Little Makers (a free play area that encourages children to imagine, create, and build). These labs are "learning environments that serve as gathering points for knowledge, tools, mentors and expertise."[3] The library relies partly on monetary donations from library patrons to support these creative projects. Promotional Maker events include

Maker Mondays as well as 3D printer certification, one-on-one sewing instruction, and knitting classes.

Providing Self-Publishing Services

A library offering self-publishing services to its community demystifies and makes transparent the creation of a book, from an abstract idea to a physical bound copy. Using tools like the innovative Espresso Book Machine (EBM), libraries can show aspiring authors that publishing a book is within their reach. An EBM, which can produce a 400-page paperback in five minutes, provides a measure of independence from the traditional book publishing process and fits perfectly with the DIY maker culture.

➤   The Sacramento Public Library (SPL) in California (www
      .saclibrary.org) installed an EBM in its community writing
      and publishing center, I Street Press, making it the go-to
      destination for patrons to self-publish and purchase print-
      on-demand books, as well as participate in writing and
      publishing classes.

   •   SPL Self-Publishing Services (www.saclibrary.org/
       Services/I-Street-Press/Pricing-en)—The SPL team offers
       a three-tiered, fee-based printing service that includes
       Print-only, Self-Publishing, and Premier Publishing.
       Writers subscribing to the Premier service are provided
       with a printed proof before the book goes into production
       and can upload published titles to the On Demand Books
       EspressNet database system for worldwide distribution.
       Self-publishers can also donate a copy of their book to be
       cataloged and added to the library's collection.

   •   SPL Print-On-Demand Services (www.saclibrary.org/
       Services/I-Street-Press/Books-to-Buy)—I Street Press
       links to the On Demand Books database and prints
       requested titles from this database for a fee. Titles in the
       database are drawn from Google Books, Random House,
       Macmillan, Simon and Schuster, HarperCollins, Penguin,
       Lightning Source, and other publishers. Self-published
       titles from I Street Press authors are also included in the
       database.

The Sacramento Public Library provides self-publishing
and print-on-demand services.

➤ The Brooklyn Public Library (New York, www
.bklynpubliclibrary.org) acquired its EBM in January 2012
to serve Brooklyn's creative community of writers, artists,
photographers, and programmers. The library also created
the Shelby White and Leon Levy Information Commons
(www.bklynpubliclibrary.org/locations/central/infocommons)
with this community in mind. The Information Commons
is equipped with a 36-seat training lab that offers classes,
workshops, and other events designed to foster individual
learning and collaborative work.

FYI

The Espresso Book Machine is a book robot available
from On Demand Books (www.ondemandbooks.
com) that prints, binds, and trims quality paperbacks
in minutes—or just long enough for the user to go
get an espresso while waiting for the process to be
completed.

Notes

1. Lauren Britton, "The Makings of Maker Spaces, Part 1: Space for Creation, Not Just
Consumption," The Digital Shift, October 1, 2012, accessed March 26, 2014, www
.thedigitalshift.com/2012/10/public-services/the-makings-of-maker-spaces-part-1-
space-for-creation-not-just-consumption.
2. "Manufacturing Makerspaces," American Libraries, February 6, 2013, accessed March
26, 2014, www.americanlibrariesmagazine.org/article/manufacturing-makerspaces.
3. "Fayetteville Free Library Makerspaces—Fayetteville Free Library U.S.," Public
Libraries Connect, accessed March 26, 2014, www.plconnect.slq.qld.gov.au/
networking/public-library-showcase/technology-trendsetters.

29

Mendeley
Reference Management and
Collaboration Service
www.mendeley.com

Overview

Mendeley is a free reference management service designed to support researchers in their efforts to discover, store, organize, and share research papers, as well as automate the process of generating bibliographic citations. Mendeley's strength as a reference manager, when compared with competing services such as EndNote, RefWorks, Zotero, and Papers (see the comparable products chart at www.mendeley.com/compare-mendeley), lies in its dual functions as reference manager and academic social network. Mendeley users can integrate its reference management application, Mendeley Desktop, with the social networking sharing and collaborative capabilities of Mendeley Web. Mendeley mobile apps are currently only available for iOS devices (iPhones, iPads, and iPod Touch), but Android app development is ongoing with an expected launch in 2015.

Managing research in Mendeley begins by searching for and adding PDFs and other documents from multiple sources (desktop, web, and academic databases), then organizing and managing these documents within Mendeley's personalized libraries; generating bibliographies using supported plug-ins (Microsoft Word and Open Office); syncing saved resources across desktops, websites, and mobile devices; and sharing saved research data within online social networks.

Founded in 2008 by German graduate students to support academic research, the service was acquired by publishing giant Elsevier in 2013 with the goal that "Mendeley will become Elsevier's central workflow, collaboration and networking platform."[1] In a bid to suppress negative feedback from Mendeley's existing customers (including librarians)

146

who questioned the future of this open and social educational data service now acquired by a proprietary business enterprise, Elsevier gave the assurance that it will continue to offer a free version of the service with 2GB of free storage space, will accelerate research and development efforts to enhance existing features, and provide seamless operability with its signature products: SciVerse, Scopus, and ScienceDirect.[2] Mendeley supports active users in North America, Europe, and Asia.

Features

➤ Researchers register on the product homepage (www.mendeley .com) by completing the online form provided, including their name, password, field of study, and academic status. Completing the online research profile increases a researcher's impact within the Mendeley network, as information is supplied on the user's biography, professional experience, education, publications, disciplines supported, research interests, organizational affiliations, awards, and consulting experience.

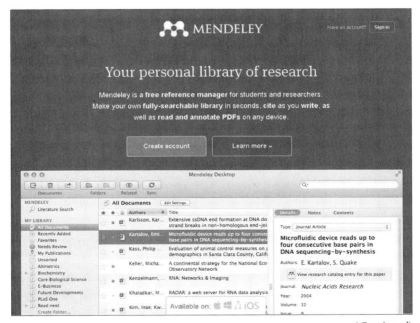

(Continued)

How Mendeley helps

Five ways Mendeley helps you

Your research, anywhere

Securely stored and accessible across devices, you can search and sort your references, documents and notes in one place - right down to the keyword you're looking for.

Read and annotate on the go

Use Mendeley online or offline to access your PDFs on the move. Highlight, annotate and add sticky notes to capture your thoughts in context.

Citation and bibliographies

Generate your citations and bibliography in the style of your choice - in just a few clicks. Compatible with Microsoft Word, LibreOffice and Bibtex.

Sharing and collaboration

Publicly or privately share reading lists, references or full-text articles. Create groups to tackle research assignments, share feedback and write papers with your collaborators.

Showcasing your work

Connect with colleagues, peers or classmates to follow their research output. Showcase your published research to millions around the world.

Mendeley is a reference management service and academic network.

➤   Mendeley Desktop, a standalone application for managing
and sharing research, is available as a free download for Mac,
Windows, and Linux users (www.mendeley.com/download-
mendeley-desktop). Mendeley Web (www.resources.mendeley
.com/Mendeley_Web/introduction), the free social network
version that supports monitoring research trends and
connecting to researchers with shared subject interests, is
available to users who register with an online account.

➤   Mendeley's basic package includes 2 GB of free storage and
backup space. There is a fair share of support documentation
(video tutorials, blog posts, and user guides) to get new users
started on the service.

➤   Mendeley's main features support the following functions:

  •   Reference and document management (organization
      of PDFs and other documents, citations plug-ins,
      annotations, highlighting, and cross-platform syncing
      across multiple devices)

  •   Knowledge discovery (access to open databases, full-text
      searches across personal papers, community tag searches,
      personalized paper recommendations, and readership
      statistics)

  •   Collaboration (public and private groups, social networks,
      and newsfeeds)

  •   General Technology (web and desktop apps, compatibility
      with most web browsers, iOS apps, library systems
      integration, and product feedback forum)

  •   Metadata extraction technology (extraction of DOIs,
      PubMed IDs, arXiv IDs, embedded metadata, and citation
      details from PDFs)

➤   Adding references to a Mendeley My Library account can be
simplified to five steps: *add, organize, discover, share* and *sync*:

  1. Add—Researchers have several options available to add
      research data to personal libraries. Search and add PDFs
      and other documents from a desktop using the drag-and-
      drop feature. Browse the web and add resources using a

bookmarklet compatible with most web browsers. Search Mendeley's open database of academic literature (over one million documents). Import and transfer research libraries created in other reference managers such as Zotero, EndNote, and Papers.

2. Organize—Manage documents in a personalized My Library by organizing into folders and adding annotations, sticky notes, and highlights. Sort documents saved in My Library by filters (authors, titles, journals, recently added, and favorites). Generate citations and bibliographies in supported plug-ins for Microsoft Word, Open Office, and BibTex. Utilize a range of citation styles (including APA, Chicago Manual of Style, Harvard, Modern Language Association, Turabian and Bluebook).

3. Discover—Integrate a bookmarklet to the toolbars of most web browsers via the Web Importer (www.mendeley.com/import), allowing the import of papers, webpages, and other documents directly to My Library when searching the web and Mendeley's supported academic databases, including ACM Portal, IngentaConnect, ScienceDirect, EBSCO, JSTOR, PubMed, Scopus, Wikipedia, Wiley Online Library, SpringerLink, and WorldCat.

4. Share—Connect with colleagues by registering with online groups in the user's areas of interest. Collaborate and share research data publicly or privately.

5. Sync—Save research data on Mendeley's cloud-based servers and personal libraries that are synchronized to enable quick access to data on the web, desktops, and mobile devices.

How Cybrarians Can Use This Resource
Research and Publishing

The Mendeley user base is extensive and comprises researchers in all types of communities, such as undergraduate and graduate students, postdoctoral researchers, professors and lecturers, commercial R&D professionals, and government researchers. For academic librarians working in institutions where publishing is a requirement for tenure and promotion, or for those wishing to pursue publishing as an avenue to contribute new research, Mendeley is a useful tool for pursuing independent work or for working collaboratively with colleagues, as it supports the following tasks:

> Saving and organizing links to online resources (books, journal articles, and websites) for quick and easy access anywhere, anytime, across all devices

> Sharing research resources with colleagues on social networks

> Discovering new publishing leads in specific subject fields by exploring the personal libraries of other Mendeley users

> Generating and sharing bibliographies using one of the standard citation styles supported by Mendeley

> Exploring the "recommend related document" feature to discover and stay current with research activity in specialized subjects

FYI

Mendeley's innovative research platform has won several awards including, in 2009, TechCrunch Europe's Best Social Innovation Which Benefits Society.[3]

Notes

1. Alice Bonasio, "Q&A: Team Mendeley Joins Elsevier," Mendeley Blog, April 9, 2013, accessed March 17, 2014, blog.mendeley.com/press-release/qa-team-mendeley-joins-elsevier.
2. Ibid.
3. "Mendeley," CrunchBase, accessed March 17, 2014, www.crunchbase.com/organization/mendeley.

30

Microsoft Office Online
Productivity Tool
https://office.live.com

Overview

Microsoft Office Online (previously known as Office Web Apps) is a free online version of Microsoft's proprietary software Microsoft Office. This freeware variant of the globally recognized office suite is packed with lightweight, web-based versions of Microsoft productivity software commonly used in the office and home environment (Word, Excel, PowerPoint, and useful add-ons Outlook, OneNote, OneDrive, an online calendar, and contact list). Microsoft Office Online provides users with the browser-based productivity tools required to create documents, spreadsheets, and presentations, record notes, send email, and save, store, and share files in the cloud.

This free offering from Microsoft invariably draws comparison with similar office suites such as Google Docs, Zoho, and Open Office. Executive vice president and chief marketing officer Chris Capossela believes the advantage that Microsoft holds is brand recognition and familiarity with the product: "[O]ffice web applications complement the Office suite and Office Mobile applications" thus enabling "customers to share and collaborate more effectively through the familiar Office experience."[1]

There is also the recognition by Microsoft that, within an increasingly mobile environment, tech-savvy customers own and have access to multiple devices and are demanding products that not only offer seamless integration between their browsers, PCs, and mobile devices, but also enhance online collaboration with social contacts. Capossela asserts that Office Online offers these advantages: "[W]e know our customers use their PC, phone, and browser in different situations depending on their needs. The browser is particularly important when

Microsoft Office Online is packed with lightweight versions of its productivity software, including Word, Excel, and PowerPoint.

you need to access and edit files while traveling, working remotely, or using someone else's PC. Together, these new tools enable new styles of community-based collaboration where multiple people can contribute simultaneously to various work through the internet."[2]

Microsoft Office Online was first released as Office Web Apps in October 2008 and rebranded in February 2014.

Features

> New users must first create a Microsoft account (https:// login.live.com) using an email address from Outlook, Yahoo, or Gmail and providing the following information: first/ last name, user name, password, country, zip code, date of birth, and telephone number. Users already registered with Microsoft can enter the same login credentials used for signing in to Windows PC, tablet, smartphone, Xbox Live, Outlook, or OneDrive.

> Office Online (https://office.com/start/default.aspx) runs within supported web browsers (Internet Explorer, Firefox,

Google Chrome, and Safari). There is no need to download or install additional software. The suite includes free templates for the creation of all types of documents and presentations (flyers, calendars, budgets, invoices, school projects, photo albums, and slideshows).

➤ Once signed into the online account, users have immediate access to free online lightweight versions of Microsoft productivity tools: Word, Excel, PowerPoint, OneNote, OneDrive, Outlook, Calendar, and People (online contacts).

➤ Documents, spreadsheets, presentations, and notebooks created in Office Online are stored in OneDrive (formerly called SkyDrive—see Chapter 33). Documents and files created can be shared with contacts using a URL link (automatically generated within the service) and on social networks Facebook, Twitter, and LinkedIn. OneDrive also facilitates working collaboratively on documents, presentations, spreadsheets, and notebooks by allowing colleagues to view changes in real time.

➤ The Microsoft Office Template website (https://odcom .officeapps.live.com/Templates) provides free online templates, including daily task lists, fitness plans, business project plans, resumes, seasonal calendars, and event flyers. These templates can be imported and saved to Microsoft Online programs.

➤ In keeping with the company's "cloud first, mobile first" marketing strategy, Microsoft has developed free Office versions for the iPad, iPhone, and Android devices. These apps feature similar integration and comparable functionality to their web versions.

How Cybrarians Can Use This Resource

Promote a Suite of Collaborative Online Productivity Tools

Office Online combines Microsoft Office's suite of productivity software (Word, PowerPoint, and Excel) with its cloud-based file sharing service OneDrive to facilitate real-time co-authoring activities. Within this web-based environment, colleagues can work collaboratively to create documents, spreadsheets, presentations and notebooks, save their work online in OneDrive, and use social networks to easily share with others in real time.

FYI

Microsoft Office Online was first released as Office Web Apps in October 2008.

Notes

1. "Microsoft to Extend Office to the Browser," Microsoft News Center, Oct. 28, 2008, accessed March 30, 2014, www.microsoft.com/en-us/news/features/2008/oct08/10-28pdcoffice.aspx.
2. Ibid.

31

Mobile Apps for Libraries
Mobile Applications
www.en.wikipedia.org/wiki/Mobile_app

Overview

The popular expression, "There's an app for that," is indicative of the pervasive nature of application software, known the world over as apps, currently being designed and developed to run on mobile devices. The widespread use of apps in an increasingly mobile world has led to the creation of profitable enterprises for developers and distributors alike. According to research firm Gartner, "by 2017, mobile apps will be downloaded more than 268 billion times, generating revenue of more than $77 billion and making apps one of the most popular computing tools for users across the globe."[1] The mobile app market is dominated by heavyweights such as Amazon, Apple, Google, and Microsoft.

Apps have become increasingly popular as more mobile subscribers are opting to download and use apps instead of visiting a vendor's native site via their web browsers. This trend is reflected in usage and download data readily available from most platforms. For example, in 2015 Apple announced that the first week of January set a new record for billings from the App Store, with customers spending nearly half a billion dollars worldwide on apps and in-app purchases.[2]

This rising popularity, global acceptance, and widespread usage of mobile apps can be attributed to a number of factors: the relative ease with which users are able to download these applications from the distributors' platforms to their target mobile devices; the nearly infinite number of freemium apps available; the relatively low prices for commercial apps; and the ability to use apps to perform real-time

Apple's App Store displays a range of apps to consumers.

tasks related to productivity, information retrieval, gaming, banking, entertainment, and online shopping.

Features

➤   Mobile apps are available (downloadable for free or for a fee) through digital distribution platforms or application stores typically developed by the owner of the mobile device operating system/platform. Popular application stores include the Amazon Appstore, Apple App Store, BlackBerry World, Google Play, Nokia Store, Samsung Apps, and the Windows Phone Store.

➤   App marketplaces or application stores are designed as online stores, allowing consumers to browse through different categories and genres of applications (free, productivity, multimedia, and games), view summaries and reviews, purchase (when required), and automatically download and install the apps on their mobile devices. Notifications and alerts about updates are also regularly available.

➤   Most app marketplaces serve as incubators for creative and innovative developers who utilize the available infrastructure to develop third-party applications. Some companies view this as a profitable venture and are quick to assert strict restrictions and regulations on app developers. For example, companies may require that all apps are subject to review, apply developer fees, or secure commissions on revenues for apps sold through their online stores.

How Cybrarians Can Use This Resource

Promoting Apps Developed for Libraries

Within the library world, the rapid development, widespread availability, and easy access to a variety of mobile apps in different genres has made discovery and promotion challenging tasks. Fortunately, there are a number of online resources available to assist in the creation, curation,

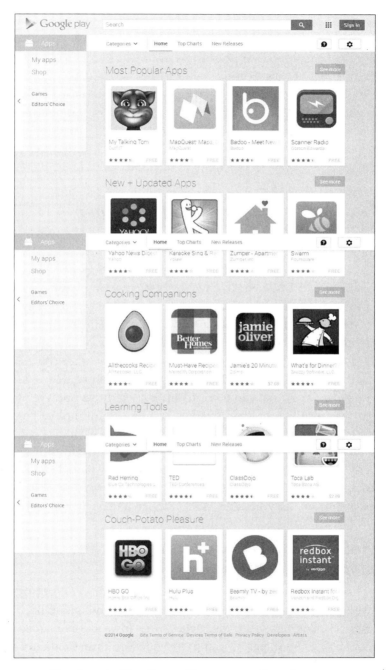

The Google Play Store offers apps to Google users.

review, and promotion of a wide range of apps relevant to library services. One such example is the library guide "Mobile Apps" (www .libguides.fau.edu/MobileApps-boca) developed by Florida Atlantic University (Boca Raton, Florida), with active weblinks to information about mobile apps useful for library users and librarians. A comprehensive index on the landing page allows direct access to mobile apps in multiple categories including Art, Museums and Fairs, Barcode Readers, Books and Articles, Health and Medical, History, Libraries, Reference, and Science. A "Best of" list recommends top-rated apps for all platforms.

Professional Development and Training for Library Users

Learning about mobile technologies to advance professional development, and promoting apps with features and functionalities that assist patrons in areas such as renewing and reserving books, booking study rooms, accessing ebooks, connecting to library social networks, organizing reading lists and course materials, and scheduling reference and research instruction sessions, are essential tasks for all librarians. *American Libraries*, the flagship journal of the American Library Association (ALA), in its July 2013 issue shared with readers a helpful guide to 40 free apps that can be easily integrated into a library "mobile strategy" and also "provide innovative services, useful mobile content, and opportunities for outreach."[3] Most of the apps listed are compatible with Android and iOS (Apple) devices and include well-known productivity apps (Amazon Books, Google Maps, Google Translate, and Dropbox) and lesser-known, but equally useful mobile apps (AccessMyLibrary, EasyBib, Free Wi-Fi Finder, and MyCongress).

Promoting and Prototyping Apps Developed by Libraries

Many libraries are designing apps to extend access to collections, services, and programs. Innovative uses include enabling online access to previously closed collections, developing instructional videos for on-the-go users, and integrating apps provided by library database vendors to allow for vetted research from mobile devices. A select sampling of these types of apps includes:

➤ Biblion: The Boundless Library, from the New York Public Library (www.exhibitions.nypl.org/biblion), available on iTunes and given the 2011 Apple Education App of the Year Award, "immerses users in rare items from The New York Public Library's vast collections, providing context while also allowing for serendipitous discoveries." Collections highlighted and promoted in this inventive manner include the 1939 New York World's Fair and *Frankenstein*.

➤ In 2012, the Castro Valley Library (www.guides.aclibrary .org/CastroValley) in California hosted programmers and designers in an app challenge or "hackathon" called the Alameda County Apps Challenge.[4] This hackathon was promoted as an event primarily geared towards encouraging participants to tap into the county's databases, conduct research, and develop apps supportive of the community. The app awarded first place in the Challenge was aptly called "BookIT," an app that enabled readers to scan a book's barcode with a smartphone in order to determine that title's availability in the library and to reserve it immediately.

➤ The Naperville Public Library (Illinois) launched a mobile app (www.naperville-lib.org/node/306), developed by Boopsie Inc., that enables patrons to easily access all the library's resources from their mobile devices. The library also developed a Mobile App Tutorial instructing patrons on how to download the app to Android and iOS devices, use the app to check out books, download ebooks and audiobooks, and access the "Ask a Librarian" reference service as well as the library's mobile databases. The app can be downloaded from the native mobile device app store, from the Boopsie website (www. naperville.boopsie.com), or scanned to a device using a QR code.

➤ The Orange County Library System, Florida (OCLS) Shake It! App (www.ocls.info/downloadables/mobileapps.asp) is available for both Android and Apple devices. Patrons in this large Florida county library system can discover titles in the catalog (audiobooks, movies, novels, and biographies) by shaking their device. The OCLS mobile-friendly resource pages provide an updated list of all apps developed by OCLS and major library vendors.

Promoting Apps Developed by Library Vendors

The following is a selection of apps developed by vendors that are widely available for all libraries to integrate into collections, services, and programs:

- ➤ OverDrive Media Console (www.app.overdrive.com)—Available for download on all major platforms, OverDrive Media Console app enables patrons to access ebooks, audiobooks, and videos from their local libraries while on the go.

- ➤ Library Anywhere (www.librarything.com/forlibraries/ index.php?page=libanywhere)—Developed by LibraryThing, Library Anywhere takes a library's catalog and homepage and instantly creates a mobile version that allows users to search the catalog, place holds on titles, renew library materials, and view library programs and events. Library Anywhere is available as a native app for Apple and Android smartphones.

- ➤ Gale/Cengage Learning AccessMyLibrary (www.solutions. cengage.com/apps)—This location services app uses GPS to find libraries within a 10-mile radius of a patron's location and provides free, unlimited access to authoritative Gale online resources.

- ➤ OCLC Developer Network website (www.oclc.org/developer/ home.en.html)—This open source code sharing network provides a virtual sandbox for developers to create and promote innovative apps that engage users, streamline workflows, improve library catalogs, and boost mobile services.

- ➤ Goodreads (https://www.goodreads.com)—Readers can discover and share books on Goodreads, described as the world's largest social network for readers and book recommendations.

➤ Mango Languages (www.mangolanguages.com)—Mango Languages' Library Edition App provides free access to more than 60 foreign language courses and 17 English courses taught in the user's native language.

➤ EBSCOhost (www.ebscohost.com)—EBSCOhost has developed iOS and Android apps to provide library users with immediate access to premium EBSCOhost databases.

➤ OneClickdigital (www.oneclickdigital.com)—This app enables users to download and transfer audiobooks from local libraries subscribed to the OneClickdigital lending platform.

FYI

In 2010, "app" was designated Word of the Year by the American Dialect Society.

Notes

1. "Gartner Says by 2017, Mobile Users Will Provide Personalized Data Streams to More Than 100 Apps and Services Every Day," Gartner Press Release, January 22, 2014," accessed February 7, 2015, www.gartner.com/newsroom/id/2654115.
2. "App Store Rings in 2015 with New Records," Apple Press Info, January 8, 2015, accessed February 7, 2015, www.apple.com/pr/library/2015/01/08App-Store-Rings-in-2015-with-New-Records.html.
3. Sanhita SinhaRoy, "40 Great Apps for Mobile Reference and Outreach," *American Libraries*, July 1, 2013, accessed March 7, 2014, www.americanlibrariesmagazine.org/blog/40-great-apps-mobile-reference-and-outreach.
4. Rebecca Parr, "Alameda County Apps Challenge Draws Tech-savvy Crowd to Castro Valley Library," *San Jose Mercury News*, December13, 2012, accessed March 7, 2014, www.mercurynews.com/top-stories/ci_22187342/alameda-county-apps-challenge-draws-tech-savvy-crowd.

32

Netvibes
Social Media Management Service
www.netvibes.com

Overview

Netvibes is the go-to service for users interested in developing free start pages aimed at documenting and recording all aspects of their daily digital lives. These start pages provide one-stop access to all of the user's digital resources (blogs, news, online videos, podcasts, pictures, and email accounts). Founded in 2005, Netvibes is recognized as the first service to pioneer this prototype of a personalized dashboard and publishing platform for the web.

With a company slogan advocating "We Dashboard Everything," Netvibes' operational philosophy is based on the premise that, within a highly interactive social web environment, dashboards should no longer be viewed as passive tools. Instead, dashboards should be used to gather business intelligence and monitor content, conversations, and trends, and this quantitative data should then be incorporated into a company's strategy to respond in real time, thus streamlining marketing campaigns and tailoring services to meet consumers' immediate needs and interests.

For individual users, creating a dashboard on Netvibes is equivalent to creating a scalable personalized workspace for monitoring trends, reading newsfeeds, adding widgets, searching and updating posts on social networks, and gathering analytics.

Netvibes currently offers industry-based dashboards and widget distribution services for some of the world's leading companies including agencies, business enterprises, and government and nonprofit organizations. Netvibes has offices in Paris, London, and San Francisco, California.[1]

Users of Netvibes create personal dashboards to monitor trends, read newsfeeds, add widgets, update posts on social networks, and gather analytics.

Features

➤ Netvibes offers a four-tiered packaged service comprising a free basic service for individuals and three subscription-based services (VIP, Premium for Individuals, and Premium for Teams). Organizations subscribed to premium services have access to advanced analytics that monitor industry trends and brand reputation.

➤ To set up personal dashboards or start pages, new users must first register with the service by providing a username, valid email address, and password as well as agreeing to the terms of service. Dashboard wizards are available for creating customized, prepopulated dashboards in one of five languages (English, French, Spanish, German, and Japanese). To streamline and access news as RSS feeds and stay current on selected topics, users have the option of browsing recommended topics from an online database of popular dashboards or searching by keyword on a topic of choice.

➤ Within these dynamic personalized start pages that are either shared publicly or maintained privately, users integrate apps or widgets (200,000 are currently available) to do the following:

- Observe trends on specific topics such as business and finance, technology, politics, travel, sports, shopping, and lifestyle

- Add functionality for specific activities and events such as weather updates, email monitoring, calculators, stock quotes, translators, calendars, maps, games, to-do lists, sticky notes, bookmarks, and HTML editors

- Conduct searches on social networks like Facebook, Twitter, BoardReader, and Google Plus and blogs on platforms such as Google, Twingly, and WordPress

- Conduct both image searches on social media tools Flickr, Picasa, Instagram, Photobucket and video searches on YouTube, Dailymotion, Metacafe, and Vimeo

- Integrate social networks to view daily postings and send and receive messages

- Add RSS feeds to read articles and receive daily news feeds on trending topics

- Share articles and newsfeeds with friends via email or social networks

➤ A mobile version of Netvibes (mobile.netvibes.com) is only accessible to registered users. This version of Netvibes for mobile devices called Dashboard Anywhere (blog.netvibes .com/new-netvibes-mobile-and-tablet-version) provides support for iOS (iPhone and iPads) and Android devices and offers user-friendly optimizations, including split and floating views, touch functions, menus with icons, and offline reading.

How Cybrarians Can Use This Resource

Self-Publishing Dashboard Platform for Social Media Monitoring and Aggregating Digital Resources

Netvibes offers the flexibility of developing a one-stop centralized personal workspace for managing social media tools, accessing social data, monitoring trends, reading newsfeeds, and gathering analytics. The following Netvibes user testimonials appeared on the website of the Centre for Learning and Performance Technologies (C4LPT), an organization that reports on learning trends, technologies, and tools:

➤ "This manages my life! It aggregates all of my RSS feeds & also has a number of tools from listing tasks to searching for photos & videos."

➤ "My personal pin board and something I would now not cope without—like your filofax in the 90's, but better. I can watch students' updates to our wiki, link to my [favorite] blogs, collect all my favorite websites and bookmarks with a Delicious widget, check my i-calendar, see updates on Twitter and watch Facebook updates when I have a break—all on one very pretty page on my desk top."

➤   "This is my online portal. I use it to read feeds, to access my most commonly used sites (like an HTML reference list) and to manage my 'to do' lists and my calendar."[2]

FYI

Netvibes offers a Universal Web App service for app developers interested in building and distributing their products on Netvibes and other supported platforms (www.uwa.netvibes.com).

Notes

1. "Netvibes—About Us," Netvibes, accessed March 7, 2014, www.about.netvibes.com.
2. "Top 100 Tools for Learning—Netvibes," Top 100 Tools for Learning—A C4LPT Resource, accessed March 7, 2014, www.c4lpt.co.uk/top100tools/netvibes.

33

OneDrive
Cloud Storage/File Hosting/
Sharing Service
https://onedrive.live.com

Overview

In 2014, Microsoft changed the name of its patented cloud storage service from "SkyDrive" to "OneDrive"—partly in response to a lawsuit brought by Britain's Sky Broadcasting Group PLC, and also to serve a marketing strategy that would help the software giant compete with popular services such as Apple iCloud, Google Drive, Dropbox, and Box. In a competitive and crowded field, Microsoft enjoys the advantage as a reputable, established company once helmed by Bill Gates. This legacy may serve the company well in a distrustful online environment where the average consumer is still wary about storing important files in the cloud, often citing privacy and security concerns.

Quick to build on this advantage, Microsoft's OneDrive offers attractive options to lure new clients. In addition to the staple 15 GB of free cloud storage (as compared with Apple iCloud's 5 GB, DropBox's 2 GB, and Google Drive's 15 GB), the service provides additional free storage for students, additional storage for referrals made by existing clients (500 MB for each referral), and automatic uploads of photos using OneDrive mobile apps on smartphones (3 GB). Considered a premier file hosting service, OneDrive allows users to upload and sync files in multiple formats (photo, video, and text) in the cloud and readily access these files from their computers, tablets, and smartphones.

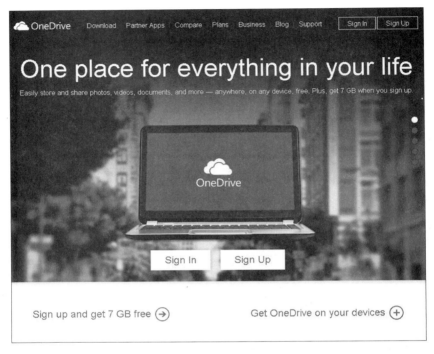

Microsoft OneDrive (formerly SkyDrive) is Microsoft's
patented cloud storage and file hosting service.

Features

> New users to the service must first register with a Microsoft
> account by providing an email address and password
> (https://onedrive.live.com). Microsoft clients who use
> Windows 8 and 8.1 have the advantage of having OneDrive
> already built into the operating system. Other users can
> download the software to desktops, tablets, smartphones, and
> Xbox consoles.

> The service supports storage of different content (photos,
> videos, documents, and surveys) in varying formats including
> Portable Document Format (PDF), Open Document Format
> (ODF), and plain text. These stored files can be readily
> accessed from PCs and mobile devices. Files are organized
> intuitively by formats that allow users to quickly search and

access them. OneDrive supports geo-location data for photos uploaded onto the service, and it will automatically display a map of tagged locations.

➤ OneDrive users have the option to keep stored files private, share these with contacts, or make the files publicly available.

➤ Users who require more than the 15 GB of free space may subscribe to paid premium plans providing 100 GB, 200 GB, and 1 TB of storage.

➤ A WYSIWYG text editor lets users view, edit, delete, and find and replace files. Deleted files (stored in the recycle bin) are kept for a minimum of 3 days and a maximum of 30.

➤ OneDrive offers seamless integration with multiple products to enable collaboration: productivity applications (Microsoft Office and Outlook), search engines (Bing), and social networks (Facebook, Twitter, and LinkedIn).

How Cybrarians Can Use This Resource

Providing Online Support for File Storage, Collaboration and Communication

At the University of Washington (UW, in Seattle), OneDrive for Business is enabled automatically for all current students, faculty, and staff.[1] This online service provides resources for file storage, collaboration, and communication with other users. UW OneDrive for Business has the following capabilities:

➤ Store files (up to 25 GB of data in the cloud with 2 GB maximum file size and including HIPAA- and FERPA-protected data)

➤ Share files with other UW users

➤ Access and synchronize files easily on desktop applications and mobile devices

➤ Create and edit Microsoft Office files in the cloud using Office Web Apps

➤ Create SharePoint sites

FYI

Microsoft's file hosting service has undergone several name changes in recent times. Known previously as SkyDrive, Windows Live SkyDrive, and Windows Live Folders, OneDrive is the latest iteration.

Note

1. "UW OneDrive for Business," University of Washington, accessed February 6, 2015, www.washington.edu/itconnect/wares/online-storage/onedrive/.

34

Paper.li
Social News Aggregator
www.paper.li

Overview

Publishing as many as 200 million articles a day, Paper.li is a content curation service enabling its users to automatically find, publish, and promote articles, photos, and videos from across the web in newspaper format. The Paper.li platform is akin to a fertile newsroom, giving self-publishers unparalleled access to articles, blog posts, and rich media on the internet along with the tools required to tailor this content to meet their publishing needs, allowing them to create an online newspaper in a manner of minutes. Paper.li initiates and completes the tasks of curating, extracting, analyzing, and presenting data based on the user's preferences.

Setting up an online newspaper within Paper.li is an intuitive three-step process. First, users select the news/content sources based on subject interest. Support is provided for multiple sources of online information including social networks (Twitter, Facebook, Google Plus, and YouTube) and RSS feeds. Second, users engage in a customization process allowing them to set parameters such as title, language, frequency, and selection of specialized topics, fonts, background images, and colors. Third, users can take advantage of Paper.li's promotional tools (tweets, daily email digests, and embeddable news widgets for websites or blogs) to engage, grow, and retain audiences reading their Paper.li newspaper.

Comparable to Flipboard (Chapter 14), which also curates content from social media networks, blogs, and other websites to blend this content into a personalized magazine, Paper.li curates similar content with an end product in newspaper form. As of this writing, there are no apps for iOS or Android devices. The developers explain their strategy

173

≡ **paper.li**

Create your online newspaper in minutes.

Automatically find, publish & promote engaging articles, photos and videos from across the web.

Promote your passion

Like 17k   +1 12k   Tweet 100K+   Share 2.8k

GET STARTED
It's FREE !

Niche publishing

Cover all the relevant news for your town or community, on an industry or event, or any topic you find fascinating.

Content marketing

Easily publish relevant, curated content daily to engage your community, build relationships and attract the right visitors to your brand.

Web monitoring

Automatically listen to signals from millions of sources to help identify influencers, competitors, experts and conversations around your brand.

We already publish over 200 million articles a day for our users. Let Paper.li do the heavy content lifting for you, too.

See how it works

💬 What our users are saying

Ekaterina Walter, Wall Street Journal bestselling author

❝ Paper.li is a fantastic tool for delivering relevant content to your community. It cultivates current connections and establishing new ones.

Estelle Metayer, Trend Spotter and Strategist

❝ Paper.li is powerful and simple to use. You can monitor peers, trends and industry news while establishing credibility as an expert along the way.

Mack Collier, #blogchat founder, Social Media Strategist

❝ I absolutely love how dead-simple it is to create a beautiful online newspaper with Paper.li. It's visually beautiful and valuable to #blogchat members.

Alastair McPheat, MD of ZeinMarketing

❝ We use Paper.li to deliver a daily paper with very little effort, providing a wealth of information to both our existing client base and prospective customers.

Paper.li is a content curation service, enabling users to automatically find, publish, and promote content from the web in newspaper-like format.

this way: "[W]ith the introduction of responsive design in October 2012, we discontinued our Apple app and no longer support it. You can still read your Paper.li on your mobile device and/or tablet and access the settings via your browser."[1] Paper.li is based at the Swiss Federal Institute of Technology-Innovation Center in Lausanne, Switzerland.

Features

➤ To create and customize personal online newspapers on Paper.li, users must first register with the service from the product homepage (www.paper.li). Unlike other curation-type services where it is optional to sign in with an existing social network account, a Paper.li account requires using the login credentials for an existing Twitter or Facebook account. The user's chosen social network account is then linked to Paper.li. An email account is also needed for notifications from the service.

➤ The basic version is free. A Pro version offers additional features such as a custom domain, custom CSS, monetized ad placement, collaborator options, email service directly to customers, exporting to RSS, and Google analytics.

➤ The basic version offers the following features:

- Twenty-five source feeds for curated content

- Editor's note providing information on the paper's intended scope and coverage, insights on topic interests, and issuing invitations to other users with similar interests to collaborate

- Scheduled updates that allow users to decide the frequency and the time of day when each new edition of the newspaper is published

- An auto-tweet option that allows users to send a tweet automatically to followers each time a new edition is published

- Email notifications to readers

- The Paper.li Publish it! bookmarklet that allows users to grab content or feeds from any webpage and seamlessly add this content to the newspaper

- Fully embedded code to display the newspaper on a website or blog by simply pasting a few lines of code

- Content blacklists

- Custom background options

- Usage statistics to track subscribers and other uses (posts, embeds) of the user's newspapers

- Access to the Paper.li dashboard, described as the centralized source for changing global settings, adding/editing content sources, adding content filters (language, paper sections, list of blacklisted persons and blacklisted websites), customizing layout and appearance, embedding layout widgets, selecting promotion channels (email, Twitter, Facebook, LinkedIn) and viewing statistics

(number of followers, number of paper views, number of embeds on blogs and websites)

➤ Creating a Paper.li newspaper and submitting the first news feed is a relatively simple process:

- Register and log in to the service.

- Enter a newspaper title and subtitle.

- Add a description or overview of scope and coverage.

- Include how often the site will be updated.

- Add content sources using the source search tool provided. Several sources and search strategies are available for adding content. These include conducting keyword searches on Twitter, Google Plus, and Facebook, searching RSS feeds by keyword or full URL, searching by Twitter hashtags (e.g. #libraries), searching a YouTube channel, or adding topics from Scoop.it.

- Complete the process by selecting the button "OK, Show Me My Paper" to view the first edition.

How Cybrarians Can Use This Resource

Creating an Online Newspaper to Promote Library Services

Paper.li provides the tools to enable the quick creation of customized online newspapers. The curation service will automatically find, publish, and promote articles, photographs, and videos from across the web, according to the user's interests. Libraries can use this service to promote and monitor library services:

➤ Web monitoring—Automatically access sources that capture all the news on the market and conversations around the library's brand.

➤ Content marketing—Publish relevant, curated content daily to engage the community, build relationships, and attract visitors.

➤ Create an online newspaper and become a trusted source of information for patrons searching for the best content in selected subject areas.

➤ Niche publishing—Build community, awareness around a cause, and audiences around shared interests.

FYI

The Paper.li blog (blog.paper.li) provides regular updates on new features and innovative applications from its community of users.

Note

1. "Paper.li—Help," Paper.li, accessed March 17, 2014, https://support.paper.li/hc/en-us/articles/204105903-Mobile-device-or-tablet-where-s-the-app.

35

Pinterest
Social Bookmarking Service
https://www.pinterest.com

Overview

Pinterest is a virtual visual discovery tool that enables users to collect, organize, manage, and share theme-based collections referred to as pinboards. Users or "pinners" have been innovative in utilizing this tool as an online social networking service to "pin" or bookmark images, videos, and other media content to boards that reflect their professional and personal interests.

As of this writing, more than 30 billion items have been pinned to profile hobbies, organize special events, plan projects, prepare travel guides, share new ideas, and manage personal libraries.[1] Visitors to the site can browse, follow, and repin boards based on their interests. Home, Arts and Crafts, Style and Fashion, and Food have been identified as popular pinboard categories on Pinterest, and not surprisingly, based on these trends, 87 percent of Pinterest users are women.[2]

Pinterest's mission as stated on its website is to "connect everyone in the world through the 'things' they find interesting." By industry standards, this undertaking has been accomplished at a rapid pace, as the site was listed as one of *Time* magazine's 50 Best Websites in 2011, despite starting off slowly in invitation-only beta mode in 2010. The California-based company has since become a powerhouse in the social networking space, and currently supports more than 70 million global users.[3]

Features

➤ Registration is required to access the full functionality of the site (https://www.pinterest.com). New users can sign up with a Facebook or email account. Registered users can log in to the service with their existing Facebook, Google, or Twitter account. Free business accounts are available for established brands, small businesses, nonprofit organizations, and bloggers.

➤ Pins (images, videos, and other media content) can be added to Pinterest in several ways (all pins link back to the original source site):

- Clicking the "Pin It" button on any existing pin

- Adding the "Pin It" button or a bookmarklet to a browser to immediately pin items while exploring websites

- Uploading a pin from a PC

- Using a Pinterest mobile app to pin from a mobile device

➤ Virtual theme-based boards are developed by pinners to collect, organize, and showcase pins on a wide range of subject areas such as hobbies, professional interests, projects, and travel plans. Boards can be private or public, and they can be shared by sending email invitations to specific persons or by posting to Facebook or Twitter.

➤ Follow buttons allow searchers to view pins and boards created by other individuals as pinfeeds on their Pinterest homepage. Users can add specific locations using place pins on an interactive map.

➤ Coding is available for publishers of websites who wish to opt out of sharing their site content. Meta tags can also be inserted in website headers: <meta name="pinterest" content="nopin"/>. Coding a website this way displays the following message to viewers: "This site doesn't allow pinning to Pinterest. Please contact the owner with any questions. Thanks for visiting!"

How Cybrarians Can Use This Resource

Promote and Market Library Services

Pinterest's philanthropic offer to host free business accounts has been utilized by popular brand companies like the Gap, Chobani, Nordstrom, and Etsy to develop virtual storefronts that promote and

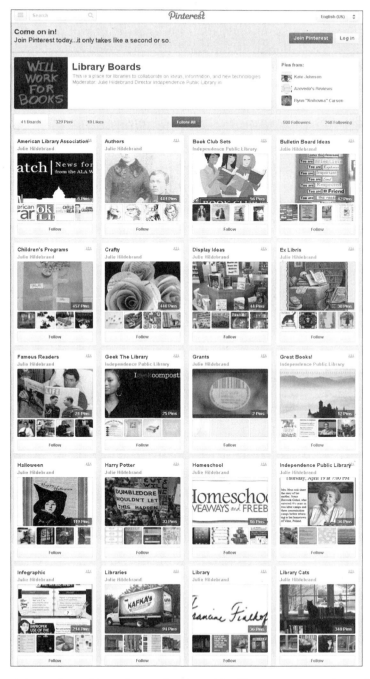

Virtual theme-based boards are developed by Pinterest users who collect, organize, and showcase pins on a wide range of subjects.

market products and services online. Educators have taken advantage of the tool to plan lessons and assign students the task of using Pinterest resources to collaborate on projects.

Libraries have also discovered ways for using this online pinboard service to promote collections, services, and programs. Edudemic, an online forum dedicated to connecting education with technology, identifies "20 Ways Libraries are Using Pinterest."[4] Innovative services include the following:

➤ Pinning book covers

➤ Showcasing historic archives and digital collections

➤ Creating collaborative boards with patrons

➤ Creating reading lists

➤ Sharing new acquisitions

➤ Promoting library activities

➤ Assisting patrons with research

➤ Generating ideas for book displays

➤ Sharing craft projects

➤ Profiling staff

Academic libraries are using Pinterest to facilitate collaboration, assist in self-curation, and create visual resource guides.[5]

The following is a select listing of libraries that have been adept at devising creative approaches to engaging their communities on Pinterest:

➤ New York Public Library, New York (www.pinterest.com/nypl)

➤ Fullerton Public Library, California (www.pinterest.com/fullertonpl)

➤ Omaha Public Library, Nebraska (www.pinterest.com/omahalibrary)

➤ Paul J. Gutman Library, Philadelphia University, Pennsylvania (www.pinterest.com/gutmanlibrary/databases-of-buildings)

➤ Smiley Memorial Library, Central Methodist University, Missouri (www.pinterest.com/librariancyn/smiley-library-new-books)

➤ Virginia Tech University Libraries, Virginia (www.pinterest.com/vtlibraries)

FYI

Compared to time spent on Twitter (21 minutes), LinkedIn (17 minutes), and Google Plus (3 minutes), the time spent on Pinterest by the average user is approximately 90 minutes per month.[6]

Notes

1. "Pinterest," Pinterest, accessed February 7, 2015, www.pinterest.com.
2. Brandon Gaille, "10 Most Popular Categories and Board Names on Pinterest," BrandonGaille.com (blog), June 22, 2013, www.brandongaille.com/10-most-popular-categories-and-board-names-on-pinterest.
3. Craig Smith, "By the Numbers: 80+ Amazing Pinterest Statistics," January 21, 2015, accessed February 8, 2015, www.expandedramblings.com/index.php/pinterest-stats.
4. Jeff Dunn, "20 Ways Libraries Are Using Pinterest Right Now," Edudemic, March 13, 2012, accessed February 15, 2014, www.edudemic.com/20-ways-libraries-are-using-pinterest-right-now.
5. Joe Murphy, "Pinterest and Academia: Association of College and Research Libraries Webcast," SlideShare, September 18, 2012, accessed February 15, 2014, www.slideshare.net/joseph.murphy/pinterest-for-academic-libraries-webcast-murphy-acrl.
6. Brandon Gaille, "10 Most Popular Categories and Board Names on Pinterest."

36

Poll Everywhere
Audience Response/Polling Service
www.polleverywhere.com

Overview

Poll Everywhere is an application that works well for soliciting real-time audience responses for live events such as conferences, presentations, and classroom lectures. This mobile resource offers a timely substitute for handheld clickers currently used to garner similar responses.

Poll Everywhere is quick and relatively simple to use. The pollster (the person conducting the survey) posts a question using the Poll Everywhere app. The audience responds by voting in real time, using their laptops, smartphones, or tablets. The live results are displayed on the web or in a PowerPoint or Keynote presentation.

Instant audience interaction and response was the driving force behind the development of the service, with the main objectives being "to poll, poll well, and poll everywhere." To date, the service has been successful at accomplishing these tasks and is currently being used everywhere, with users running the gamut from large corporations (McDonald's, Google, Starbucks) and notable education institutions (Virginia Tech University, Duke University, University of Notre Dame, the University of North Carolina at Chapel Hill) to small-scale businesses and nonprofits.

Established in April 2007, Poll Everywhere is a private company with its headquarters in San Francisco.

Features

➢ Poll Everywhere (www.polleverywhere.com) is offered as both a freemium and premium product. The service is free for audiences of 25 members or less, and this free service can be upgraded to paid premium plans available for businesses,

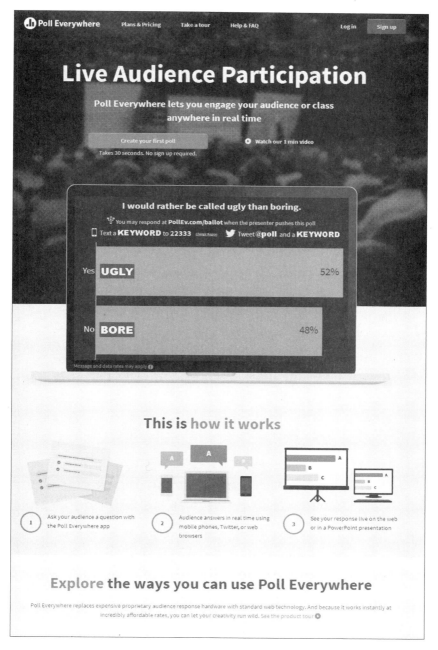

The Poll Everywhere interface presents several options
for audiences to respond to online polls.

nonprofits, and higher education and K–12 institutions. Premium services offer advanced features and functionality such as larger polling sizes, custom keywords, response segmentation, presenter moderation, multiple accounts, and analytical reports.

➤ Registering to create a poll is optional, and pollsters have ready access to an intuitive dashboard where polls can be created in the following sequence:

- The user types poll questions, and chooses whether the answers will be open-ended, multiple choice, or images for audience members to click on. For both freemium and premium plans, there is no limit on the number of poll questions, and these questions can be imported from external sources.

- Audience members respond to the poll, voting in real time with their laptops, smartphones, or tablets and posting their responses using one of several options displayed on the screen:

  - Sending a text message to the numeric code provided

  - Submitting a response directly to the pollster-created PollEv.com webpage for the event (for example, www .pollev.com/pollster name)

  - Sending a tweet to @poll on Twitter

  - Sending a response to a private webpage

- Polls are updated instantly, displayed onscreen, and can be downloaded as slides within Microsoft PowerPoint or Apple Keynote.

- Results can be shared via email, Facebook, and Twitter, or embedded as a widget on a webpage.

How Cybrarians Can Use This Resource
Analytics: Data Gathering and Sharing

Poll Everywhere was invented as a tool for corporate and professional use and can be readily adopted by librarians to poll audiences at webinars, conferences, and classroom lectures. The service is flexible as it allows you to use open-ended or closed questions; integrates modern technology for quick response time via text messaging, web URLs, and social media; enables storing of data in the cloud; and permits the sharing of poll results with peers. These features combine to transform polling, often characterized as a tedious exercise, into a more end user-driven, engaging experience.

FYI

The Poll Everywhere blog (www.polleverywhere.com/blog) is regularly updated with information on new features, current research, and customer stories about innovative product use.

37

Popplet
Visualization Service
www.popplet.com

Overview

Popplet is a visualization tool for capturing, organizing, and sharing ideas. Available on the web and as an app for iPads and iPhones, Popplet is marketed as a resource suitable for both the home and school environment. In the classroom, students use Popplet for visual learning by creating "popples," mind maps to capture facts, record thoughts, and add images to demonstrate the relationships between these discrete pieces. This tool has been described as a visualization aid to "help a new generation of digital natives emerge with skills in organizing information and thinking about how ideas—and the world we live in—are all connected."[1] In the office or when traveling, professionals use Popplet to generate ideas, organize their thoughts during brainstorming sessions, record notes, plan new projects, and collaborate in real time.

Popplet is a fertile platform for ideas that has enabled users in different communities to visually map out their workflow or contribute new ideas around a central concept using mind maps, charts, and online presentations. Everyday uses for the tool include tasks such as creating a sitemap for a web design project, sharing revision notes on literature studies for an English lesson, or designing a project to address global climate concerns. This broad appeal can be attributed to Popplet's main features, the simple intuitive interface of its web-based version and app, a shallow learning curve, and the ease with which users can start thinking visually to create popples or boards, add content (text, images, videos, and weblinks), collaborate in real time, and share their creations with others.

Popplet was developed by Notions Inc., headquartered in New York.

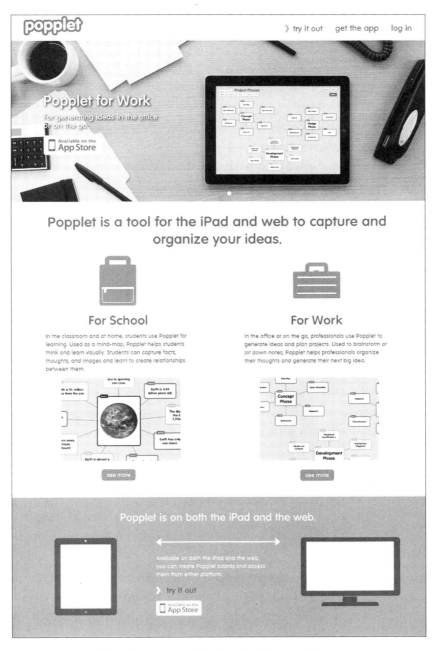

Popplet is a visualization tool for capturing,
organizing, and sharing ideas.

Features

➤ New users can create an account online by first registering on the Popplet homepage (www.popplet.com), providing their name, email address, and password, and agreeing to the terms of service and privacy policy.

➤ For new Popplet users, a free version of the service is available for use on the web, Apple iPad, and iPhone. This free basic version offers access to the creation of five popplets with a registered account, use of all the Popplet features including presentation mode, the ability to embed popplets into webpages, and the ability to share and collaborate on popplets with other registered users. Paid plans are offered as monthly and yearly subscriptions with no restrictions on the number of popplets created.

➤ A Popplet Lite version for iPads and iPhones is free and provides a basic introduction to how the app works on mobile devices. Users have access to only one free popplet and are encouraged to purchase the full app version to have access to unlimited creation of popplets on a mobile device.

➤ Popplet's simple intuitive interface allows users to quickly create mind maps, charts, and presentation slides using the following features:

- Customizable backgrounds and border colors, text size and alignment, name tags, comments, and duplication options

- Integrated content from external sources such as images from Flickr, videos from YouTube, and maps from Google Maps

- Capability to save to local drives, export as JPEG, PDF, or hi-res PNG format, or print a hard copy

- External VGA display support to enable presentation mode (slideshows) for large audiences

- Automatic resizing of boards (popples) to fit text, photos, and drawings

- Capability to pan and zoom views as well as click-and-drag to move text
- Ability to invite collaborators to enable real-time creation
- Private or public viewing on social networks Facebook or Twitter and via email invitation
- Code generation (URL link) and ability to embed this link on blogs and websites
- Ability to sync popplets between the app and web version
- Multilanguage support (Japanese, Korean, and Hebrew)

➤ Popplet users can discover other popplets created by registered users by browsing a public gallery (www.popplet .com/app/#/public) categorized as Most Popular and More Recent. Users can view these publicly accessible Popplets to gain inspiration for their own background themes, topics, and layouts.

➤ The Popplet blog (www.blog.popplet.com) is the main resource for sharing ideas on innovative uses, promoting new features, profiling clients, and sharing tips and tricks on using the tool. An integrated tutorial and informative user guide are available to assist new users. (www.bit.ly/ 1i14RYK).

How Cybrarians Can Use This Resource
Promoting Visualization Tools to Enhance Learning
Visual thinking and learning strategies are fast becoming a necessity for creative professionals and students as they search for innovative models and solutions to brainstorm and organize ideas, create infographics, relate compelling stories, show hidden connections, or record information. Popplet as a visualization tool supports these creative efforts, providing a platform to conceptualize and explore ideas, create mind maps, record thoughts, plan projects, and collaborate with others.

The Learning in the Libraries blog, maintained by the University of Minnesota Libraries, was developed to discuss tools and methods to enhance learning. On one blog post, Popplet was highlighted as a content creation tool, used to develop a tutorial to assist students in the undergraduate Biomedical Engineering Seminar in evaluating articles from peer-reviewed journals.[2]

FYI

Popplet was recognized as one of the best websites for teaching and learning in 2012 by the American Association of School Librarians (AASL).

Notes

1. "Popplet," Popplet, accessed March 27, 2014, www.popplet.com.
2. Jon Jeffryes, "Popplet," Learning in the Libraries (blog), April 25, 2011, blog.lib.umn .edu/learninglibraries/2011/04/popplet.html.

38

Project Gutenberg Self-Publishing Press
Self-Publishing Platform
www.self.gutenberg.org

Overview

Project Gutenberg, developers of the first online platform for the distribution of free ebooks, has progressed to the next logical step and created a free self-publishing portal for authors. This project, which provides a platform for contemporary authors to upload and distribute their self-published works, is in sync with the growing independent do-it-yourself (DIY) movement, and it both vindicates and promotes a cause for many independent authors who have been clamoring for such platforms to publish their works.

The original Project Gutenberg fulfilled a need for a centralized platform to provide online access to and downloading of a growing collection of public domain ebooks (now estimated at 46,000 texts). This allied project, Project Gutenberg Self-Publishing Press, is a boon for contemporary authors wishing for "a cloud service ... to share their works with readers."[1] Readers can access the site to search, view, and download works without registering with the service. However, it is mandatory for authors to first register with this service in order to upload their works and participate fully in the online social networking community.

Project Gutenberg Self-Publishing Press was officially launched on July 4, 2012 and currently hosts approximately 3,000 published books on its virtual shelves.[2]

Features for Authors

➤ Registration is not required for reading or downloading publications. Registration is required, however, for authors to upload their books, post comments, and add ratings and reviews. There is no fee for using the service.

➤ A "How To" video tutorial is available on the homepage (www.self.gutenberg.org) and provides tips on creating an account, searching for contemporary publications, creating a profile, and uploading publications.

➤ Uploading and publishing ebooks can be easily accomplished by following these steps when logged in to the service:

- From the homepage (www.self.gutenberg.org), click on the "upload" tab.

- Enter bibliographic information including title, volume, author, language, category, subject, file type, name of publisher, date of publication, summary, and table of contents.

- Upload author photo, book cover art, and ebook file (supports PDF, MP3, or video).

- Check the box to agree to the terms of service and submit for publication approval. The approval process takes up to 48 hours.

➤ Described as a place where "readers and authors meet," the Project Gutenberg Self-Publishing Portal provides for built-in, two-way interaction between authors and readers. Every ebook published has its own Book Details Page (information on file size and type, book summary, reproduction date, author's biography and QR code with URL link to the book's homepage), Star Ratings, and Reader Comment area.

➤ Submission Guidelines (www.self.gutenberg.org/view/submission-guidelines-.aspx) and a Self-Publishing Checklist (www.self.gutenberg.org/view/self-publish-check-list.aspx) are two online resources available for authors wishing to publish with the service.

Features for Readers

➤ Registration is not required for reading or downloading ebooks. However, registration is required to post a comment or review.

➤ Readers can easily search for publications by typing keywords into the ebook finder search engine prominently displayed on the homepage, or alternatively they can browse the collection by author, title, subject, and language. Filters and an advanced search tool are provided for refining searches.

➤ Books can be easily saved, downloaded, printed as PDF files, or added to a personalized virtual bookshelf or online reading list. All Project Gutenberg ebook downloads are compatible with iPads, Kindles, Nooks, Kobo devices, and other select digital readers.

How Cybrarians Can Use This Resource

Promote as a Free Self-Publishing Tool to Authors

Online self-publishing is one of the fastest growing publishing options being explored by independent authors. This trend has

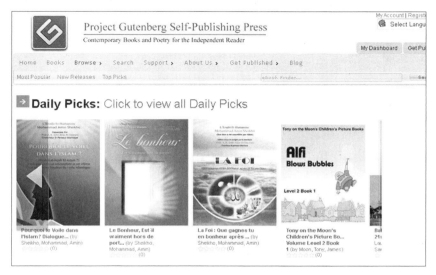

(*Continued*)

Project Gutenberg eBooks are downloadable in PDF file format and are compatible with the iPad, Kindle, Nook, Sony Reader, Kobo, and most other reader devices.

25 Most Recent Publications

Tony on the Moon's Children's Picture Book - Tony on the Moon : Ogg Gets Sick ; A series of illustrated story books for children, Level 3 Book 1

Title: Tony on the Moon's Children's Picture Book - Tony on the Moon : Ogg Gets Sick ; A series of illustrated story books for children, Level 3 Book I

Author: Moon, Tony, James

Publisher: Dodgy Publications

Volume: Level 3 Book I

Language: English

Subjects: Non Fiction, Education, Children's literature

Collection: Children's Book Series

Description: This series is arranged in levels of reading difficulty ranging from 1 to 5. The easiest is level 1, the hardest level 5. All these books are royalty free and can be copied used printed and distributed, scrawled on walls, acted out in plays and told (very slowly) to your pet dog, if you don't have a dog a cat will do, but hamsters do not listen as they only speak Spanish. They are designed to be easily read on a computer and can be printed on standard A4 size paper (landscape format) There is no bad language or offensive words anywhere in these books.

Project Gutenberg Self-Publishing Portal

Free Public Access to eBooks by Project Gutenberg Self-Publishing.

The purpose of Project Gutenberg Literary Archive Foundation is to encourage th voluntary creation and distribution of electronic books. Project Gutenberg Self-Publishing's purpose is to create a cloud service for contemporary writers to share their works with readers.

From Project Gutenberg, the first producer of free eBooks, now comes the free Au Community Cloud Library, a social network Self-Publishing Portal. This Portal allow to share their works with readers as well as allows readers to provide comments, re and feedback to the authors. Every eBook has its own Details Page, Star Ratings, a Reader Comment area.

There is no charge for using this service. Registration is not required for reading or downloading the publications or comments. However, registration is required to upl book or post a comment. All postings are monitored and offensive or indecent post be removed.

Project Gutenberg Origins

For the next Millennium the digital press will change the literary world as much for n times as did books from the Gutenberg Press.

In 1971 Michael Hart founded Project Gutenberg, a global coordinated volunteer e digitize and distribute the great works of history.

Mission Statement: "The Purpose of Project Gutenberg is to encourage the creation distribution of electronic books."

Until now, Project Gutenberg has focused mostly on the re-creation of classic literat paper books into digital books rather than the distribution of new authors and mater have spent as much of our time on finding books and doing copyright research as w eBook creation and distribution. This Self-Publishing Portal is our first project focus on distribution rather than creation.

Project Gutenberg's Self-Publishing Portal is a place where living authors can upload and share their writing.

gained widespread appeal, as independent DIY authors are discovering that self-publishing offers promotional, marketing, and distribution resources comparable to those presently offered by traditional publishers, yet with retention and ownership of copyright as obvious and added advantages.

Many librarians who have been following trends in the publishing industry are now actively integrating Project Gutenberg Self-Publishing Press in their portals (blogs, webpages, and library guides), promoting it as a dual function platform where contemporary writers can publish their works and share ideas with their readers within an interactive social networking space.

FYI

In 1971, Michael S. Hart founded Project Gutenberg, a globally-coordinated volunteer effort to digitize and distribute the greatest literary works of all time.

Notes

1. "Project Gutenberg Self-Publishing Press: Authors Community," Project Gutenberg Self-Publishing Press, accessed February 6, 2015, www.self.gutenberg.org/Catalog/6/Author-s-Community.
2. Ibid.

39

Quick Response (QR) Codes
Barcode Scanning and
Generator Software
www.en.wikipedia.org/wiki/QR_code

Overview

Quick Response codes, better known as QR codes, are two-dimensional barcodes readable by smartphones and other mobile devices. Initially designed for the automotive industry to assist in tracing manufactured parts, QR codes have quickly been adopted and adapted in other industries (advertising, publishing, shopping, entertainment) and of course libraries. This adoption can be attributed in part to key QR code features that offer an advantage over other standard barcodes: easy creation and reproduction, readability (in any direction), portability, error correction capability, and increased storage capacity.[1]

For commercial enterprises and nonprofit organizations, QR codes are considered essential modern day marketing tools. They can be embedded with information pointing users to websites, contact information (vCards), text messages, geo coordinates, video trailers, social networks, and URLs. Empowered users are downloading free QR code readers to their mobile devices not only for accessing consumer discounts, special promotions, contests, and new products and services, but are also using the freely available, easy-to-use apps to generate their own QR codes in order to personalize items such as coffee mugs, T-shirts, and calendars.

In similar fashion, the publishing industry has readily adopted QR codes to bolster marketing and other promotional efforts in their bid to increase sales. Simon & Schuster in 2012 unveiled a campaign to embed

Quick Response (QR) codes are two-dimensional barcodes
readable by smartphones and other mobile devices.

QR codes in all book jackets on hardcover books and trade paperbacks. On scanning these codes, readers are immediately directed to the author's website where they can sign up for alerts, browse the author's other publications, or watch a video interview with the author. Libraries are also very much on board with what is considered a low-budget marketing technique, and librarians are using QR codes to promote services and collections to tech-savvy patrons.

Features

➤ QR codes readers and scanners are available as free or purchased apps for the following mobile operating systems: Google Android, BlackBerry OS, Microsoft Windows Phone, and Apple iOS (iPhone, iPod, and iPad). The majority of these apps are equipped with real-time, auto-detect scanning capabilities, with the user simply opening the reader on their device of choice and pointing the device directly at the readable QR code. Codes scanned in this way are immediately resolved, and users are automatically directed to the embedded content.

> QR code scanners are multifunctional, enabling users to scan QR codes, standard barcodes, and text (using OCR recognition), create PDF files with a "Scan to PDF" feature, and scan and share photos and files via email, MMS/SMS, Facebook, and Twitter. The QR Reader for iPhones and iPads is an example of this type of advanced QR code reader.

> Many QR code readers and scanners, such as the Kaywa Reader (Chapter 24), also include QR code generator suites allowing users to quickly generate QR codes in a number of different formats. QR codes generated in this way can serve multiple functions: redirecting users to embedded URLs, storing contact information, viewing calendars, generating text messages, and embedding geographic locations.

> The following is a list of free QR code generators:

  - Kaywa (qrcode.kaywa.com)
  - QRStuff (qrstuff.com)
  - QR Droid Zapper (qrdroid.com)
  - QR Code Generator using Google's Chart API (createqrcode.appspot.com)

> Free QR code reader apps (available in most app stores) that can be marketed to patrons for mobile use include:

  - i-nigma (www.i-nigma.mobi)
  - Kaywa (qrcode.kaywa.com)
  - NeoReader (get.neoreader.com)
  - RedLaser (www.redlaser.com)
  - Scanlife (www.scanlife.com)

How Cybrarians Can Use This Resource

Promote QR Codes during Professional Development Workshops

> Albertsons Library at Boise State University (Idaho) created an informative research guide using LibGuides

(covered in the first volume of *The Cybrarian's Web*; www
.guides.boisestate.edu/QRcodes) to inform patrons about QR
codes. This guide includes information on how QR codes are
being used at the library, tips on creating effective codes, and
evaluations and recommendations on QR code readers and
scanners.

➤ The George T. Potter Library at the Ramapo College of New
Jersey created a portal using LibGuides to provide general
information on QR Codes and case studies of QR Codes
at work in libraries. (www.libguides.ramapo.edu/content
.php?pid=327381).

Real-World Examples of How Libraries are Using QR Codes to Enhance Services and Collections

Library Success: A Best Practices Wiki (www.libsuccess.org/index.
php?title=QR_Codes), maintained by Meredith Farkas, lists innovative
uses of QR codes in libraries:

➤ Directing patrons to virtual and audio library tours

➤ Linking to mobile versions of library websites, reference
services, library collections, blogs, and Facebook and Twitter
pages

➤ Creating on-the-spot reservations for group study rooms

➤ Placing codes on end stacks to lead patrons to online subject
guides

➤ Placing codes on books to recommend related titles and link
to book reviews

➤ Embedding codes in DVDs to link to video trailers

➤ Embedding codes in catalog records to offer basic information
about items such as location and call number

➤ Adding codes to library exhibits that link to related
multimedia

➤ Using codes to promote library events

➤ Adding codes to library signage

Utilize Social Media Tools to Demonstrate Innovative Ways of Using QR Codes

➤ The Seeley G. Mudd Library at Lawrence University in Appleton, Wisconsin created a page on Flickr (www.tinyurl .com/k3boek6) to demonstrate the use of QR codes in helping patrons access information.

➤ Pinterest boards are visually appealing exhibits that can be used to demonstrate practical uses of QR codes in libraries (www.pinterest.com/joycevalenza/library-qr-codes).

FYI

Up to 4,296 characters of alphanumeric data can be encoded in a QR code.[2]

Notes

1. Denso Wave, "QR code.com: Answers to your Questions about the QR Code," QRCode.Com, accessed March 17, 2014, www.qrcode.com/en.
2. Ibid.

40

Readability
Web and Mobile Reading Application
https://www.readability.com

Overview

In a competitive web environment, ads are considered valuable revenue generators, and are worthy of the investment in having them strategically and conspicuously embedded on webpages. Due to the clutter often caused by the volume of ads on webpages, many readers are attracted to the idea of a clutter- and pop-up-free online reading experience. Readability was developed to provide this function. As stated on the company's website, the Readability story "started with the desire for a better, smarter, more readable web."

As a free web and mobile reading platform, Readability aims to deliver the rare reading experience of connecting readers directly to writers, by removing clutter and creating webpages with clean comfortable reading views. The application is compatible with web browsers, iPhones, iPads, Amazon Kindles, Android devices, and BlackBerry smartphones, giving readers the flexibility of syncing articles across devices to read anywhere, anytime.

Released in 2009 by Arc90, a New York-based design and technology shop, Readability was first launched as a JavaScript-based reading tool to transform webpages into customizable reading views. This original Readability codebase is now embedded in a host of applications, including Apple's Safari 5 browser (the Safari Reader feature), the Amazon Kindle, and iPad applications like Flipboard and Reeder.

Features

➤ Readers register for this free service on the Readability homepage (https://www.readability.com) by providing a

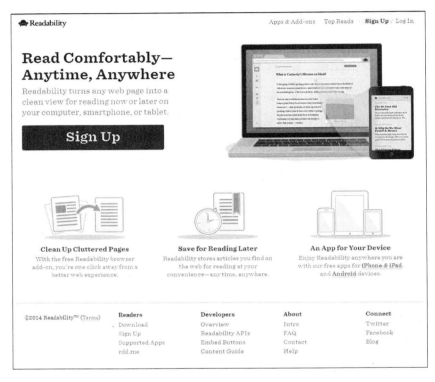

Readability is a web-based and mobile reading platform
that removes clutter from webpages.

username, email address, and password, and accepting the
terms of service.

➤ To start reading without the distractions of embedded and
pop-up advertisements, registered readers must download the
Readability software available as an add-on on supported web
browsers or as a separate app for mobile devices.

➤ The Readability browser add-on and app installs buttons that
allows readers to

• Read Now—unclutters the viewed page

• Read Later—adds the page currently reading to a list

• Send to Kindle—allows Kindle users to instantly send any
web article to their device in an uncluttered reading view

➤ Readers have access to the following features to customize and enhance their reading experience in an uncluttered format:

- Customize the reading view by adjusting font size and type, background and text color, and column width of the reading screen

- Save articles in a Reading List to read later or archive

- Obtain reading recommendations from people being followed as well as from Reading Picks compiled by the Readability staff

- Add articles to a reading list by copying and pasting up to 20 URLs into the body of an email and sending this list to a personalized Readability email address

- Share favorite articles on social networks (Twitter and Facebook)

- Export recommendations and reading lists in machine-readable format to support backing up of data or importing into another service

➤ Web publishers can opt out of the Readability service by emailing the service (contact@readability.com) with attached proof that they own the website domain.

➤ The Readability App Gallery (https://www.readability.com/apps) provides access to tools, apps, and services across multiple platforms.

How Cybrarians Can Use This Resource

Promoting a Service that Enhances Patrons' Reading Experience

With trends showing an increase in the ownership and popularity of ebook readers, it makes sense for librarians to promote tools such as Readability, which are designed to provide an uncluttered reading experience. This application can be promoted as offering immediate advantages to avid ebook readers:

➤ Providing an efficient way to save web content for current or future reading

➤ Improving the reading experience by integrating web content as clipped articles in a visually appealing format.

➤ Enhancing the online reading experience by enabling customization features such as adjustment of background, text color, and font size.

FYI

Readability offers a "Shorten Any Link and Read Comfortably" service called rdd.me (https://www .readability.com/shorten), which generates shortened URLs for lengthy news articles.

41

Scoop.it
Social News Aggregator
www.scoop.it

Overview

Similar in intent and purpose to other online curation tools Diigo (Chapter 9), Pinterest (Chapter 35), and Storify (Chapter 45), the Scoop.it curation platform assists professionals, businesses, nonprofit organizations, and educational institutions in the task of publishing content online. Using the tool's intuitive user interface, Scoop.it curators search for and discover content online using smart searches and feedback from a proactive Scoop.it community, edit this content by adding personalized perspectives and ideas, and, with assistance from Scoop.it's one-click publishing feature, share this content online as postings on social networks, websites, blogs, and splash pages.

In an information overload environment where "content is king," there is a commonly held perception that mathematical algorithms and human intervention—by way of curation—are equally required to efficiently and effectively organize content on the web in a smart and meaningful way. Scoop.it as a content curation service delivers on its promise to effect this synergy by "combining big data semantic technology that helps curators quickly find relevant content with an easy-to-use social publishing platform" and organize, manage, repackage, and share this information within their online communities of interest and social media channels.[1]

Launched to the public in November 2011, Scoop.it has been consistently ranked as one of the top tools for publishing by curation. The service attracted more than 75 million people during its first 18 months in existence. Scoop.it is headquartered in San Francisco and also has offices in Toulouse, France.[2]

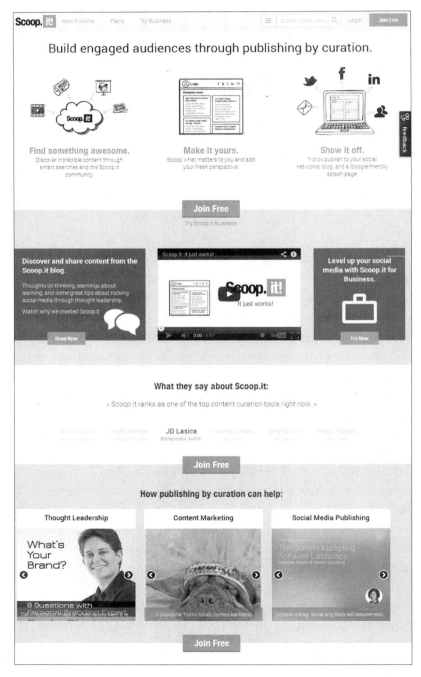

The Scoop.it curation platform assists professionals, businesses, nonprofit organizations, and educational institutions in publishing content online.

Features

➤   Scoop.it curators must register with the service (www.scoop .it) to have online access to the free account. Users can sign up with an existing Facebook, Twitter, or email account. With a free Scoop.it account, users create a Scoop.it webpage or "topic," with immediate access to Scoop.it's content suggestion engine, and connect the page to their social network accounts (Twitter, Facebook, LinkedIn, and WordPress). To create additional topic pages and take advantage of optimized features including social sharing capabilities, enhanced customization, analytics and weekly newsletter reports, scheduling features, and subdomain hosting services, users must subscribe to one of Scoop.it's premium plans.

➤   Once registered with the service, Scoop.it curators have immediate access to the following features and can initiate the process of curating, managing, and sharing content:

- Create a topic—For content curators, the first task is assigning a name for the chosen topic in the online template provided. A topic (for example, Social Media in Libraries) is one of the webpages or curated boards created on Scoop.it to store information harvested from the web. The topic URL mimics the subject selected (e.g., www.scoop.it/socialmediainlibraries). Curators then select the language and keywords relevant to the topic. These keywords are used by the Scoop.it suggestion engine to return relevant results (curated content or news items).

- Discover—Scoop.it discovers and curates content from the web relevant to the topic page with the assistance of several sources: the system's internal suggestion engine, an embedded bookmarklet to add content on the fly when searching the web, and "rescooping" from the Scoop.it community of active curators who share similar interests.

- Enhance—Newly curated content can be enriched by adding text to convey context or personal perspective.

- Publish and Share—Curators can publish harvested content on topic pages (SEO-friendly customizable content hubs) and share this content to blogs, websites, and social media channels (Facebook, Twitter, LinkedIn, WordPress, Google Plus, Tumblr, and Yammer).

➤ Scoop.it's "curate on the go" apps are available for the iPhone and iPad (App Store) and for Android devices (Google Play).

How Cybrarians Can Use This Resource

Digital Curation Tool

Curatorial tools are actively being developed to allow searchers to easily discover trusted, reliable, relevant content and share information with global audiences via social media channels. The popularity of social curation tools such as Scoop.it can be readily attributed to integrated social networking features that provide users with a sense of community through the sharing of similar interests in online forums.

Librarians are making use of Scoop.it and other curation tools to complete the following tasks:

➤ Post simultaneously to diverse social networks.

➤ Proactively market and customize Scoop.it pages with library branding.

➤ Aggregate library-related topics from various content sources on one centralized topic page or digital magazine, and share this content with users by embedding in blogs or library websites. Select examples include the following:

- 21st Century Libraries: All Things 21st Century Libraries Related (www.scoop.it/t/21st-century-libraries)

- School Libraries: What's New or Innovative in School Libraries (www.scoop.it/t/school-libraries)

- Transforming Our Practice—School Libraries, Ideas for School Librarians Looking to The Future (www.scoop.it/t/transforming-our-practice-school-libraries)

FYI

As traditionally used by reporters, the word "scoop" connotes originality, importance, surprise, secrecy, and exclusivity. A scoop is typically a new story, or a new aspect to an existing or breaking news story.

Notes

1. "Scoop.it: About Us," Scoop.it, accessed March 30, 2014, www.scoop.it/aboutus.
2. Ibid.

42

Scribd
Digital Library/Self-Publishing Platform
https://www.scribd.com

Overview

Scribd, a shortened form of scribbled, is the modern day subscription-based digital library providing unlimited access to a collection of professionally published ebooks and user-contributed written works. Described as the "Netflix for ebooks," Scribd does for ebooks what Netflix does for movies, offering a flat monthly "all you can read" premium subscription service to a digital marketplace. The collection—more than 500,000 ebooks and audiobooks from hundreds of publishers—comprises all genres including *New York Times* bestsellers, literary classics, and nonfiction works. In a bid to expand its competitive subscription service, Scribd signed an exclusive agreement in December 2013 with Smashwords (one of the world's largest distributors of independent ebooks) to add its extensive catalog of more than 225,000 ebook titles from 70,000 authors and publishers to the Scribd service.[1,2]

In fulfilling a dual role as digital library and self-publishing platform, Scribd offers independent authors a creative platform to upload written works (literary and academic) for an established global audience of more than 80 million monthly readers in nearly 200 countries. As of this writing, more than 60 million books and documents have been uploaded to the service.[3]

Scribd is supported on most mobile devices and is also accessible from any web browser. Readers with multiple devices are able to automatically sync content across these devices and not only continue seamlessly where they left off reading, but also read downloaded content offline.

Founded in 2007 by Trip Adler and Jared Friedman, Scribd was originally conceived as a platform for publishing academic papers. Its headquarters is in San Francisco, California.

Features for Readers

➤ Scribd's subscription reading service provides readers unlimited access to ebooks on their iPhone, iPad, and Android devices as well as in their web browsers at a flat-rate subscription service of $8.99 per month as of February 2015. A free one-month trial is offered to all new readers (www.scribd.com/subscribe).

➤ All readers can browse and search the digital library, read free content, and access previews of subscription content without signing up for an account. New users have the option of signing in to the service with their Facebook account. Registering with the service and creating a free account offers the following:

- Saving and accessing ebooks and user-generated content within a personalized My Library

- Sharing reading interests and activities with registered Scribd users and with friends on social networks (Facebook, Twitter, and Google Plus)

- Following other readers/authors on Scribd to stay current with their reading and publishing activities

- Viewing book summaries as well as related and recommended titles

- Adding comments, ratings, and keywords to ebooks and documents

- Syncing saved books and other data across multiple mobile devices

- Reading downloaded content offline

- Self-publishing independent works (www.scribd.com/publishers)

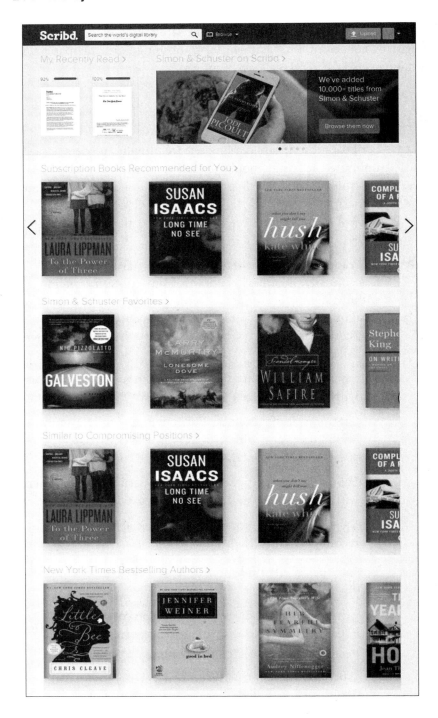

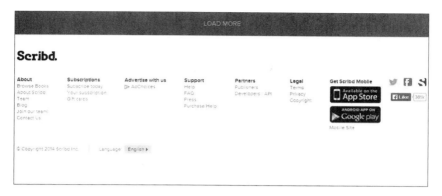

Readers browse and search Scribd's digital library, read a wide variety of free publications, and access previews of subscription content.

➤ Readers can access titles in all genres from such publishers as Simon & Schuster, HarperCollins, E-Reads, Kensington, Red Wheel/Weiser, Rosetta Books, Sourcebooks, and Workman. Readers also have access to user-contributed, independent works including creative writing (short stories and essays), articles, news stories, instruction manuals, and comics.

➤ Readers can discover new titles through browsing by genre: Biography, Historical Fiction, Food & Wine, Sci-fi/Fantasy/Paranormal, Dystopia, Travel, Romance, Mystery, Sports & Adventures, Humor, Health, Business, and Science & Nature. Popular titles can also be chosen within unique categories such as Scribd Selects (editorial picks), *New York Times* Bestselling Authors, Oprah's Book Club, and Award-Winning Children's Literature.

Features for Authors

➤ Scribd's robust publishing platform (www.scribd.com/ upload-document) is designed to help independent authors quickly and intuitively publish, market, distribute, and sell books and other content to an expanding global audience. In addition to traditional books, academic papers, magazines, and newspapers, Scribd supports the publishing of non-traditional content such as recipes, poetry, manuals and how-to-guides, catalogs, presentations and speeches, legal and historical documents, infographics, travel guides, sheet music, comics and study guides. Source files can be uploaded from a computer or from multiple cloud and file storage services (Dropbox, OneDrive, Google Drive, Evernote, and GitHub).

➤ Other options for authors who want to publish their work on Scribd include the following:

- Customizable author profile page

- Scribd's patent-pending conversion technology for turning documents into formatted HTML5 webpages

- Content indexed and searchable in Google and other search engines

- Distribution of content on Facebook, Twitter, and other social networks

- Content accessible and readable on iPhones, iPads, Android, and other mobile devices

- Detailed analytics on readership of all content

- Author-set pricing and competitive royalty terms for works sold on Scribd's subscription service

How Cybrarians Can Use This Resource

Promote as a Self-Publishing Platform to Independent Authors

Scribd's dual function self-publishing service and digital library combines the best of both worlds for authors and readers alike. For aspiring authors, this resource provides the tools to upload, publish, and distribute their works online with the option of selling these titles or making them freely available. Librarians can promote this service as

Scribd's robust publishing platform helps independent
authors intuitively publish, market, distribute, and sell
books and other creative works.

a self-publishing platform to independent local authors. The service can be promoted to readers as an online discovery portal to search for works (fee-based and free) from both established and emerging authors.

FYI

The Scribd blog (blog.scribd.com) is an informative source for book reviews, recommended titles, updates on recent acquisitions, and listings of new publishing partners.

Notes

1. Lesley Van Every, "Scribd Signs Global Deal with Smashwords to Offer Readers 225,000 Books by Independent Authors," Scribd, December 19, 2013, accessed March 5, 2014, https://www.scribd.com/doc/192561226/Scribd-Partners-with-Smashwords.
2. "Scribd: About Us," Scribd, accessed February 5, 2015, www.scribd.com/about.
3. Ibid.

43

Smashwords
Digital Library/Self-Publishing Platform
https://www.smashwords.com

Overview

In a digital marketplace where the do-it-yourself (DIY) movement has gained rapid momentum and widespread acceptance, Smashwords has actively solicited and garnered acceptance as one of the leading self-publishing and distribution platforms for independent authors and publishing houses. As Smashwords founder Mark Coker explains, it was indeed this spirit of independence and a determination to bypass a publishing industry "ill-equipped to serve all authors" that fueled his desire to develop Smashwords. Smashwords as an independent enterprise allows him to "take a risk on every author, and … let readers decide which books are worth reading." Readers have responded positively to this publishing house since its founding in 2008, and the service has successfully launched multiple bestsellers and amassed an extensive ecollection of more than 340,000 titles.[1]

Smashwords' meteoric rise as publisher and distributor can be attributed to its extensive reach in the publishing industry: authors, publishers, literary agents, retailers, and readers. For authors, publishers, and literary agents, Smashwords provides the tools and resources required for promotion, distribution, metadata management, pricing, and sale of published works. Written works published on the service include fiction and nonfiction, poetry, memoirs, monographs, research reports, and essays. For retailers, Smashwords offers an extensive catalog of "vetted, well-formatted ebooks from over 100,000 authors and publishers around the world."[2] For readers, Smashwords' well-designed and

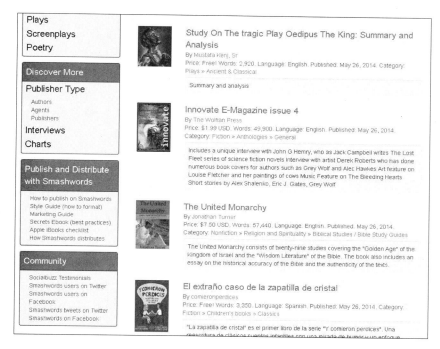

Smashwords is a self-publishing platform and distributor
for independent authors and publishing houses.

easily navigable web interface offers the tools for search and discovery
of independent voices whose works are available as free or reasonably
priced downloads.

Many of Smashwords services are aligned to what is presently being
offered by Scribd's ebook subscription and self-publishing platform
(see Chapter 42). This strategic alliance with its forecasted lucrative profit margins was the driving force that pushed a collaborative
venture between the two services in December 2013. Within such
an alliance, Scribd markets Smashwords titles on its platform and
assists Smashwords authors in marketing and distributing their works.
Smashwords is based in Los Gatos, California.

Features for Readers

➤   New readers can register with the service for free from
     the product homepage (https://www.smashwords.com).
     Registering offers the advantage of accessing a personal

online library to save purchased, free, or sampled titles, write reviews, add comments and ratings, and access discounts and publisher coupons.

➤ Smashwords offers ready access to a graphical user interface designed to facilitate keyword searching or browsing by genre (Fiction, Nonfiction, Essay, Plays, Screenplays, and Poetry).

➤ Readers have quick access to downloads of DRM-free multiformatted ebooks from independent authors. Formats supported include EPUB, MOBI, PDF, RTF, and TXT. These titles can be read online within a web browser or downloaded as ebooks on a number of supported mobile devices, including Apple's iPad, iPhone, and iPod Touch, Amazon's Kindle and Kindle Fire, Barnes and Noble Nook, and Kobo eReader. Smashwords provides its readers with the tools to download free titles from its online digital library. Smashwords users can share sample texts from the library via email or on social networks including Facebook, Twitter, Google Plus, Pinterest, Reddit, Delicious, and StumbleUpon.

Features for Authors

➤ All potential authors must first register with the service on the product homepage (www.smashwords.com/signup). A confirmation email will be sent to the email address provided. When registered, an author can publish a new book using the following workflow:

- Click on the "Publish" link on the homepage (authors must be signed in to the service to access this link).

- Download the Smashwords Style Guide (https://www .smashwords.com/books/view/52) for simple instructions on how to format a manuscript as a Microsoft Word document prior to upload. The Style Guide is available in multiple languages, including German, French, Spanish, Dutch, Italian, and Bengali. Smashwords also accepts direct uploads of professionally-designed EPUB files.

- Complete an online publication form by providing metadata on the book title, release date, synopsis (long and short description), language of book, pricing and sampling guide, subject category, and tags/keywords.

- Select the ebook format: EPUB, MOBI (Kindle), Palm Doc (PDB) PDF, RTF, plain text and HTML.

- Select the cover image.

- Select the file. The file type must be Microsoft Word .doc (10 MB maximum size file) or EPUB (20 MB maximum size file)

- Sign the Publishing Agreement.

- Click the "Publish" link again to complete the process.

➤ Authors must sign a publishing contract that guarantees earnings from the proceeds of their works and assures their input in marketing, determining the percentage of books available for sampling, and setting the sales price of works uploaded to Smashwords.

➤ Smashwords offers guaranteed assistance in marketing and distributing books and other works to global ebook distributors: Apple iBooks, Barnes & Noble, Kobo, Sony, Oyster, and Baker & Taylor.

➤ Smashwords authors have access to an online dashboard of marketing, distribution, and metadata management tools that display sales data. Authors can also benefit from a series of workshops on ebook publishing hosted on the Smashwords YouTube Channel (www.youtube.com/user/Smashwords).

➤ The service also provides authors with online access to personalized pages with a personal domain (URL). To assist with marketing and promotion of works, authors can use the Interviews feature (https://www.smashwords.com/interviews) to publish their own Q&A interview. Interviews published on the Smashwords website are linked to and discoverable from the author's profile page and book page, and they can

be shared on social networks. The Smashwords Coupon
Generator is useful for creating and issuing book promotional
coupon codes.

Features for Independent Publishers

➤   As the ebook publishing and distribution platform for
hundreds of small, professional, independent publishers,
Smashwords offers a number of online tools and resources
to assist in this process (https://www.smashwords.com/
about/publisherdocs). Publishers have access to the following
resources:

- A free co-branded ebook store at Smashwords from which
they can list an unlimited number of titles

- Automatic creation of author profile and book pages

- Distribution of titles to major ebook retailers

How Cybrarians Can Use This Resource

Expanding Ebook Collections

In an environment where libraries are proactively searching for
ways to expand ebook offerings to meet increasing patron demands,
Smashwords offers a unique opportunity for libraries to augment their
print collections. The Douglas County Libraries (DCL) in Colorado,
already well-established as a leading library innovator in developing its
own ebook lending platform, announced in January 2013 its plans to
"double the number of ebooks available to patrons" by offering "10,000
ebook titles from Smashwords." The deal held obvious advantages for
the DCL, as director James LaRue was "eager to connect ... readers to
fresh streams of digital content," and "Smashwords' average price per
title [about $4] allows us to do that more readily than we could from
the big publishers [now charging as much as $84 per ebook]." Mark
Coker, founder of Smashwords, believed the purchase was both relevant
and required "at a time when many ebook publishers are turning their
backs on libraries ... our [Smashwords] authors and publishers are
embracing libraries."[3]

Promoting Access to a Self-Publishing Platform

Smashwords and its companion service Scribd (see Chapter 42) can be promoted as platforms to provide independent authors with the free tools required to publish, market, and sell their ebooks and other user-generated content.

> # FYI
>
> On the Smashwords FAQ page, there is a brief statement on the origin of the service's name: "Smashwords is a manufactured name, capturing the angst that many writers experience during the creative process of writing, revising and editing. The word connotes the success on completion of a work exemplifying words such as 'Smash hit' or the phrase, 'Absolutely Smashing!'"[4]

Notes

1. "About Smashwords," Smashwords, accessed February 5, 2015, https://www.smashwords.com/about.
2. "Smashwords Support Center FAQs," Smashwords, accessed February 15, 2015, https://www.smashwords.com/about/supportfaq.
3. Gabe Habash & Andrew Albanese, "10,000 Smashwords Ebooks Acquired by Douglas County Libraries," *Publishers Weekly*, January 7, 2013, accessed January 17, 2014, www.publishersweekly.com/pw/by-topic/industry-news/libraries/article/55375-10-000-smashwords-e-books-acquired-by-douglas-county-libraries.html.
4. "Smashwords Support Center FAQs," Smashwords, accessed January 17, 2014, https://www.smashwords.com/about/supportfaq.

44

Snapchat
Photo and Video Sharing Service
https://www.snapchat.com

Overview

Photo and video sharing app Snapchat gained notoriety, instant media blitz, and an immediate increase in consumer demand when its founders, Stanford University students Robert Murphy and Evan Spiegel, refused an unprecedented Facebook offer to purchase the service for $3 billion in November 2013.[1] Facebook's lofty bid for the service was viewed as a reactive move by the social networking giant to retain a steadily retreating audience of teens and young adults who have been showing their waning interest in the world's largest social network by flocking to newer mobile services such as Instagram (Chapter 21), and WhatsApp (Chapter 57).

In addition to offering traditional features comparable to other photo and video sharing applications such as Instagram and Vine (Chapter 53), Snapchat is renowned for providing a unique mainstay feature that has broadened its appeal to teenagers and young adults. Photos or videos taken with the service called "snaps" are instantly delivered to a single individual or controlled group of recipients. The sender can set a time limit from 1 to 10 seconds as to how long recipients can view these snaps. After this time has elapsed, snaps disappear and are erased from the recipient's device.

It is not surprising that this ephemeral service (and others like it such as Wickr and Silent Circle), which integrates some measure of digital privacy and messaging freedom, has been "snapped" up by millennials. The Pew Research Center reports, in fact, that "26 percent of 18–29 year-olds" with mobile phones are using the service.[2] Snapchat's popularity notwithstanding, and somewhat ironically given the features of its services, the company has been plagued with issues relating to hacking, privacy, security, and pornography. In May 2014, the Federal Trade Commission (FTC) charged the mobile messaging app developer with multiple counts of "deceiving consumers" for its misleading promises about the disappearing nature of messages sent through the service, the amount of personal data collected, and the security measures taken to protect that data from misuse and unauthorized disclosure.[3] The company, to its credit, has stated publicly that it has entered into a consent decree with the FTC that addresses the commission's concerns, and has voluntarily resolved the majority of issues raised by improving the wording of the app's privacy policy and investing heavily in security and countermeasures to prevent abuse.[4]

Snapchat co-founder Evan Spiegel explains the reasoning behind the development of this self-destructing app, which by all accounts has signaled a new era in the sphere of private social sharing, "[S]pontaneity, now punishable by career ruin, has been abandoned. Instead, everyone is busy curating a perfected online image. People are living with this massive burden of managing a digital version of themselves … it's taken all of the fun out of communicating."[5] Snapchat, according to Spiegel, is one attempt to bring that fun back into the digital world.

Features

➤ New users must first download the app available on the App Store (for iOS devices) and Google Play (for Android devices) before registering for the service. Registering entails providing an email address, password, and date of birth, acknowledging

Snapchat allows photos and videos taken by users, or snaps,
to self-destruct once viewed by recipients.

terms and conditions, verifying the account, selecting a username, including a mobile phone number to enable the search feature, and adding a list of contacts.

➤ Registered users have immediate access to the service and can start sending Snaps to an individual or select group using the following steps:

- Take a snap (photo or video). Options are available for saving the image or video on the user's device photo gallery.

- Add a caption or ink drawing, if desired, to the snap.

- Set the timing for the image or video to self-destruct.

- Send it to other Snapchat users.

- Receive a text message indicating when the snap has been viewed and whether the recipient has taken a screenshot of it.

- After the set time expires, the image is automatically deleted from recipient's device.

➤ Snapchatters have some measure of control over privacy through the Settings menu.

➤ Age verification is mandatory to use the service. In June 2013, Snapchat released SnapKidz for users under 13 years of age. SnapKidz allows children within this age group to take snaps and add drawings. However, unlike the version created for teens and adults, there are no options for sending or deleting Snaps; users are restricted to saving them on their local devices. The kid-friendly option is currently available for iOS and Android devices.

➤ In October 2013, Snapchat launched Snapchat Stories, a feature that allows users to link discrete images and videos as a continuous stream and share these 'stories' with friends for 24 hours before the stream is automatically deleted.

➤ In January 2015 Snapchat debuted Discover, a feature that allows users to find and consume content from major media companies including CNN, ESPN, and National Geographic.

How Cybrarians Can Use This Resource

Marketing Library Services

Snapchat, launched in 2011, is a relatively new type of messaging service, and the library community is still exploring its potential value for patrons. As Pew Research Center statistics have shown, teenagers and young adults are using the service, and their high level of use is noteworthy for public libraries searching for ways to expand outreach services, initiate conversations, and build relationships with this demographic.

One can easily see how Snapchat Stories might be used as a marketing tool by libraries wishing to promote their collections, services, programs, and special events.

The blog "Librarian Enumerations" (www.librarianenumerations .wordpress.com) highlights how well-known companies are using Snapchat to market products and services to their customers, and it shares some novel ideas on how libraries can follow the corporate lead to creatively use this service to engage patrons. Innovative ideas offered on this blog include patrons taking photographs of library items in exotic locations while traveling abroad and promoting "hidden" library services by shooting behind-the-scenes videos of book repairs or book processing.[6]

FYI

In May 2014, Snapchat reported that its users were sending 700 million photos and 500 million Snapchat Stories daily.[7]

Notes

1. Scott Martin, "Snapchat Turned Down More Than $3B From Facebook," *USA Today*, November 13, 2013, accessed January 17, 2014, www.usatoday.com/story/tech/2013/11/13/report-facebook-offered-snapchat-3-billion/3517929.
2. J. J. Colao, "Pew Study Suggests That Snapchat Has 26 Million U.S. Users," *Forbes*, October 28, 2013, accessed January 17, 2014, www.forbes.com/sites/jjcolao/2013/10/28/pew-study-suggests-snapchat-has-26-million-u-s-users.

3. "Snapchat Settles FTC Charges That Promises of Disappearing Messages Were False," Federal Trade Commission Press Release, May 8, 2014, accessed May 17, 2014, www.ftc.gov/news-events/press-releases/2014/05/snapchat-settles-ftc-charges-promises-disappearing-messages-were.

4. "Our Agreement with the FTC," Snapchat (blog), May 8, 2014, blog.snapchat.com/post/85132301440/our-agreement-with-the-ftc.

5. J. J. Colao, "Snapchat: The Biggest No-Revenue Mobile App since Instagram," *Forbes,* November 27, 2012, accessed January 17, 2014, www.forbes.com/sites/jjcolao/2012/11/27/snapchat-the-biggest-no-revenue-mobile-app-since-instagram.

6. Paige Alfonzo, "Snapchat for Your Library," Librarian Enumeration (blog), December 9, 2013, www.librarianenumerations.wordpress.com/2013/12/09/snapchat-for-your-library.

7. Ingrid Lunden, "Snapchat has raised $485 Million More from 23 Investors, at Valuation of at Least $10B," accessed February 6, 2015, www.techcrunch.com/2014/12/31/snapchat-485m.

45

Storify
Social News Aggregator
https://storify.com

Overview

The vast amount of content currently available on the web and the challenge encountered by ardent web searchers who wish to easily access and manage this information has led to an increase in the development of content curation tools with built-in algorithms to sift, sort, organize, and manage this content around a specific theme or topic. The process of collecting and displaying information in meaningful ways is not a new phenomenon and has long been employed in museums and libraries. The contemporary and widespread interest in web-based curation tools has resulted in the rapid development and distribution of new tools including Diigo (Chapter 9), Flipboard (Chapter 14), Paper.li (Chapter 34), Pinterest (Chapter 35), Scoop.it (Chapter 41), and—as described here—Storify. These tools empower an active community of content creators and curators eagerly seeking innovative means to minimize the time spent sifting through surplus information online, accelerate the process of discovering relevant content, and gather the collective intelligence of the web.

Storify was developed to "help make sense of what people post on social media." Storify curators, a mixed group of established and new journalists, bloggers, and editors, "curate the most important voices and turn them into stories."[1] They accomplish this task in three simple steps. First, media in all formats (social network feeds, images, videos, URL links, and articles) is collected from the web. Second, content from these external sources is compiled into a cohesive narrative or storyline. Third, this compilation or collection is published and shared as a digital story on the Storify landing page, while also being embedded in blogs and websites.

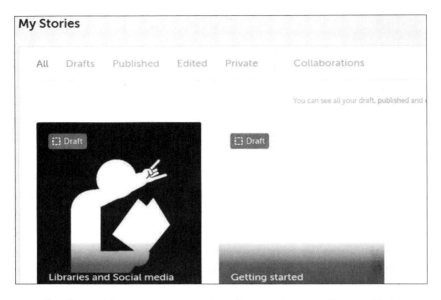

Storify enables content creators to import elements from multiple media sources in the process of storyboarding.

Media organizations including the *New York Post*, BET, Weather Channel, *Detroit News*, and the Daily Beast are experimenting with Storify as a new way to report on trending stories, and established brands like GE, Scholastic, and Cinemax are using the service to market products and relay a unified message to target audiences. Colleges and universities including the University of California, University of Texas, and Harvard University are also using Storify as a recruitment tool for new students and for promoting programs and services. Storify was acquired by Livefyre in September 2013 and is based in California.

Features

➤ New Storify users can log in with an existing Facebook or Twitter account or register for a new account on the product homepage (https://storify.com/signup). Storify is a free service with an option to upgrade to Storify Enterprise, a premium service. Optimized premium subscription features, ideal for large media organizations and publishers, include real-time updates, custom story display, enterprise level technical support, private stories, PDF exports, SEO compatibility, multiple editors/collaborators, and Google analytics.

➤ Once registered with the service, Storify subscribers have access to the following tools and features:

- Creators can search and add content related to a story's theme from multiple sources, including content from social networks such as Twitter, Facebook, Google Plus, YouTube, Flickr, and Instagram; animated GIFs available on Giphy or Google; and embedded URLs; and can reuse elements from published Storify stories. This search for disparate social media elements is simplified within the Storify editor or dashboard, where curators can use the drag-and-drop feature to add, delete, and reorder discrete elements from social media to best illustrate their stories.

- Storify users can add narrative and context by writing a headline, introduction, and description, inserting text, and adding headers, hyperlinks, and styled text between elements at any point in the story.

- Storify stories can be embedded anywhere on the web using the copy-and-paste feature to embed codes. These stories can be shared with contacts on social networks and widely distributed in a viral marketing push by notifying persons quoted in the stories created.

- Searchers have access to the Storify front or landing page, which displays the top stories curated by Storify users and the service's editorial staff in multiple categories.

- The Storify bookmarklet, when installed in the bookmarks bar in a web browser, allows users to curate items from their favorite websites.

How Cybrarians Can Use This Resource

Curation of Online Content from Multiple Social Networks

Storify enables curators to import content from various forms of media and use it to create and share social stories, with the ultimate goal of bringing together media scattered across the web into a coherent narrative. As libraries continue to use diverse social media channels to promote events, programs, collections, and services, it is sometimes difficult to unify these discrete channels to produce a cohesive message.

Storify can simplify this process and can be utilized as a centralized social dashboard, useful for collating data feeds from multiple social networks—live streams from Twitter, YouTube videos, postings on library blogs and Facebook, and images from Flickr and Instagram—onto a single landing page, with very little effort required. In addition to accommodating postings from multiple social networks, Storify has the advantage of promoting viral distribution of these social stories by facilitating strategic placement and embedding of this content into user guides, blogs, and library webpages.

FYI

Time magazine rated Storify as one of the 50 Best Websites of 2011. Storify has also won the Best News Technology Award (2011) and the Social Media Award (2012) at the respected South by Southwest Conference.

Note

1. "Storify: About Us," Storify, accessed January 17, 2014, https://storify.com/about.

46

TED (Technology, Entertainment, Design)
Global Conference/Idea Sharing Platform
www.ted.com

Overview

TED—an acronym for Technology, Entertainment, Design—is a non-profit organization devoted to spreading ideas through conferences using the unusual rigid format of short, powerful talks lasting 18 minutes or less. TED began in 1984 as an annual conference where technology, entertainment, and design converged, and its popularity has turned this gathering into a global phenomenon, with events held in North America, Europe, and Asia, attracting people from varied sectors of community life.

In addition to the lively format, the medium of transmission (live streaming and archived video collections) and eclectic mix of topics offered by celebrated speakers—politicians, celebrities, technology experts, scientists, philosophers, musicians, religious leaders, and philanthropists—are main attractions of TED events. Topic coverage is extensive—technology, entertainment, design, business, science, and global issues—and past presenters include Bill Clinton, Al Gore, Richard Dawkins, Bill Gates, Bono, and Google founders Larry Page and Sergey Brin. Since 2006, TED Talks have been offered for free viewing online on Ted.com, and in the fall of 2012 the service reached an important milestone when it was reported that TED Talks had been viewed one billion times.[1]

Of note to educators and information professionals are the independently run TEDx programs that individuals, organizations, and communities worldwide host as local, independent TED-like events. The

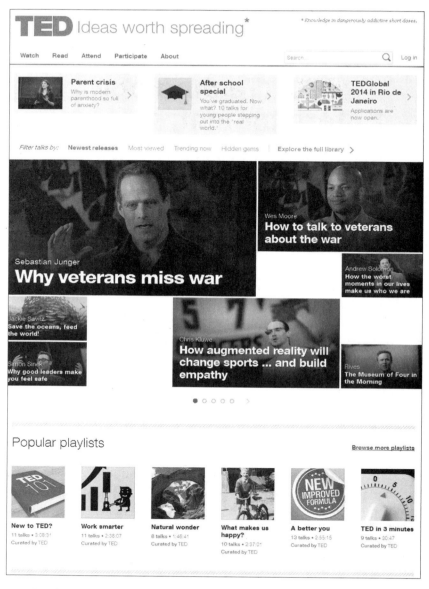

TED (Technology, Entertainment, Design) is a nonprofit organization devoted to spreading ideas through powerful talks published online.

newest initiative, TED-Ed, offers educators access to online original, animated video lessons that can be customized for use in the classroom. These two programs are examples of TED's philanthropic mission:

"Our agenda is to make great ideas accessible and spark conversation…everything we do—from our TED Talks videos to the projects sparked by the TED Prize, from the global TEDx community to the TED-Ed lesson series—is driven by this goal: How can we best spread great ideas?"[2] TED has headquarters in New York City and Vancouver, British Columbia.

Features

➢ The mainstay of the TED organization is the development of its website TED.com, which showcases its programs and initiatives and serves as a public service forum to promote the spread of good ideas. This website has won several awards, and as of May 2014 more than 1,700 TED Talks had been posted online, with an average of 17 new page views per second.

➢ All persons over the age of 13 can join TED.com by providing basic contact information (first and last name, email address, and country of residence). Once registered, users are free to set up a profile and join an interactive community in rating and commenting on TED Talks, participating in conversations, providing translation services, or by getting involved in a local, independently-organized TEDx event.

➢ Registered viewers are encouraged to view as many TED Talks as they wish for free and to share what they learn with others both on- and offline. There are several filters available for searching for content: Today's Talk, Newest Releases, Most Viewed, Trending Now, and Hidden Gems. Viewers can explore the online offerings and limit searches by topic (technology, entertainment, design, business, science, and global issues), event, language, and rating (funny, jaw-dropping, persuasive, ingenious, persuasive, courageous, fascinating, inspiring, beautiful, and informative). The TED.com website is regularly updated with new user-requested features and now includes an enhanced video player, mobile-friendly pages, and a "Watch Later" feature.

➤   TED programs and initiatives include the following:

- TEDx (https://www.ted.com/about/programs-initiatives/tedx-program)—TEDx was created in the spirit of TED's mission of "ideas worth spreading." This program supports independent organizers who wish to create a TED-like event in their own communities. For example, TEDxRiodelaPlata was organized in Buenos Aires, Argentina on September 27–28, 2013, and the event hosted 1,000 attendees, 200 volunteers, 18,000 online live stream viewers, and 25 speakers and performers.

- TED Prize (https://www.ted.com/about/programs-initiatives/ted-prize)—The TED Prize is awarded annually to a leader with a fresh, bold vision for sparking global change. The TED Prize winner receives $1,000,000 and access to the TED community's wide range of resources and expertise to make his or her dream become a reality. The TED Prize has helped to combat poverty, open dialogue on religious intolerance, improve global health, tackle child obesity, advance education, and inspire art around the world.

- TED Fellows (https://www.ted.com/about/programs-initiatives/ted-fellows-program)—The TED Fellows program nurtures the vision and passion of 40 leaders and trailblazers, giving momentum to their ideas. TED Fellows are selected across all disciplines based on the strength of their achievements, their potential for global impact, and their character. The TED Fellowship offers access to an exclusive private network of change-makers, unique skills-building workshops, and the mentorship of world-renowned experts. TED Fellows also present at TED Talks events.

- TED-Ed (http://ed.ted.com)—TED-Ed is the newest of TED's initiatives in "lessons worth sharing." The TED-Ed platform allows users to take any TED Talk, TED-Ed Lesson, or YouTube video and easily customize or flip the content by adding, questions, notes, and other supplementary resources. Educators can then distribute these lessons publicly or privately.

- Open Translation Project (https://www.ted.com/ participate/translate)—Launched in 2009, the Open Translation Project is a global volunteer effort to add subtitles to TED Talks, and make these translations available to a global audience. To date, the project has enjoyed notable success with 19,000 volunteers providing 68,000 translations in more than 100 languages.

- TED Books (https://www.ted.com/read/ted-books)— Shorter than a novel but longer than a magazine article (under 20,000 words), TED Books are original ebooks published with content from TED Conferences and available by subscription to readers.

- TED Institute (https://www.ted.com/about/programs- initiatives/ted-institute) The TED Institute is the professional development forum of the TED organization.

How Cybrarians Can Use This Resource

Providing Access to a Platform of Innovative Ideas Worth Sharing

The TED community is committed to the concept of "ideas worth sharing." This mission is exemplified in the latest initiative, TED-Ed's Lessons Worth Sharing. Relevant to information professionals and educators, this program can be promoted as a resource sharing network, enabling librarians and educators to create and share lessons built on existing videos.

Librarians and educators can utilize this platform and create innovative, flipped lessons as outlined in the following steps:

1. On the Ted-Ed homepage (http://ed.ted.com), select "Create a Lesson."

2. In the search box, enter keywords to search TED-Ed content, TED Talks, or TED-related YouTube videos.

3. Select the video or lesson to be customized.

4. Launch the Lesson Editor.

5. Flip the video by adding a title, context for the video, questions, notes for discussion, and supplementary resources.

6. Preview and publish the lesson as listed within the TED-Ed Community or select the option for the lesson to be unlisted or private.

Professional Development

Librarians can take advantage of local TEDx conferences and subscribe to feeds on the TED.com website to keep up with trends and new ideas in subject areas such as technology, entertainment, design, business, science, and global issues.

FYI

In March 2012, Netflix announced a deal to stream collections of TED Talks on its service. The content will be available to subscribers in the U.S., Canada, Latin America, the U.K., and Ireland.

Notes

1. "TED: History of TED," TED, accessed February 7, 2015, https://www.ted.com/about/our-organization/history-of-ted.
2. "TED: Our Organization," TED, accessed March 27, 2014, https://www.ted.com/about/our-organization.

47

Text 2 Mind Map
Visualization Service
https://www.text2mindmap.com

Overview

Mind maps are popular tools for organizing thoughts and ideas as they allow visualization of discrete elements within a complex project. Text 2 Mind Map is a resource developed specifically to simplify the process of creating mind maps. Requiring no registration, Text 2 Mind Map allows users to craft customized mind maps directly on the company's landing page. When completed, the mind maps can be downloaded as PDF or image files and shared (as view-only versions) on social media networks Facebook and Twitter.

This free and easy-to-use tool should be viewed as a quick solution for effortlessly creating simple mind maps online. The limited set of features does not permit robust editing, support the importing of external data, or allow for many layout options. When compared with other free concept mapping tools like Bubbl.us, Coggle, FreeMind, LucidChart, Mind42, XMind, and Popplet, therefore, Text 2 Mind Map's most effective use appears to be as a research and project planning tool. Inherent advantages lie in its interactivity and the infrastructure provided for real-time collaboration.

Text 2 Mind Map was developed in 2008 in Stockholm, Sweden. As of this writing, no applications have been developed to support installation on mobile devices.

Features

➤ Text 2 Mind Map offers free and subscription accounts for its users. Subscription accounts vary from a Mini private account (save and manage up to 12 mind maps) to the Pro account

241

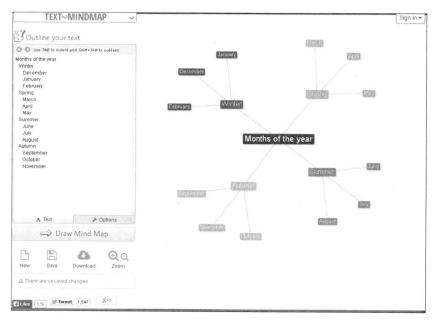

New users can immediately draw, view, and edit mind maps using the interactive template on the Text 2 Mind Map landing page.

(save and manage unlimited mind maps). Subscription account holders also have access to advanced features such as exporting and printing maps without advertisements, along with increased security and encryption functionality.

➤ New users can immediately convert text into visible mind maps by using the editable, interactive template on the site's homepage (https://www.text2mindmap.com). An email address is required to save mind maps, and these can be downloaded to a desktop or computer as a PDF or JPEG file.

➤ Text 2 Mind Map provides support for the following keyboard shortcuts:

- CTRL + Enter = Draw mind map
- CTRL + S = Save
- CTRL + D = Download

- CTRL + T = Show/hide text area
- CTRL + "+" = Zoom in
- CTRL + "-" = Zoom out

➤ A user's guide found on the product page provides basic instructions on creating interactive mind maps.

➤ Limited formatting options are provided for changing font type, size, and color, the color of branches/nodes, and the color and width of line connectors.

How Cybrarians Can Use This Resource

Promote as a Free Visualization Tool to Assist in Research

Dedicated users are using this free diagramming tool to structure and visualize ideas as they brainstorm and conceptualize projects, itemize tasks, take notes, revise a class assignment, or collaborate with peers to make decisions and solve problems.

Librarians are promoting mind maps and other concept maps as tools for researchers to assist in framing a research question, planning a research paper, taking class notes, or reviewing for a class exam. Although not using Text 2 Mind Map as the main production tool, the University of Massachusetts Libraries (Amherst, Massachusetts) created a subject guide for users with guidelines on using the free mind mapping tool Bubbl.us (https://bubbl.us) to construct a thesis state-ment.[1] Librarians at Clark College Libraries (Vancouver, Washington) developed an instructional video on how to use mind maps, including the popular online tool Popplet (Chapter 37) as brainstorming tools to complete research projects.[2]

FYI

Text 2 Mind Map's homepage features an updated feed of live tweets posted by clients who regularly use the application.

Notes

1. "Beyond Google: Integrating Library Resources into your Research Strategy: a Template for Librarians and Faculty." The University of Massachusetts Amherst Libraries, accessed May 17, 2014, www.guides.library.umass.edu/beyondgoogle.
2. "Brainstorm and Create Mind Maps," Clark College Libraries, accessed May 17, 2014, www.library.clark.edu/?q=content/brainstorm-and-create-mind-maps.

48

TodaysMeet
Microblogging Service
https://todaysmeet.com

Overview

Using microblogging services like Twitter at conferences to connect with and have conversations with one's audience in real time has become a common activity for presenters. Backchannel conversations on services like Twitter—where audience members ask each other questions, pass notes, and provide immediate feedback—and the connections forged in this manner are valuable, as they allow presentations to be tailored to the audience's immediate needs. TodaysMeet is a resource marketed as an alternative to Twitter in this arena.

This web-based service can be used to quickly create online chat rooms that enable presenters to establish live streams and communicate directly with an audience during a presentation. The attendees can immediately offer feedback, share insights, and ask questions. These isolated virtual chat rooms are specifically designed to provide unlimited access to backchannel conversations.

Launched in 2007, the basic TodaysMeet service is free, but as is common practice with most startup companies promoting products and services in beta mode, the developers have openly conceded that they may offer paid upgrades for advanced features in the future.

Features

➢ No registration is required to use TodaysMeet, and all chat rooms created on the service are private, accessible only to invited participants.

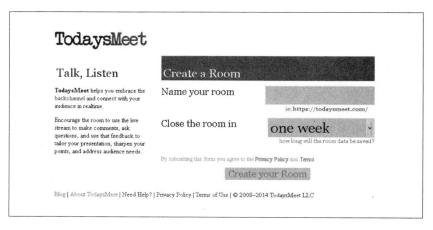

TodaysMeet allows users to quickly create online chat rooms.

➤　Using the service to create online chat rooms can be accomplished in three relatively simple steps:

1. Use the online web form provided on the homepage (https://todaysmeet.com) to enter the name of the chat room. A web link based on the name entered (for example, https://todaysmeet.com/LibraryConference) is immediately generated to be copied and emailed to participants. Room names must be 127 characters or less and not already in use.

2. Select a time period for saving data generated during the session before the room is closed (varies from one hour to one year).

3. Click the "Open Your Room" button. The presenter is then able to view chat posts on an interactive online screen. Invited participants must activate the link sent to them by email and enter their names before posting messages and comments (limited to 140 characters) in the text box provided.

➤　The Room Tools menu offers advanced options such as the flexibility to toggle to projector view, create a QR code for the session, generate an embed code for websites and blogs, view a memo of the date and time that the room is scheduled to close/expire, and access the speaker color feature to easily differentiate individual speakers.

➤ Transcripts are available for all TodaysMeet sessions, and these can be copied and saved into a word processor (WordPad and MS Office) or as a text or PDF file.

How Cybrarians Can Use This Resource

Host a Virtual Conference, Workshop, or Meeting and Connect with Attendees Anywhere

Most webinars and conferences now promote a Twitter hash tag (for example, #CIL2015) to encourage virtual and on-site attendees to post information and feedback on presentations. TodaysMeet is a worthy alternative for encouraging this type of two-way interaction. For the presenter, the immediate advantage is the ability to connect and host live conversations with attendees. For attendees, there is instant gratification in participating in an open and uncensored forum where they can share their insights and obtain immediate responses to comments and questions.

Librarians can promote the recently launched subscription-based TodaysMeet Teacher Tools (https://todaysmeet.com/about/teachertools) to teachers and lecturers as a digital platform for hosting classroom discussions online. This meeting portal offers users:

➤ Unlimited access to transcripts of online sessions hosted

➤ The option to temporarily close or pause the conversations in a meeting room

➤ The option to mute conversations

➤ The ability to control and limit accessibility to meeting rooms

➤ The ability to add topics or prompts to streamline discussions

FYI

The TodaysMeet Blog (blog.todaysmeet.com) provides tips and tricks for using the service as well as announcements of new and enhanced features.

49

Tumblr
Microblogging/Social
Networking Service
https://www.tumblr.com

Overview

Tumblr is a free microblogging and social networking service offering a suite of tools with customizable functionality that enable bloggers to effortlessly share content such as text, photos, quotes, links, music, video and audio files, and chat posts. The service's intuitive web-based dashboard permits sharing of this content from a web browser, mobile device, or email.

In a content-driven environment where creators are eagerly looking for tools to seamlessly communicate and connect within their communities, Tumblr has emerged as a popular go-to service in a lucrative market that includes other blogging services such as LiveJournal, Blogger, and WordPress. This advantage is a result of the social network's advanced features and functionalities, developed specifically to offer bloggers a social platform to create blogs quickly and effortlessly in real time, post multimedia content, follow subject-specific blogs, add tags, schedule posts, and share content directly on their Facebook and Twitter accounts.

Originally founded by David Karp in 2007, the New York-based blogging service was purchased by Yahoo! in 2013 for $1.1 billion.[1] The relatively low learning curve required to develop microblogs and share content (in all formats) on this service makes it attractive for new users, the majority of whom are reportedly young bloggers (38 percent under age of 25, and 68 percent are under 35).[2] Tumblr currently hosts more than 220 million blogs and 100 billion posts. Tumblrs have been developed in every imaginable subject area including art, poetry, fashion, food, music, publishing, books and bookstores, and, of course, libraries.

Features

➤ Users must first register on the product homepage (https://www.tumblr.com), providing an email address, password, and username to use the service. The simple registration process is designed to enable new Tumblrs to quickly create an account, customize a blog, and begin posting.

➤ The web-based dashboard is the primary platform available for managing and sharing blog content. Within this dashboard, users can accomplish the following tasks:

   • Create blog posts using myriad formats (text, images, quotes, links, audio, video, and chat posts)

   • Customize the layout and appearance of their microblogs using themes from an in-house directory or editing existing HTML

   • View live feeds of recent posts from blogs they follow

   • Mass edit posts and tags simultaneously

   • Assign privacy settings or short URLs to posts and blogs

   • Search for and "like" other Tumblr blogs

➤ Tumblr provides multiple platforms for sharing content:

   • Seamless news feed syndication allows Tumblrs to share posts on Twitter and Facebook

   • Using the custom email address assigned to each blog created on the service, Tumblrs can share posts via email

   • Using the "call in" posts feature, Tumblrs can dial an established telephone number (1-866-584-6757) and record an audio post

   • Tumblrs can post content from desktops, laptops, or mobile apps available for iPhone, iPad, Windows Phone, and Android devices

➤ "Share on Tumblr" bookmarklets allow users to quickly share content discovered while browsing other websites

➤ "Follow Tumblr" buttons allow new and existing Tumblr users to follow and promote content

Tumblr's dashboard is a popular platform for
managing and sharing blog content.

➤ As a consumer curation tool, Tumblr offers an easy way to
repost content (articles, images, videos, and text files) with a
click of the "Reblog" button

➤ Interactive feedback, opinions, and answers can be obtained
from the Tumblr community by ending a post with a question
mark and checking the option "Let people answer this" before
clicking "Publish"

➤ Tumblr's configurable post queue can automatically publish
posts on a designated schedule

How Cybrarians Can Use This Resource

Networking with a Community of Librarians on Tumblr (Tumblarians)

"Tumblr is rife with libraries. They're everywhere,"[3] according to Molly
McArdle. This opening line to McArdle's *Library Journal* article leads to
an in-depth review of libraries and librarians using the microblogging
service. At the time, in June 2013, McArdle estimated that there were
500 library- and archives-related blogs on Tumblr, which she attributed
to the same pull factors cited by other user communities: "ease of use in
adding and posting content in all formats, social features comparable
to Twitter, and the 'cool factor.'" This growing community of librarians on Tumblr has led to the coining of a new self-descriptive term
"Tumblarians," librarians who are flocking to the service that is part
social network and part microblogging service.

Tumblarians cite the following benefits in using the service:

➤ Hosting conversations, mainly through reblogging and comment functionality, and obtaining feedback on the library profession (#libraries, #librarians, #Tumblarians)

➤ Curating posts relevant to libraries and librarians

➤ Networking and sharing of information about libraries and librarianship with various communities such as publishers, booksellers, major media outlets, educators, and patrons

➤ Flexibility afforded as both a formal and informal social space, easily juxtaposing personal with professional information

➤ Sharing of resources and innovative ideas for library services such as book displays, library instruction, and ebooks

Libraries on Tumblr

➤ Arlington Public Library, Virginia (www.arlingtonvalib.tumblr.com)

➤ Darien Library, Connecticut (www.darienlibrary.tumblr.com)

➤ Library & Technology Services, Wellesley College, Massachusetts (www.wellesleycollegelibtech.tumblr.com)

➤ The New York Public Library, New York (www.nypl.tumblr.com)

➤ Queens Library, New York (www.queenslibrary.tumblr.com)

➤ Smithsonian Libraries, Washington, DC (www.smithsonianlibraries.tumblr.com)

Librarians on Tumblr

➤ Erin Downey Howerton and Bobbi Newman, "This is What a Librarian Looks Like" (www.lookslikelibraryscience.com)

➤ David Lee King, Digital Services Director, Topeka & Shawnee County Public Library (www.davidleeking.tumblr.com)

➤ Daniel Ransom, Librarian for Research and Electronic Resources at Holy Names University's Paul J. Cushing Library, Oakland, California (www.thepinakes.tumblr.com)

➣   Gina Sheridan, St. Louis, Missouri
     (www.iworkatapubliclibrary.com)

➣   Kate Tkacik, E-Resources Librarian at the Foundation Center–
     San Francisco (www.thelifeguardlibrarian.tumblr.com)

Tumblrs on Library Training and Professional Development

➣   Library Advocates, from ALA's Washington Office
     (www.libraryadvocates.tumblr.com)

➣   iPads and Tablets in Libraries
     (www.tabletsinlibraries.tumblr.com)

➣   Library Journal (www.tumblr.libraryjournal.com)

FYI

The average Tumblr user creates 14 original posts each month and reblogs three posts. Half of the posts on Tumblr are photos; the balance are split between text, links, quotes, music files, and videos (www.tumblr.com/about).

Notes

1. Chris Isidore, "Yahoo Buys Tumblr, Promises to Not 'Screw it Up'," *CNN Money*, May 20, 2013, accessed February 21, 2014, www.money.cnn.com/2013/05/20/technology/yahoo-buys-tumblr.
2. Molly McArdle, "The Library Is Open: A Look at Librarians and Tumblr," *Library Journal*, June 25, 2013, accessed February 21, 2014, www.reviews.libraryjournal.com/2013/06/in-thebookroom/post/the-library-is-open-a-look-at-librarians-and-tumblr.
3. Ibid.

50

TweetDeck
Social Media Management Service
https://tweetdeck.twitter.com

Overview

Since its launch in 2006, the social networking and microblogging service Twitter, which allows users to create, send, and read messages or posts known as "tweets," continues to gain notoriety and popularity worldwide. Twitter is currently ranked as one of the ten most visited websites, with 288 million monthly users and an average of 500 million tweets per day.[1] In 2011, five years after Twitter's launch, co-founder Biz Stone touted the service as "more than a triumph of technology," viewing it as a "triumph of humanity."[2] One only has to look at tweets posted about recent global events—the Arab Spring, the Iranian election, Venezuela's insurgency, crises in Ukraine and Iraq, the devastating effects of Ebola in Africa, and the onslaught of natural disasters—to find tangible evidence and confirm that Stone's views still hold true as Twitter's continued presence in online interactive communication helps to foster and connect communities around the globe.

Given Twitter's role in the social networking sphere, it is not surprising that many applications have been built to integrate with the Twitter platform. TweetDeck, Twitter's native social media dashboard for management of Twitter accounts, is one such tool. Like other Twitter applications, TweetDeck integrates seamlessly with Twitter's API to allow Twitterers to send and receive tweets and view profiles. This management dashboard service is ideal for real-time tracking, organizing, and social engagement.

The one disadvantage in using TweetDeck is that Twitter has discontinued support for TweetDeck AIR, TweetDeck for Android, and TweetDeck for iPhone, along with the suspension for support of popular social networks Facebook and LinkedIn. Twitter rationalized the

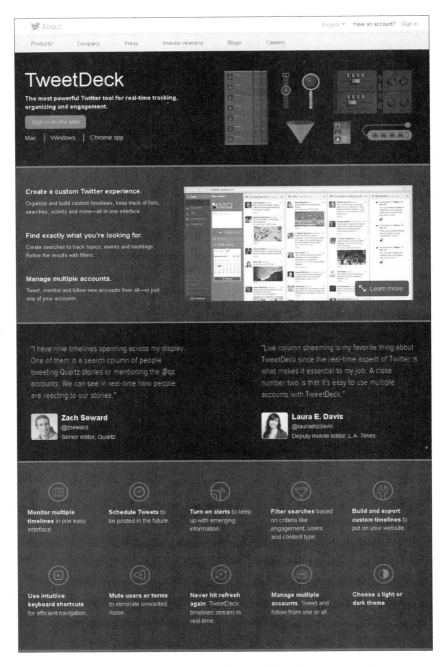

TweetDeck is Twitter's native social media dashboard
for the management of Twitter accounts.

move in a statement reiterating the service's "need to focus our development efforts on our modern, web-based versions of TweetDeck."[3] TweetDeck is currently only available as a web and desktop application.

Features

➤ Effortless sign-in with an existing Twitter account (https://tweetdeck.twitter.com)

➤ Monitoring of multiple timelines in one easy intuitive interface/dashboard

➤ Scheduling of tweets for future postings

➤ Ability to turn on alerts to keep up with trending information in specific fields

➤ Use of filter searches based on criteria such as engagement, users, and content type

➤ Ability to build and export custom timelines to embed on blogs and websites

➤ Use of intuitive keyboard shortcuts for efficient navigation

➤ Ability to mute users or terms (keywords) to eliminate unwanted data

➤ Ability to refresh timelines

➤ Option to manage tweets and follow multiple accounts simultaneously from one account

➤ Choice of dashboard themes

How Cybrarians Can Use This Resource

Streamline Multiple Library Twitter Accounts

As a social media management service, TweetDeck provides the tools for organizations to track online, real-time conversations within Twitter. The service's flexibility and customizable layout allows users to monitor and keep current with trends on Twitter, across multiple topics and accounts. Within libraries, TweetDeck can be used to customize the Twitter experience—building custom timelines, lists, searches, and filters—and to manage and streamline multiple Twitter accounts within a centralized platform that ensures standardized service and messaging to local and global communities.

Librarian blogger Diane Schrecker shares her experience of using TweetDeck's web version in a project to highlight the collections at the Instructional Resource Center (IRC) at the Ashland University Library in Ohio. As a "return on this particular investment" in using the service, she "hopes to see an increase in followers for the IRC Twitter feed and an increased awareness and use of the IRC and its collections."[4]

FYI

The TweetDeck Blog (https://blog.twitter.com/tweetdeck) offers tips, news, and updates about TweetDeck features, functions, and new services.

Notes

1. "About Twitter," Twitter Website, accessed February 8, 2015, https://about.twitter.com/company.
2. Biz Stone, "Tweet Preservation," Twitter Blog, April 14, 2010, https://blog.twitter.com/2010/tweet-preservation.
3. "An Update on TweetDeck," TweetDeck Blog, March 4, 2013 https://blog.twitter.com/2013/an-update-on-tweetdeck.
4. "TweetDeck Newbie", Library Cloud Blog, Monday July 7, 2014, www.librarycloud.blogspot.com/2014/07/tweetdeck-newbie.html.

51

Udutu
Course Management System
www.udutu.com

Overview

Udutu offers online learning solutions designed to help small and large organizations build and distribute online training courses. The company's free online course authoring software and accompanying complementary technical network supports institutions wishing to build interactive online courses. The company also offers a full-featured, hosted Learning Management System (LMS) for a fee.

For large corporations, small businesses, and educational institutions desiring to provide learning and training opportunities for managers, employees, faculty, or students, Udutu serves as a practical, feasible online LMS solution. The online course authoring component of the service requires limited technical expertise and is fully supported within most operating systems and web browsers. The "What You See Is What You Get" (WYSIWYG) interface seamlessly integrates all media types (graphic, sound, and video formats) and permits import of existing curricula and PowerPoint presentations to develop interactive courses.

Udutu's commitment to provide eLearning solutions to an expanding customer base stems from the company's conviction that "web-based online learning is one of the hot emerging industries of this decade" and that tools should be developed to "make it easy for anybody to create and deliver online learning."[1] The company has offices in Canada (Victoria, British Columbia) and the U.S. (Santa Cruz, California).

Features

➢ Trainers can register for a free Udutu Course Authoring account by providing an email address, password,

Udutu offers online learning solutions for small and large organizations that want to build and distribute training courses.

organization name, first name, last name, and promotion code (www.myudutu.com/myudutu/main/admin/EditCustomer.aspx?uc=1).

➤ The minimum system requirements for accessing the cloud-based authoring software are as follows: Internet Explorer (5+), Firefox (1+), or Macromedia Flash Player (8+), with minimum screen resolution of 1024 x 768.

➤ Udutu's free course authoring tool package offers the following features and capabilities to support developing interactive online courses:

• Cloud-based authoring software

• Online help resources

- Monitored customer support (info@udutu) available seven days a week

- Real-time collaboration

- Customizable theme templates

- HTML5 screen templates

- Interactive assessment templates

- Advanced interactive templates

- Prebuilt, game-like scenario templates

- Simple or complex branching from objects or screens

- Optimized media

- Embed third party videos (YouTube)

- Link to course screens, documents, or external websites

- Import PowerPoint as HTML or as Flash (iSpring)

- Import complex flash zip files from other tools (Captivate, Raptivity, etc.)

- Import any web-compatible content from other sources

- Save content objects to a library

- Publish watermarked preview links to courses

- Publish to Facebook, iOS, HTML5

- Publish an iPad-compatible version

- Extract courses and deploy on any web server or SCORM (Shareable Content Object Reference Model) LMS

- Extract courses and burn to DVD

- Add additional course authoring users

- Review course authoring history

- Section 508 compliance

➣ A full-featured, fee-based, hosted LMS available as a free 90-day trial provides access to the following features:

- Private LMS accounts

- Customized branding

262 The Cybrarian's Web 2

- Customized groupings and ad-hoc virtual classrooms for learners to ensure closed access
- Curriculum tracking that facilitates online courses and tests
- Unlimited monitoring of learner progress with extensive reporting capabilities

How Cybrarians Can Use This Resource

Promoting Access to a Virtual Learning Environment (VLE)

Designed with the goal of providing educators with the best tools to manage and promote learning, Udutu offers free authoring tools to build and distribute online training courses. The company's extensive list of global clients in all sectors (Georgia Department of Education, Harley-Davidson, Canadian Pacific Railway, Microsoft, and Pearson) is evidence of its viability in supporting elearning needs. Cybrarians can promote Udutu to teachers and students within their local library communities. Registered members have immediate access to the cloud-based system in order to experiment, build, test, and extract interactive online courses.

FYI

The Udutu Testimonial page (www.udutu.com/index .php/testimonials) provides examples of organizations and institutions actively engaged in Udutu projects.

Note

1. "Udutu," CrunchBase, accessed May 17, 2014, www.crunchbase.com/organization/udutu.

52

Unglue.it
Crowdfunding Platform
https://unglue.it

Overview

Using the tag line "Give Ebooks to the World, Unglue.it," a new type of crowdfunding service for ebook enthusiasts and authors was launched on the web on May 17, 2012. The service's initial campaign urged site visitors to make monetary pledges towards five books they wished to "unglue" and free from copyright and other legal restrictions. The idea behind this new service is as simple as it is innovative, and it attempts to respond to questions like the following: What if you could give a book to everyone on earth? Get an ebook and read it on any device, in any format, forever? Give an ebook to your library? Own Digital Rights Management (DRM)-free ebooks legally? Read free ebooks on all devices and know their creators had been adequately compensated?[1]

Unglue.it is marketed as the platform where individuals and institutions can work collectively to pay authors and publishers to publish ebooks and other types of digital content free under a Creative Commons license. If supporters pledge and raise the dollar amount chosen by the book's rights holder before a stipulated deadline, the book is released as "unglued" in electronic editions under the Creative Commons license and can be freely downloaded by anyone in the world, including libraries. Unglue.it is a service provided by Gluejar, Inc.

Crowdfunding, collectively pooling contributions or pledges to support a cause, has gained traction in recent times with civic-minded sites such as Indiegogo, Kickstarter (Chapter 25), and Fundly leading the way. Complete strangers from all over the globe, drawn by a common cause, coalesce on the internet to work together and solicit funds to start a project, support an invention, or launch a professional career. Based on current trends showing worldwide support for crowdfunding services, there is the promise that Unglue.it's unique ebook distribution platform will continue to grow exponentially, given its civic mission.

Features for Authors

➤ Registration on Unglue.it (https://unglue.it) is free. However, when pledge campaigns have been successfully completed, Gluejar Inc. deducts commission fees from the funds raised.

➤ To start a campaign, authors need to establish that they are the rights holder for the books they wish to unglue, work with the Gluejar team to sign all the required legal agreements, set revenue goals, and obtain tips on running and publicizing campaigns.

➤ Authors can take advantage of one of three types of ungluing campaigns:

  • Pledge Campaign—Supporters pledge monetary contributions to unglue a book. When the revenue goal is reached, the unglued ebook is released with a Creative Commons license, and the author retains the copyright. Supporters' credit cards are charged only when the funding goal is reached.

  • Buy-to-Unglue Campaign—Each copy of an ebook sold on the service propels the author towards achieving the established revenue goal and ungluing date, when the book is released under a Creative Commons license.

  • Thanks-for-Ungluing Campaign—This campaign targets ebooks that have already been unglued and released under a Creative Commons license. Pledgers continue to reward authors of unglued works by opting to continue making financial contributions.

➤ Each unglued ebook is issued a dedicated webpage with bibliographic information (author, title, publication date, and brief description), the date the campaign succeeded, the number of successful pledges, a listing of project supporters, the revenue goal, and the amount of money raised.

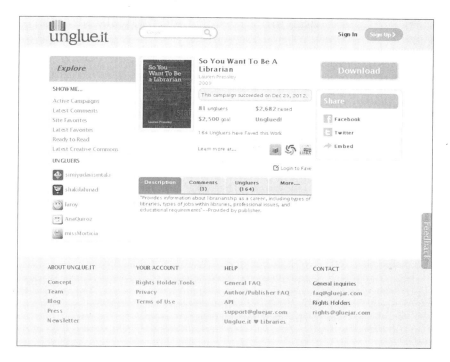

On Unglue.it, each unglued ebook is issued a dedicated webpage.

➤ For authors, support is provided in the form of FAQ pages for Rights Holders (https://unglue.it/faq/rightsholders) and online access to Rights Holder Tools (https://unglue.it/rightsholders).

Features for Readers and Campaign Supporters

➤ On the Unglue.it homepage, readers can search for and download unglued books, as well as view and support active campaigns. Books can be downloaded as MOBI or EPUB files. There are instructions to download titles directly to ereaders (Kindle, Nook, and Kobo), desktop computers, and iOS and Android devices.

➤ Visitors to the site have the option of searching the website's database to identify books they want unglued. Once a title is found, it can be added to a wish list. The more wish lists a book is on, the more appealing it is for rights holders to launch an Unglue.it campaign.

> Users have access to a widget (embedded HTML code) that can be added to a personal website or blog to share an active ungluing campaign. There are also social media sharing links (Facebook and Twitter) on Unglue.it's landing page.

> For those wishing to make a monetary pledge, there is a "Support" button on all active campaign pages. A registered account is required in order to pledge. When ungluing campaigns are successful, pledgers are acknowledged in the unglued ebook as follows:

  • A donation of $25 lists the supporter's name in the book's acknowledgement section.

  • A donation of $50 lists the supporter's name and link to his/her profile page in the Benefactors section.

  • A donation of $100 lists the supporter's name, link to his/her profile page, and a personal dedication of 140 words or less in the Bibliophiles section.

How Cybrarians Can Use This Resource

Host or Pledge Support for an Unglue.it Campaign

Librarians can promote and market this platform to local authors and other information professionals as a platform for self-publishing, downloading, and sharing free ebooks. Lauren Pressley, author of *So You Want to Be a Librarian,* hosted a successful campaign on Unglue.it. The campaign reached its target goal of $2,500 on December 29, 2012 with the support of 81 ungluers.

On the book's dedicated webpage, Pressley presents a compelling case on "Why Should Librarians (and Those Who Want to be Librarians) Unglue?" She comments, "Unglue.it is something every librarian should be paying attention to. Part crowdsourcing, part open access, part answer to the ebook problem, it's a solution to some of the most critical issues libraries are facing today. Ungluing a book gives it to the world, so that anyone can access the ebook without Digital Rights Management (DRM), without worrying about how many devices they've put it on, and without worrying about legality and compensation issues. Libraries can provide access to unglued books for free, forever, in any format—no need to worry about changing contract terms or pricing."[2]

Libraries actively supporting Unglue.it campaigns include the Leddy Library University of Windsor (Ontario, Canada), the University of Alberta Libraries (Edmonton, Canada) and the Z. Smith Reynolds Library (Wake Forest University, Winston-Salem, North Carolina).

Library Activism and Advocacy: Support the Unglue.it for Libraries Program

The developers of Unglue.it, including Eric Hellman (President of Gluejar Inc. which provides the Unglue.it service), openly admit that "we love libraries because we're from the library world and want libraries to have books they can share with patrons without DRM, without device restrictions, without tracking of patrons, [and] without license expirations."[3]

Libraries are encouraged to participate in and support the Unglue.it for Libraries project using the following steps and guidelines:[4]

1. Create a library page on Unglue.it then review and sign the Library License Agreement.

2. Once approved, buy library licenses for any ebook with a "Buy-to-Unglue" campaign.

3. Libraries can immediately lend these ebooks to patrons using the Unglue.it free distribution platform. The library license gives download access to a single patron for a circulating period of 14 days.

4. The license continues until the ebook is unglued, then the book becomes freely available in the public domain. Using this method of licensing, libraries can augment existing ebook collections by adding books released during successful campaigns.

5. Catalogers are encouraged to register with the Unglue.it Catalogers' List and utilize their skills to add high quality MARC records to OCLC and SkyRiver databases. These MARC records are available at no cost to participating libraries to download to online catalogs.

FYI

Unglue.it's first successful campaign was the release of Ruth Finnegan's *Oral Literature in Africa* (https://unglue.it/work/142306/#).

Notes

1. "Unglue it: FAQs Basics," Unglue.it, accessed June 3, 2012, https://unglue.it/faq/.
2. "Sarah Pressley, "So You Want to be a Librarian," Unglue.it, accessed February 17, 2014, https://unglue.it/work/76348.
3. "Unglue it: About," Unglue.it, accessed February 17, 2014, https://unglue.it/about.
4. "Unglue it for Libraries" Unglue.it, accessed February 17, 2014, https://unglue.it/libraries.

53

Vine
Video Sharing Service
https://vine.co

Overview

Vine is Twitter's mobile video-sharing app, developed to enable users to create and share short looping video clips. Like tweets that are restricted to a maximum of 140 characters, each recorded Vine has a maximum clip length of six seconds. This brevity, as explained by Twitter, should inspire creativity as videographers easily capture motion and sound.[1] Videos created using the app can be immediately posted on Vine's social network or shared on other social networks such as Twitter and Facebook.

As innovative as Twitter was for instant messaging, Vine is a ground-breaking service for novice videographers wishing to capture and share unique films. The service is designed to record separate short films and link these together without much editing for a final clip totaling six seconds. Each short video plays in a continuous loop and is viewable directly on Vine's online network. The app's intuitive interface, home screen, and social networking capabilities are similar to Instagram's (Chapter 21). In fact, Vine is often labeled as the "Instagram for videos."

The Vine app is freely downloadable from the App Store (iOS), Google Play (Android), and Windows Phone Store (Windows Phone). Vine was acquired by Twitter in October 2012 for a reported $30 million and within seven months of purchase (April 9, 2013), Vine became the most downloaded free app available in the App Store.[2] Vine's popularity and extensive usage is in keeping with a recent Pew Research Center report that indicates photos and videos have become an integral part of the online social experience. Pew findings reveal that more than half of

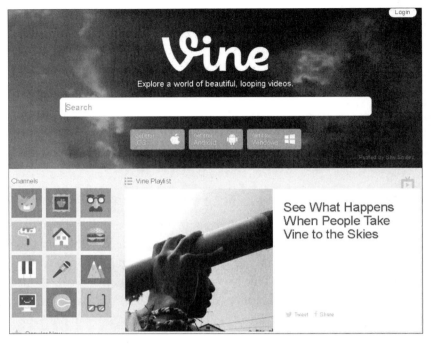

Vine is Twitter's video-sharing app, designed to enable users
to create and share short, looping video clips.

internet users post or share photos or videos online, with 54 percent of
adult internet users acknowledging that they had posted original photos or videos online.[3]

Features

➤   New Vine users register on the product homepage (https://
    vine.co) by completing an online form with their name,
    email address, password, and telephone (optional) as well as
    agreeing to the terms of service and privacy policy. All new
    users are assigned a profile page to set a profile photo and
    add brief biodata. Options are available to add Vine contacts
    from Twitter or invite contacts via text or email. Facebook
    and Twitter can be directly linked to a Vine account to allow
    seamless sharing of Vines created on the service.

➤   A tutorial is available to guide new users in recording their
    first video or vine. The concept is unique, restricting users to

filming very short, separate clips to form a full six-second video. Vine records (with audio) only when users tap and hold the screen with their fingers for a maximum of six seconds. This step is repeated until a six-second (or less) looping video is created. A progress bar tracks the length of each clip, and built-in camera tools assist with editing the short clip.

➤ Vines can be revined (similar in function and intent to retweeting in Twitter), "liked," tagged with keywords, and commented upon.

➤ Both the Search and Explore options on Vine's web-based and app versions allow Vine users to view popular video posts, highlighted in the Vine Playlist, Editor's Picks, Featured Viners, Trending Posts, or Posts on the Rise. Users can also browse videos arranged by channels or wide ranging categories such as Comedy, Art, DIY, Style, Animals, Family, Beauty and Fashion, Food, Health and Fitness, Nature, Music, News and Politics, Special FX, and Sports.

➤ In 2015 Twitter launched the VineKids app. "Through adorable animated characters, kids can watch videos that are appropriate for a young audience." (blog.vine.co/post/109591575386/say-hello-to-vine-kids).

How Cybrarians Can Use This Resource

Creating Social Videos to Promote Library Services

By limiting videos to six seconds, Vine aims to capture the essence of sound, motion, and images in new and compelling ways. Libraries have adopted this new format to promote and market library services. Ellyssa Kroski in "15 Cool Ways Libraries Can Use Vine to Create Social Videos" shares innovative ideas on how libraries can use videos created with Vine:[4]

➤ Highlight new acquisitions

➤ Showcase library exhibits

➤ Offer micro library tours

➤ Spotlight library events

➤ Offer instruction and tips

➤ Introduce library staff

➤ Showcase collections

➤ Spotlight a Makerspace or other unique space

➤ Aggregate video content

➤ Profile patrons and their work

FYI

Vine was listed among *Time* magazine's 50 Best Android Applications for 2013. (www.techland.time .com/2013/07/01/50-best-android-apps-for-2013/ slide/vine)

Notes

1. Michael Sippey, "Vine: A New Way to Share Video," Twitter Blog, January 24, 2013, https://blog.twitter.com/2013/vine-a-new-way-to-share-video.
2. *Wikipedia*, s.v. "Vine (Service)," accessed March 27, 2014, www.en.wikipedia.org/wiki/Vine_(service).
3. Maeve Duggan, "Photo and Video Sharing Grow Online," Pew Research Internet Project, October 28, 2013, accessed March 24, 2014, www.pewinternet .org/2013/10/28/photo-and-video-sharing-grow-online.
4. Ellyssa Kroski, "15 Cool Ways Libraries Can Use Vine to Create Social Videos," OEDb Open Education Database, July 23, 2013, accessed March 24, 2014, www.oedb.org/ilibrarian/10-cool-ways-libraries-can-use-vine.

54

Voki
Avatar Creation Service
www.voki.com

Overview

Voki is a service that provides users with the online tools to create customized speaking avatars. Avatars are graphical representations of persons (or their alter egos) and are commonly used as characters in social media profiles, gaming, virtual worlds (such as Second Life), computing, and online community forums. Using Voki, avatars can be fully customized and transformed into historical figures, cartoons, animals, and selected individuals or personae. Avatars created on Voki are given a voice via recordings with the help of a device's microphone, using the service's dial-in number, or uploading an audio file. Voki characters created in this way can be shared via email, on social media networks, and embedded on websites.

Although the basic Voki service is free, two Voki subscription-based plans—Voki Classroom and Voki Presenter—are marketed primarily as educational tools, for educators and students. Voki Classroom is a classroom management system enabling students to complete class work and assignments within the Voki digital environment. Voki Presenter is a presentation tool designed to enhance the way teachers teach, interact with, and engage students by allowing the insertion of Voki characters into presentations.

The Voki range of products was developed exclusively for personal, noncommercial use. For commercial clients wishing to enhance and improve social engagement and online communication using customizable avatars, an alternative product SitePal is available as a paid subscription. Voki is created and managed by Oddcast and is based in New York City.

Voki is a service that allows users to create customized speaking avatars.

Features

➤ The basic Voki service is free. All new users must first register for a Voki account on the product homepage (www.voki.com) by providing a name, email address, and password. Account holders must be at least 13 years old.

➤ When registered with the basic service, Voki users have access to the following features:

  • Create, save, and edit avatars

  • Access to 200 characters (some restrictions apply)

  • Create and edit audio messages (up to 60 seconds)

  • Options for adding backgrounds and themes

  • Post Voki avatars on blogs or websites

➤ Using Voki's user-friendly web-based interface, users can quickly create and share Voki characters on social networks by following this process:

- Click the "Create" tab from any Voki page.

- Select a character from one of several available styles: Classic, Animals, Edgy, Oddballs, VIP, World, and Digimon.

- Customize the avatar by changing its physical appearance, clothing, and accessories. The Voki editor supports the following formats: JPG or JPEG files (background image files) as well as WMA, PCM, MP3, and WAV (audio) files.

- Add voice using one of several options: via telephone (using the service assigned telephone number and passcode), recording on a microphone, typing text that is converted to speech, or uploading a file from an external source.

- Choose a background from an online library or upload a background file from a computer.

- Share the avatar with friends via email, post to social networks (Twitter, Facebook, Google Plus, WordPress, or Blogger) or copy HTML code provided to embed the avatar on a blog or website.

➤ The Voki app is available for Apple and Android mobile devices.

How Cybrarians Can Use This Resource
Online Educational Tool

The Voki website serves as a virtual toolbox complete with online resources on how cybrarians can use this tool in classroom and other teaching environments. Resources include:

➤ Learn About Voki page—tutorials, FAQs, getting started tips, and user guides (www.voki.com/learn.php)

➤ Voki blog (blog.voki.com)

➤ Instructional videos (https://www.youtube.com/watch?v=pZwQTm_5s6Q&feature=youtu.be)

➤ Lesson Plans and Activities (www.voki.com/lesson_plans.php)

FYI

Voki is a combination of the words "vox" and "Loki."
Vox is the Latin term for voice, and Loki is a god from
Norse mythology—described by some sources as a
trickster with the ability to change his shape.

55

Wattpad
Social Networking Service
https://www.wattpad.com

Overview

Wattpad was built on the premise that great stories can bring people together; all that is required to make this bonding a reality is a story-telling platform to connect the writer with the reader. Conceived as such a storytelling platform in 2006, Wattpad has grown into the "world's largest [online] community for discovering and sharing stories," with readers reportedly spending more than nine billion minutes on the service every month, collecting stories for their reading lists, forging connections with writers, voting for their favorite titles, and sharing their views with friends and other readers.[1]

For writers on Wattpad, the service offers an opportunity to publish and share their work with more than 35 million readers, many of whom are willing to provide literary criticism and other feedback. Writers can experiment with articles, monographs, and serialized works in genres such as romance, mystery, and science fiction, and readers can access and read these literary pieces on- or offline, within their browsers or using the Wattpad app developed for iPhones, iPads, BlackBerry, Kindle, and Android devices. The service is based in Toronto, Canada.

Features

➤ Readers and writers can register for the service for free on the product homepage (www.wattpad.com). Accounts can be created using an email address and password or users can register with an existing Facebook account.

➤ Readers can search for stories and add them to their personal libraries. Work of potential interest can be readily discovered by browsing staff picks and reader recommendations in the following categories: Featured, What's Hot, Undiscovered Gems, and What's New. Stories are easily accessible when organized into reading lists.

➤ Each reader can create a maximum of 10 reading lists, and each list is limited to 200 stories. Reading lists are public to other Wattpadders, unlike personal libraries, which can be designated as private. Readers can follow as many as 1,000 of their favorite writers in order to receive updates and messages or add comments to titles. Users who reach the limit must unfollow some writers before they can add new ones.[2]

➤ Writers can self-publish stories to share with the Wattpad community of readers using the built-in "What You See Is What You Get" (WYSIWYG) editor. Within this editor, there are options to add tags, place a story in a specific category, select a rating, and attach copyright information.

➤ As a storytelling and online sharing community, the service offers meaningful advice on how to share and promote stories on Wattpad:

- Follow other writers, read their work, and offer feedback

- Engage in conversations with readers, being responsive to comments about stories

- Register with a Wattpad Club (www.wattpad.com/clubs) such as the Editorial Exchange or the Multimedia Designs Club

- Link other social media networks (notably Facebook and Twitter) to a Wattpad profile and use these networks to promote works

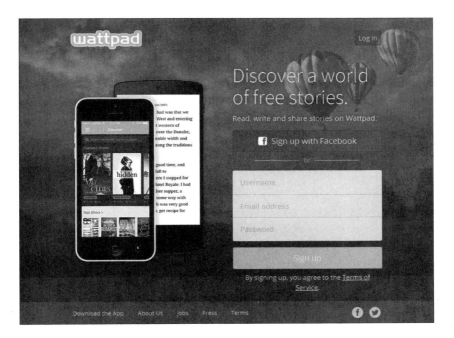

Wattpad is the world's largest online community
for discovering and sharing stories.

How Cybrarians Can Use This Resource

Market Wattpad as a Self-Publishing Platform to Authors

Cybrarians can use Wattpad to give aspiring writers a platform to promote their literary works to local and global communities. Promotional strategies include the following:

➤ Indexing Wattpad as a resource for writers in subject guides

➤ Liking Wattpad's Facebook page (https://www.facebook.com/wattpad)

➤ Following Wattpad's Instagram page (http://instagram.com/wattpad#)

➤ Linking to Wattpad's Twitter feeds (https://twitter.com/wattpad)

➤ Creating a Wattpad Pinterest board (www.pinterest.com/pin/84231455504044114)

➤ Writing reviews of works published in Wattpad and posting these reviews on library blogs

FYI

The Watty Awards is an annual contest voted on by Wattpad community members to recognize the best submissions in a number of genres.

Notes

1. "About Wattpad," Wattpad, accessed February 6, 2015, www.wattpad.com/about.
2. "Wattpad Help Center," Wattpad, accessed November 3, 2014, http://support .wattpad.com/hc/en-us/articles/201415410-How-do-I-follow-other-people-

56

Weebly
Web Hosting Service
www.weebly.com

Overview

Named by *Time* magazine as one of the 50 Best Websites of 2007, Weebly is a web-hosting service that compares favorably with competing services Blogger, Google Sites, and WordPress.[1] Weebly's trademarked drag-and-drop website building capabilities have been the mainstay of the product's popularity with its clientele, as this feature allows nonprofessionals with little or no technical expertise to quickly create websites. The additional features available to build blogs and support ecommerce have also proven to be significant in retaining Weebly's extensive customer base. Since the service launched in 2007, more than 20 million individuals and businesses have used it to establish an online presence.[2]

Weebly is available in 11 languages and supports the integration of all types of content elements including text, photos, maps, video, and audio. Websites are built in real time within a web browser and without the need to install additional software. Websites created are hosted within the cloud and can be accessed across multiple platforms and devices. The company has its headquarters in San Francisco, California.

Features

➤   Weebly's free service (www.weebly.com) offers all the basic features and functionalities required for new users to build high-quality websites. Free accounts have unlimited storage space on the cloud, but each individual file can be no more than 10 MB in size.

➤   The three-tiered premium plan (Starter, Pro, and Business) offers advanced features not available on the free version. These include customized domain names, built-in site analytics, site searches, password protection, technical support, and integrated ecommerce capabilities.

➤   Weebly's core advantage over its competitors is its innovative drag-and-drop website editor. Content elements such as text, videos, photos, maps, and slides are important building blocks of all websites. Adding elements to a website built using Weebly is as simple as clicking on that element and dragging and dropping it on to a webpage. No advanced HTML coding or special technical skills are required.

➤   Weebly supports the creation of blogs with full comment moderation features, the ability to add tags to all posts created, integration of different types of content, and the flexibility of either immediately publishing posts or saving them as drafts, to edit or publish at a later date.

➤   Online access is provided to a library of design templates for selecting a website theme. Within the Weebly editor, there is also the option of customizing the templates or building new ones using custom HTML and CSS style sheets.

➤   Weebly automatically generates a mobile version of each website built using the service. When this mobile version is enabled, visitors accessing websites from smartphones and other mobile devices are presented with content optimized for mobile viewing.

➤   Weebly offers easy integration of social networks (Facebook, Twitter, Pinterest, and Google Plus) for sharing information with friends and followers.

➤   Weebly website developers have three options for choosing a website domain/address:

1. Use a free sub-domain of Weebly.com (e.g. http://your name.weebly.com)

2. Purchase and register a new domain directly from Weebly

3. Configure an existing domain to work with the Weebly site

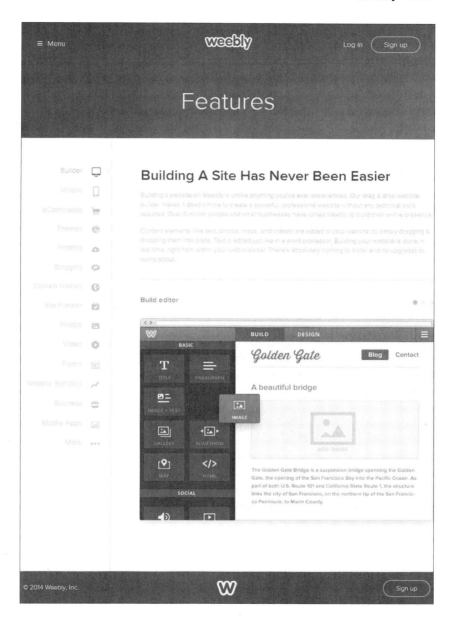

Weebly is known for its trademarked drag-and-drop
website building capabilities.

➤ Weebly apps are available for iPhones and Android devices. These apps allow website developers to multitask, managing their websites from mobile devices and posting and sharing content on the go using their social networks.

How Cybrarians Can Use This Resource

Promote the Weebly for Education Program

Weebly has extended its service to educators through the Weebly for Education program (www.education.weebly.com/ed-features.php). The password-protected environment and user-friendly website editor are popular features among teachers, as with other user communities. Weebly is a great example of a free resource that cybrarians can promote to educators to assist in creating classroom websites, student eportfolios, and websites for assigned projects.

FYI

Weebly's Beginners Guide and hosted webinars (www.kb.weebly.com/first-steps.html) provide all the basic information users need to build their sites.

Notes

1. Maryanne Murray Buechner, "Weebly: Build a Web Site," Time.com, July 8, 2007, accessed January 11, 2014, www.content.time.com/time/specials/2007/article/0,28804,1633488_1633608_1633636,00.html.
2. "About Weebly," Weebly, accessed February 6, 2015, www.weebly.com/about.

57

WhatsApp
Instant Messaging Service
www.whatsapp.com

Overview

WhatsApp Messenger is a mobile messaging app that allows users to exchange instant messages and group chats (SMS), send photos and videos, and share locations on their smartphones. This multifunctional, cross-platform app is supported on Android, BlackBerry, iPhone, Microsoft Windows Phone, and selected Nokia platforms.

In a modern mobile environment where instant messaging (texting) is increasingly popular, users are often compelled to pay monthly subscription fees to internet service providers (ISPs) to communicate via text messaging. WhatsApp has emerged as a credible alternative in this highly competitive arena, offering a client-friendly bundled service with low subscription rates—currently free for the first year followed by $0.99 paid annual subscription service—accessible on all major smartphones. As of this writing, WhatsApp is not supported on tablets or desktop computers.

Smartphone users registering with the service can share content with anyone who has downloaded and installed the app on their device and can immediately send instant messages in an ad-free environment. This shrewd marketing strategy has led to unprecedented growth in the company's client base. The service, launched in 2009, is currently serving some 500 million subscribers, and on December 31, 2013 set "a new record of 18 billion messages processed in one day."[1]

This expansive database of users coupled with a viable business model was perceived by industry insiders as WhatsApp's sell-off appeal, leading them to promote the company as the perfect candidate for potential merger and acquisition by established venture capitalists and

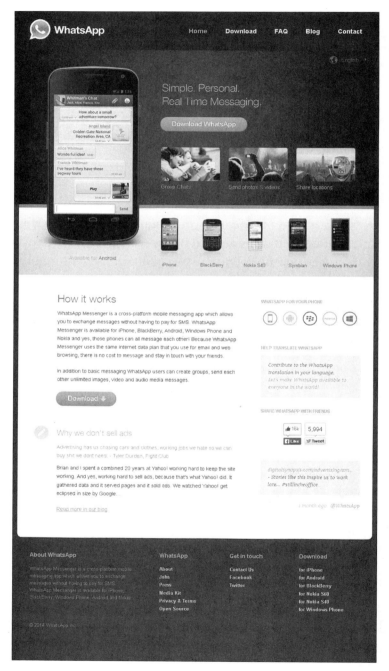

WhatsApp users have immediate access to
apps on most major mobile platforms.

entrepreneurs. Social networking juggernaut Facebook, which had already shown a predilection for gaining a strong foothold in the lucrative mobile services industry by successfully purchasing mobile photo sharing app Instagram (Chapter 21) for $1 billion, acquired WhatsApp in February 2014 for $19 billion.

Commenting on this extremely costly acquisition, Facebook CEO Mark Zuckerberg wrote on his personal Facebook page: "Our mission is to make the world more open and connected. We do this by building services that help people share any type of content with any group of people they want. WhatsApp will help us do this by continuing to develop a service that people around the world love to use every day … We also expect that WhatsApp will add to our efforts for Internet.org, our partnership to make basic internet services affordable for everyone."[2]

In an attempt to secure the mobile messaging service's long-term viability and future potential to "connect one billion people," Zuckerberg assured existing users that "WhatsApp will continue to operate independently within Facebook and the product roadmap will remain unchanged."[3]

Features

➤ This real-time messaging app is supported on most major mobile platforms. On the product homepage (www .whatsapp.com), users have immediate access to download the app for the following smartphones: Apple iPhone, Android, BlackBerry, Nokia, and Microsoft Windows Phone. When installed, WhatsApp creates a user account using the subscriber's phone number, thus there is no need to create a username and password.

➤ In addition to basic messaging, WhatsApp users can do the following:

   • Create groups, add or remove group participants, change the group subject, set a group icon, and broadcast group messages

   • Send unlimited images, video files, and voice notes to contacts

- Set a profile photo
- Send instant messages to other WhatsApp users
- Immediately access existing contacts
- Save messages and push notifications when offline
- Share locations and exchange contacts
- Customize wallpapers and notification sounds, set landscape mode, add message timestamps, and email chat history

How Cybrarians Can Use This Resource

Implement IM and SMS Reference Services

Text messaging is becoming the preferred communication mode among colleagues, family, and friends. This communication form is so pervasive, in fact, that most web users expect instant messaging (IM) and text messaging (SMS) services to be instantly accessible and available when visiting educational, commercial, and organizational websites. To keep up with this trend, libraries are offering around-the-clock, chat-based Ask a Librarian reference services, and many librarians are taking advantage of professional development opportunities to learn how to implement IM and SMS reference services in their libraries.

Several factors must be considered before integrating these services with traditional reference services. These include assessing the library patron population (target audience), evaluating the internal human resources needs (scheduling and training staff), examining the technological requirements (software and hardware availability), promoting best practices, marketing to patrons, and continually assessing and evaluating services once they have been implemented. A list of libraries offering SMS reference services can be found at the Library Success Wiki (www.libsuccess.org/Libraries_Offering_SMS_Reference_Services).

FYI

In January 2015, the service introduced WhatsApp Web, giving users the ability to view/mirror all conversations and messages from their mobile devices within the Google Chrome web browser (blog.whatsapp.com).

Notes

1. "On Dec 31st We Had a New Record Day: 7B msgs inbound, 11B msgs outbound = 18 billion Total Messages Processed in One Day! Happy 2013," WhatsApp (Twitter Feed), January 2, 2013, accessed February 22, 2014, https://twitter.com/WhatsApp/status/286591302185938946.
2. "Mark Zuckerberg's Full Statement on Facebook Buying WhatsApp," The Guardian, February 20, 2014, accessed February 22, 2014, www.theguardian.com/technology/2014/feb/20/mark-zuckerberg-statement-facebook-buying-whatsapp.
3. Ibid.

58

Wikispaces
Wiki Hosting Service
https://www.wikispaces.com

Overview

Notwithstanding its critics, Wikipedia is often cited—along with Facebook, YouTube, and Twitter—as an example of a Web 2.0 service that has been successfully implemented and has steadily gained acceptance across diverse groups of users. For some, this resource continues to be one of the top reference sources for information on a particular topic, and it is often one of the first sources returned in a Google, Yahoo!, or Bing search. Wikipedia's continued growth as a leading collaborative reference resource has led to the development of similar tools devoted to enhancing collaborative work online.

Wikispaces is a good example of a service built on a collaborative platform, like Wikipedia, that provides free wiki hosting services to educators, businesses, and nonprofits. On Wikispaces, distinct groups from various communities work within dedicated web spaces and have access to tools to collaboratively edit and share projects and ideas online. Wikispaces appeals to a wide cross section of users, as it is based on the commitment to create a product that is not "engineer-focused, hard to use and buried under busy user interfaces," opting instead for simplicity and ease of use, to enable users to "focus on building content, talking with other members, and growing [their] community."[1] Competing services include PBworks, Wetpaint, Wikia, and Google Sites.

Launched initially by Tangient LLC in March 2005, Wikispaces was acquired in March 2014 by TSL Education, a U.K.-based online network for teachers, and now hosts wikis for more than 14 million persons working in shared communities ranging from small classrooms to large corporations and educational institutions.[2] Customers include Denver Public Schools, Chippewa Falls School District, Arizona State

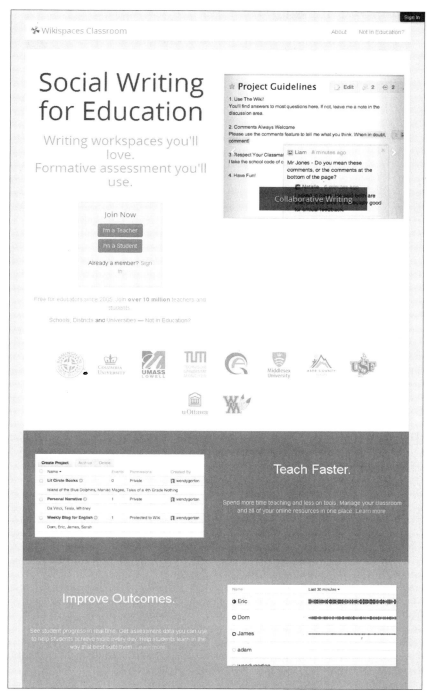

(Continued)

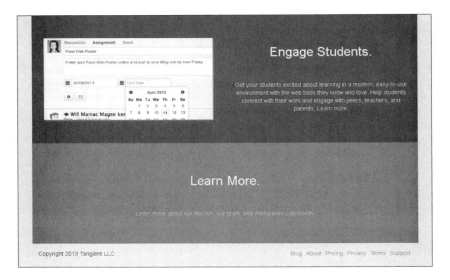

Wikispaces provides wiki hosting services to
educators, businesses, and nonprofits.

University, City University of New York, Harvard School of Public
Health, U.S. National Archives & Records Administration, and the
Beijing International School.

Features

➤ Online registration on the product homepage (https://www
.wikispaces.com) is required, and new users must provide
a username, password, email address, and occupation. The
basic service is free for individuals and small groups, and it
allows for creating one wiki, with five team members; access
to standard features; use of the visual editor; and an ad-free
interface.

➤ Wikispaces Classroom (www.wikispaces.com/content/
classroom) is free for educators and has all the features
students and teachers require to read, write, and work
collaboratively. Wikispaces Plus is a premium service suitable
for family, team, or group work. Wikispaces Super provides
a "super-powered" wiki with features for large projects

(unlimited members, SSL security, custom domain name, custom themes, and permissions).

➤ Wikispaces provides the tools to build a wiki that is easy to use and can be readily adopted within varied communities, as it supports the integration of widgets (videos, calendars, and visitor counters) and other media.

➤ Using the creative tools provided, Wikispaces communities have the freedom to publish pages that are sustainable, regularly updated, collaboratively developed and maintained. The service supports the organization of team members into project-related teams with assigned webpages, file storage space, and custom permissions. This collaborative interface enhances discussion and feedback, allowing the creation of online forums to respond to questions and the ability to add comments on individual pages.

➤ Working online within supported web browsers, Wikispaces members can immediately create pages and workspaces using guidelines they establish. Guest authors can be authorized to edit pages with or without creating an account, and Wikispaces pages are supported in several languages.

➤ Dedicated to building the world's easiest to use wiki service, Wikispaces offers an intuitive interface that demands little technical knowledge. The visual editor allows quick editing and customization of layout, design, and themes, access to page templates, and tags or keywords. The wiki automatically logs changes, updates, and revisions, providing complete page histories for users to easily compare page drafts or revert to earlier versions.

➤ The Wikispaces App for iPads is available at the Apple App Store.

How Cybrarians Can Use This Resource

Promoting Wikis as Online Collaborative Resources

Within the library community, there is demonstrable evidence that wikis are value-added tools. One such example is the popular Library

Success: a Best Practices Wiki (www.libsuccess.org/Main_Page), maintained by Meredith Farkas and acclaimed as a librarian's one-stop online resource for innovative projects and idea sharing. Librarians can promote Wikispaces Classroom as a free wiki hosting service for educators, as presently there are millions of teachers and students using the service. This service provides the following benefits:

➤ Enhancing students' use of social media tools (students have separate logins)

➤ Developing collaborative writing spaces

➤ Managing classroom online resources in one centralized location

➤ Viewing student progress in real time

➤ Providing feedback on assigned projects

➤ Facilitating discussions with students and providing a forum for them to host conversations with their peers

➤ Enhancing student learning in a modern, easy-to-use environment with creative collaborative tools

FYI

The Wikispaces blog (www.blog.wikispaces.com) keeps community users regularly updated on new features, tips and tricks, hosted events, customer feedback, and product reviews.

Notes

1. "Wikispaces: About," Wikispaces, accessed March 29, 2014, www.wikispaces.com/About.
2. Ibid.

59

XPRIZE
Philanthropic Competition
www.xprize.org

Overview

XPRIZE is a nonprofit organization that develops, manages, and monitors large-scale public competitions intended to encourage technological developments that have "the potential to positively impact humanity." The core philosophy driving the organization is the belief that incentive campaigns with monetary awards worth millions of dollars can spark innovation by tapping into that "indomitable spirit of competition" and entrepreneurial drive, "bringing about breakthroughs and solutions that once seemed unimaginable."[1]

Prizes are generally awarded to a team of individuals, companies, or organizations that have shown the potential to capture the imagination of the public, spur innovation, and accelerate the rate of positive change across the globe in the five prize areas: Energy and Environment, Exploration, Global Development, Learning, and Life Sciences. As of this writing, the philanthropic thrust of the organization has been realized, with several successful projects designed and monetary prizes awarded. These awards include the $10 million Ansari XPRIZE for private, suborbital space flight; the $10 million Progressive Insurance Automotive XPRIZE for creating safe, affordable, production-capable vehicles that exceed 100 MPG energy equivalence (MPGe); and the $2 million Northrop Grumman Lunar Lander XCHALLENGE for advanced rocket development. Active prizes currently in development include the $30 million Google Lunar XPRIZE, the $10 million Qualcomm Tricorder XPRIZE, the $2.25 million Nokia Sensing XCHALLENGE, and the $2 million Wendy Schmidt Ocean Health XPRIZE.[2]

The XPRIZE Board of Trustees consists of visionaries drawn from all sectors of society who "recognize the power of prize philanthropy to create fundamental change in the world" and comprises notable individuals such as James Cameron, Larry Page, Arianna Huffington, Ray Kurzweil, Ali Velshi, and Wendy Schmidt.[3] The foundation has its offices in California.

Features

➤ The XPRIZE large-scale monetary award is given to a team that achieves a specific goal set by the XPRIZE Foundation in one of five different prize groups:

- The Energy and Environment Prize Group incentivizes development of projects that aim to end addiction to oil and stem the harmful effects of climate change. It includes breakthroughs in clean fuels, renewable energy, energy efficiency, energy storage, carbon reduction, and sustainable housing.

- The Exploration Prize Group expands the use of space, the ocean, and other under-explored frontiers in order to improve life on Earth and extend life beyond the confines of land.

- The Global Development Prize Group focuses on finding solutions to address major challenges in the areas of agriculture, capital, health, and water use.

- The Learning Prize Group envisions a future with unprecedented, individually-tailored opportunities for lifelong learning, literacy, autonomy, and career readiness, as well as the development of tools for uplifting entire populations from the vicious cycle of poverty. The ultimate goal is to empower a universally educated population, with equal access to information and knowledge regardless of age, gender, race, nationality, or socioeconomic status.

- The Life Sciences Prize Group focuses on stimulating innovative breakthroughs in molecular biology, stem cell research, bionics, organogenesis, synthetic biology, and artificial intelligence in order to improve health care and extend healthy living.

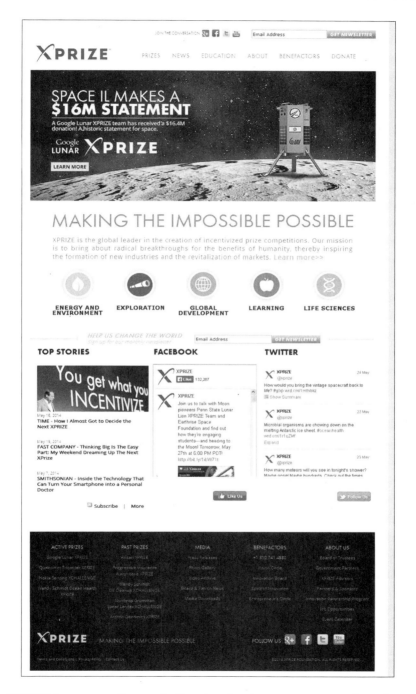

XPRIZE is a nonprofit organization that develops, manages, and monitors large-scale public competitions encouraging technological development.

➤ XPRIZE LOOP (https://www.xprize.org/donate) is an avenue
available for donors to support XPRIZE's competitions. There
are varying membership levels for supporters wishing to make
a philanthropic investment:

- EXPLORE ($10/month)—Members receive the XPRIZE
newsletter, exclusive XPRIZE memorabilia, and invitations
to XPRIZE LOOP events.

- DISCOVER ($20/month)—Members receive the XPRIZE
newsletter, exclusive XPRIZE memorabilia, invitations
to XPRIZE LOOP events, quarterly prize development
updates, access to insider videos, and free admission to
select XPRIZE ticketed events.

- DISRUPT ($30/month)—Members receive the XPRIZE
newsletter, exclusive XPRIZE memorabilia, invitations to
XPRIZE LOOP events, quarterly prize development updates,
access to insider videos, free admission to select XPRIZE
ticketed events, publicity as a member on XPRIZE social
media, presale access to an XPRIZE LOOP prize design
workshops where winning concepts are presented to the
XPRIZE team, and a book authored by a XPRIZE benefactor.

➤ Individuals can volunteer to speak at an XPRIZE event as
an expert in one of the incentivized areas of competition:
Energy and Environment, Exploration, Global Development,
Learning, and Life Sciences.

How Cybrarians Can Use This Resource

Promoting a Philanthropic Campaign to Promote Lifelong Learning, Literacy, Autonomy, and Career Readiness

The XPRIZE mission of bringing about "radical breakthroughs for
the benefit of humanity" through incentivized competitions is a noble
effort. This philanthropic campaign can be promoted by librarians to
individuals and units across all disciplines to develop innovations and
technologies that ultimately assist in overcoming global challenges.

Librarians as advocates can be particularly instructive and
instrumental in bringing worldwide attention to the Global Literacy

XPRIZE Campaign, which currently focuses on the following global problem:

> With [more than] 60 million children not receiving primary education, basic education and literacy is a significant global Grand Challenge. The XPRIZE Foundation believes a technological breakthrough is needed in the tools and toys for learning and thinking. These include accessibility, quality, scalability, and customization of systems and techniques to learn, both inside and outside the educational establishment. A Global Literacy XPRIZE has been conceptualized to rethink learning by harnessing innovation and technology and by placing the capability and desire to become educated into the hands of the learner. The prize has the potential to change what people think is possible regarding the means and methods used to teach and learn.[4]

FYI

The Google Lunar XPRIZE aims to create a new "Apollo" moment for this generation as well as spur continuous lunar exploration with $30 million in incentive-based prizes. To win the grand prize ($20 million) a private team must land safely on the surface of the Moon, travel 500 meters above, below, or on the Lunar surface, and send back two "Mooncasts" to Earth before the contest deadline of December 31st, 2016. (www.googlelunarxprize.org/prize-details).

Notes

1. "XPRIZE: Who We Are," XPRIZE, accessed May 17, 2014, www.xprize.org/about/who-we-are.
2. "About XPRIZE," XPRIZE, accessed May 17, 2014, www.googlelunarxprize.org/about/about-x-prize.
3. "XPRIZE: Board of Trustees," XPRIZE, accessed May 17, 2014, www.xprize.org/about/board-of-trustees.
4. "XPRIZE: Learning Prize Group," XPRIZE, accessed May 17, 2014, www.xprize.org/prize-development/learning#prize-group-in_development.

60

Yammer
Social Networking Service
https://www.yammer.com

Overview

Marketed as the leading enterprise network for businesses, Yammer was developed as a collaborative platform to get "work done smarter and faster." More than 200,000 companies worldwide use Yammer's private social network to establish secured connections to work on team-based projects, organize events, launch campaigns, and share information and ideas across diverse departments and disparate geographic regions.

Yammer's full range of features is ideally suited to business enterprises and nonprofit organizations wishing to establish an internal network that streamlines communication channels, increases productivity, and connects disengaged workers. Starting a Yammer Group on a project can provide the support and infrastructure required for team members wishing to work together, by creating a flexible, virtual workspace that helps them establish and meet deadlines, share documents, and organize feedback.

For individuals working in dispersed departments within an organization, there is the opportunity to create a profile highlighting skill sets and expertise on specific subject areas, then share this information with colleagues through an internal database. For workers at all levels of the organization or project group, there are opportunities to participate in open conversations on current projects, post questions for solutions to work-related problems, upload documents to a central shared location, and post URL links to valuable resources.

Founded in 2008, Yammer was acquired by Microsoft Corporation in 2012. The company has its headquarters in Redmond, Washington.

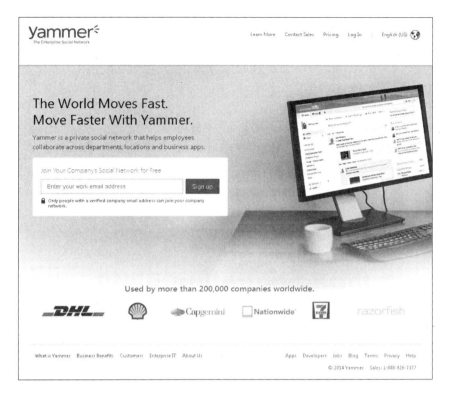

Yammer is marketed as the leading enterprise
social network for businesses.

Features

➤ Yammer offers freemium and premium subscriptions. Premium packages—Office 365 and the SharePoint Online/ Yammer Enterprise— include advanced integration with established business applications (SharePoint, Microsoft Office, OneDrive, and Skype), additional administrative and security controls, and customer support and engagement services.

➤ The freemium Yammer Only service offers access to basic enterprise networking features:

• Real-time conversations, public or private, via inbox messaging

- Employee profiles integrating picture, contact information, and expertise
- Member directories to search for co-workers within the organization
- Full-text universal search to quickly find documents, conversation threads, internal notes, and tagged messages across the Yammer network and integrated business apps
- Yammer Groups to share files, announcements, updates, company events, and polls, as well as co-edit content
- Praise tab and leader boards to view accomplishments, rewards, and projects completed
- Detailed organizational chart
- Automatic translation of foreign languages

➤ Yammer mobile provides on-the-go access with apps developed for iOS (iPhone and iPad), Android, and Windows Phone.

➤ Yammer supports integration with third-party applications such as Klout, GitHub, and Zendesk to improve engagement and boost productivity.

How Cybrarians Can Use This Resource
Integrating a Business-Oriented Social Network into the Library Work Environment

As an enterprise-driven social network, Yammer has a proven track record of providing a service that, if successfully implemented within organizations (including libraries), can streamline communication, increase productivity, and connect disengaged workers. Another major selling point is the service's efficacy in circumventing work disruptions in instances where employers relocate offices and staff, recruit new employees, or promote existing employees.

Within fast-paced mobile environments, Yammer "helps organizations become more agile … putting information at employees' fingertips and giving them a voice and a place where they can ask questions and post comments" on how the process is affecting current workflow.[1]

FYI

Yammer's YouTube video (https://www.youtube.com/watch?v=MMEoWMJf1uY) provides valuable insights on how the service has been successful in transforming work environments for businesses.

Note

1. "Yammer on Tour (London Baby!)," *The Running Librarian* (blog), March 7, 2013, www.therunninglibrarian.co.uk/2013/03/yammer-on-tour-london-baby.html.

61

Zinio
Digital Publishing Service
www.zinio.com

Overview

With a database of more than 5,500 magazines from publishers of all genres and a readership of 200 million, Zinio is marketed as "the world largest digital newsstand."[1] It is a claim that is hard to challenge, as this multifunctional distributor of digital magazines currently hosts a majority of the publishing industry's most highly rated magazines, among them *Bloomberg, Consumer Reports, The Economist, Esquire, GQ, Maxim, Macworld, National Geographic, Newsweek, Outdoor Photographer, PC Magazine* and *Smithsonian.*

The company's success can be attributed in part to its foresight in recognizing the needs of 21st-century readers, often described as wired, device agnostic, and wanting seamless and effortless access to information. Zinio has been proactive in responding to these diverse needs by building a digital platform capable of delivering its product (magazines) on traditional PCs and laptops as well as mobile devices, enabling readers to shop, download, and read subscription-based and free content online, offline, and synced across multiple devices.

Of note to libraries is the partnership between Recorded Books and Zinio to offer the Zinio for Libraries service, which offers patrons online access to a library of "complete digital magazines."[2] Patrons can check out library subscription titles, with no holds, checkout periods, or limits placed on the number of titles borrowed. Patrons can then download and read these magazines on a browser or via the Zinio app, available on most mobile devices.

Zinio's Digital Magazines for Libraries service offers online patrons access to the library's subscription magazines.

Features

➤ On the Zinio homepage (www.zinio.com), new readers must first create an account before shopping for magazines, reading the free articles available, and accessing a custom library of selected titles.

➤ The homepage is regularly updated with automatically generated magazine splash cover pages of Top Sellers, Featured Listings, and New Arrivals.

➤ Readers can limit searches to specific content by selecting from a wide range of categories such as Art & Photography, Entertainment, Lifestyle, News, Science & Technology, Sports, and Travel.

➤ A "Download the App" button on the main webpage allows readers to immediately download the Zinio app to read content on their mobile devices. Links are provided to iTunes (iPhones and iPad), Google Play (Android devices), and Windows Phone Store.

➤ In support of its "read on any device" marketing strategy, Zinio has invested heavily in developing a mobile app that is multifunctional as well as user- and reading-friendly. Key app features allow:

- Syncing personal libraries across all devices
- Connecting with social networks to share content with friends and followers
- Automatic downloading of content
- Reading magazines offline and on the go
- Accessing support for interactive and multimedia features on select titles

How Cybrarians Can Use This Resource

Promote the Zinio for Libraries Service

The publishing industry and other library-supported industries have undergone significant changes within the last decade. The push factor—the rapid evolution of emerging technologies—has led to the parallel development of digital publishing alongside traditional publishing, and the appearance of Zinio and other publishing platforms in the digital domain.

Zinio's partnership with Recorded Books to provide Zinio for Libraries demonstrates how libraries are perceived as instrumental in providing access to these innovative digital platforms and, in doing so, meeting the needs of a new type of library reader. The nonrestrictive—no holds, checkout periods, or limits on titles borrowed—approach combined with the added bonus of syncing titles across multiple mobile devices is guaranteed to appeal to patrons seeking access to ecollections. This service is currently available to public libraries in the U.S., U.K., Australia, and Canada, and a website with prerecorded webinars has been developed to promote the service (www.recordedbooks.com/index.cfm?-fuseaction=rb.byki_webinar).

Libraries that have implemented the Zinio for Libraries service include:

➤ Broward County Library, Florida (https://www.rbdigital.com/browardfl/service/zinio/landing?)

➤ Plainfield Public Library District, Illinois (https://www.rbdigital.com/plainfieldil/service/zinio/landing?)

➤ Boston Public Library, Massachusetts (https://www.rbdigital.com/bostonma/service/zinio/landing?)

➤ Eugene Public Library, Oregon (http://www.rbdigital.com/eugeneor/service/zinio/landing?)

➤ West Hartford Public Library, Connecticut (http://www.westhartfordlibrary.org/books_dvds_more/download_audiobooks)

FYI

The Ziniophile blog (blog.zinio.com) is regularly updated with editorial contributions, industry news, and information on new Zinio apps and features.

Notes

1. "Zinio: Meet Zinio," Zinio, accessed February 6, 2015, www.corp.zinio.com.
2. "Zinio: The World's Largest Newsstand is now Available for your Library," Recorded Books, accessed February 16, 2014, www.recordedbooks.com/index .cfm?fuseaction=rb.zinio

Appendix I

Tips and Teaching Tools for Keeping Up-To-Date with Emerging Technologies and New Resources

The Internet of Things,[1] big data, augmented reality, wearable technology, web-scale IT, 3D printing, APIs, cloud computing, and mobile strategies are all new tech-driven concepts that beg the following questions: How do we as cybrarians stay current with all these quick-fire technologies and fast-paced changes in the digital workplace? Where can we find an online clearinghouse to discover new tools? What resources should we consult to learn about best practices applicable to our work environment?

This book and similar publications are logical resources to start the process of keeping current. Personally, I have discovered over the years that the core of any learning strategy is a commitment to learning, a willingness to experiment, and a caring and sharing attitude. This strategy can be spelled out in one simple formula: *Learning + Experimenting = Sharing + Innovation.*

Here are useful pointers for keeping up:

➤ Social Media Tools

- Set and regularly evaluate social media goals. Focus on social media platforms that work best for communities served. Develop a social media policy.

- Effectively manage and constantly monitor social media tools by scheduling social media tasks into the daily routine, such as posting quality content, networking, fostering new connections, and participating in online discussions.

- Use social networking services like Pinterest, Instagram, LinkedIn, Facebook, Tumblr, and Twitter to promote collections, services, products, and special events, connect with the library community in the areas of reference and instruction, highlight patrons' skills, and market the library's brand and message. Monitor and utilize the latest features that are developed and integrated into these social networks.

- Utilize content curation tools such as Diigo, Flipboard, Paper.li, Storify, Scoop.it, and Pinterest to sort through complex content on the web, organize this content around a specific theme or topic, and publish and share with library users.

- The mobile revolution is here. Recent studies have shown that the majority of our clients are now spending more time with their mobile applications than they do browsing the web. Optimize the library's website for mobile devices, curate library-related mobile content and apps for patrons, and establish a multifaceted tech tool/gadget program.

➤ Personal and Professional Commitment

- Make a personal commitment to conduct research and learn about the emerging technologies, then follow through.

- Take advantage of professional development opportunities, many of them free and available on the web. On the *Cybrarian's Web* companion website (www .cybrariansweb.com), I provide links to such opportunities. Network with colleagues, as they are often the ones who are aware of what is available.

- Network with industry players at the forefront of developing emerging technologies. This may require a *can do* attitude that borders on brazen and takes you to areas outside your comfort zone.

- Have the capacity to learn constantly and quickly.

- Read the professional literature—especially outside a particular field of enterprise and expertise—and be prepared to conduct research and publish the results.

Finally, here are links to resources that should help you stay current. Good luck!

Recommended Resources for Keeping Up
General Resources
ALA Library Matters: Impact Research (www.ala.org/research/libraries-matter)

ALA Transforming Libraries (www.ala.org/transforminglibraries)

Huffington Post (www.huffingtonpost.com)

ITI NewsLink (http://www.infotoday.com/newslink)

Library Success: A Best Practices Wiki (www.libsuccess.org/index.php?title=Main_Page)

Library Technology Guides (www.librarytechnology.org)

Lifehacker (www.lifehacker.com)

Mashable (www.mashable.com)

OCLC Web Junction (www.webjunction.org)

Pew Research Center (www.pewinternet.org)

ReadWriteWeb (www.readwriteweb.com)

TechCrunch (www.techcrunch.com)

Tech Soup for Libraries (www.techsoupforlibraries.org)

Wired (www.wired.com)

TED: Ideas Worth Spreading (www.ted.com)

Blogs
ACRL TechConnect (www.acrl.ala.org/techconnect)

ALA TechSource (www.alatechsource.org/blog)

David Lee King (www.davidleeking.com)

Free Range Librarian (www.freerangelibrarian.com)

iLibrarian (www.oedb.org/blog)

Information Wants to be Free (www.meredith.wolfwater.com/
wordpress)

Librarian in Black (www.http://librarianinblack.net/librarianinblack)

Library Future (www.libraryfuture.com/blog)

Library Stuff (www.librarystuff.net)

Lita Blog (www.litablog.org)

Stephen's Lighthouse (www.stephenslighthouse.com)

Tame the Web (www.tametheweb.com)

Note

1. The Internet of Things (IoT) is characterized as advanced connectivity of devices, systems, and services within our physical world. One select IoT example is enabling smartphone users to use their device to control household appliances, cars, and other remote objects.

Appendix II

Social Media Tools, Apps, and Other Resources—Brief Summaries

Adobe: Adobe Systems Incorporated is an American multinational computer software company focused on the creation of multimedia and creativity software products.

Amazon CreateSpace: Amazon CreateSpace provides innovative tools and professional services to enable independent authors to self-publish and distribute their works on their own terms.

Aurasma: Hewlett Packard's augmented reality platform.

BrandYourself: A web-based platform that provides personal Search Engine Optimization (SEO) and online reputation management services within the Google search engine.

Camtasia: Camtasia Studio and Camtasia for Mac are software suites for creating video tutorials and presentations using screencasting technology.

Codecademy: An online interactive education platform that offers free coding classes in programming languages (Python, PHP, jQuery, JavaScript, and Ruby) and markup languages (HTML and CSS).

Coursera: A for-profit educational technology company offering massive open online courses (MOOCs).

Digital Public Library of America: A U.S.-based project aimed at developing a large-scale public digital library that provides free online access to digital holdings of America's libraries, archives, and museums.

Diigo: A social bookmarking website.

Dropbox: A free file sharing, storage, and synchronization service.

Ebook: An electronic book consisting of text and images read on electronic devices.

Ebook Readers: Designed specifically for reading, these devices display digitized versions of books that enable easy, on-the-go reading.

Evernote: A suite of software and services designed for note-taking and archiving.

Flipboard: A social network aggregation service that collects content from social media and other websites and presents this content in a digital magazine format.

Google Drive: File storage and synchronization service provided by Google.

Google Glass: Google's patented wearable computer with an optical head-mounted display. Using natural language instructions, Glass users (referred to as "Glassholes") command this device to explore the internet, capture photographs, record videos, check and send emails, and make video calls.

Google Hangouts: A combined instant messaging and video chat service enabling Google subscribers to send and receive instant messages, photos, videos, and emoji (animated GIFs) as well as initiate free video calls (one-on-one or group).

GoToMeeting: Citrix's web-hosted video conferencing service.

Hootsuite: A social media management dashboard providing the tools to manage and measure the performance of multiple social networks.

Infogr.am: A data visualization service used to create and market infographics.

Instagram: An online photo/video sharing and social networking service that enables users to take pictures and videos, apply digital filters, and share this content on popular social networks.

Issuu: A digital publishing platform developed to simulate the experience of reading a print publication online.

Jumpshare: A real-time file sharing service that permits users to upload, store, and share files online.

Kaywa Reader: A two-dimensional (2D) barcode reader used to scan Quick Response (QR) codes leading to URLs, SMS messages, contact information (telephone number, email), and text, audio, or video files. Also offers a generator for creating QR Codes.

Kickstarter: A crowdfunding platform that solicits public funding to develop creative projects in multiple genres: Art, Comics, Dance, Design, Fashion, Film, Food, Games, Music, Photography, Publishing, Technology, and Theater.

Learnist: A crowdsourced collection of digital works referred to as learnboards.

LiveBinders: A social bookmarking service that curates content, saves this content in varied formats (videos, text files, images, and webpages), and organizes and displays this saved information as virtual three-ring binders.

Makerspaces: A community-operated do-it-yourself (DIY) workspace where individuals with common interests in diverse subject areas can meet, socialize, and collaborate.

Mendeley: A free reference management service that supports researchers in their efforts to discover, store, organize, and share research papers, and also automates the process of generating bibliographic citations.

Microsoft Office Online: A free online version of Microsoft's proprietary Microsoft Office software.

Mobile Apps: Application software designed and developed to run on mobile devices (smartphones and tablets), laptops, and PCs.

Netvibes: A personalized publishing platform useful for monitoring trends, reading newsfeeds, adding widgets, searching and updating posts on social networks, and gathering analytics.

OneDrive: Microsoft's patented cloud storage service (formerly known as SkyDrive).

Paper.li: A content curation service that enables users to search and discover online content (articles, photos, and videos) and publish this content in digital newspaper format.

Pinterest: A virtual visual discovery tool that enables users to collect, organize, manage, and share theme-based collections referred to as pinboards.

Poll Everywhere: An application for soliciting real-time audience responses during live events such as conferences, presentations, and classroom lectures.

Popplet: A visualization tool for capturing, organizing, and sharing ideas.

Project Gutenberg Self-Publishing Press: A publishing platform that allows independent authors to upload, promote, and distribute their self-published works.

Quick Response (QR) Codes: Two-dimensional barcodes readable by smartphones and other mobile devices.

Readability: A web and mobile reading app that offers an efficient way to save web content for online and offline reading and improve the reading experience by providing this content in clipped, uncluttered format.

Scoop.it: An online curation service that offers a platform to discover, edit, publish, and share content online as postings on social networks, websites, blogs, and splash pages.

Scribd: A multifunctional product serving the dual role of digital library, providing access to a collection of professionally-published ebooks and user-contributed written works, and self-publishing platform, offering independent authors a creative platform to upload written works.

Smashwords: An ebook self-publishing and distribution platform for authors, publishers, literary agents, and retailers.

Snapchat: An ephemeral photo and video mobile sharing app that allows users to capture videos and pictures called snaps that self-destruct after being viewed by recipients.

Storify: A social networking service that allows users to create stories by curating and publishing content from social networks.

Technology, Entertainment, Design (TED): A nonprofit organization devoted to spreading ideas through conferences using the unusual rigid format of short, powerful talks of 18 minutes or less.

Text 2 Mind Map: A visualization tool developed specifically to simplify the process of creating mind maps.

TodaysMeet: A microblogging service used to quickly create chat rooms during presentations, enabling presenters to establish live online streams and communicate directly with audience members.

Tumblr: A microblogging and social networking service offering tools that enable bloggers to effortlessly share content from an intuitive, web-based dashboard via an internet browser, mobile device, or email.

TweetDeck: Twitter's native social media dashboard for management of Twitter accounts.

Udutu: A course management system that offers online learning solutions designed to help small and large organizations build and distribute online training courses.

Unglue it: An ebook crowdfunding service where individuals and institutions can collectively work together to pay authors and publishers to distribute ebooks and other types of digital content free to the world under a Creative Commons license.

Vine: Twitter's mobile video-sharing app, developed to enable users to create and share short looping video clips with a maximum clip length of six seconds.

Voki: A service that provides users with the online tools to create customized avatars.

Wattpad: An online community for discovering and sharing stories that connects readers and writers, providing the latter with opportunities to publish online and share their works with readers willing to give feedback.

Weebly: A web-hosting service with trademarked drag-and-drop website building capabilities that allow nonprofessionals with little or no technical expertise to create websites.

WhatsApp: A cross-platform mobile messaging app.

Wikispaces: A wiki hosting service for educators, businesses, and nonprofits.

XPRIZE: A nonprofit organization that develops, manages, and monitors large-scale public competitions intended to encourage technological development in five prize areas: Energy and Environment, Exploration, Global Development, Learning, and Life Sciences.

Yammer: A social networking service developed for businesses and other enterprises.

Zinio: A multiplatform distribution service for digital magazines.

Appendix III

Referenced Websites

Chapter 1

Yolo County Library System (www.yolocounty.org/general-government/
general-government-departments/library)

Bedford Free Public Library (www.bedfordlibrary.net)

OverDrive (https://www.overdrive.com)

Chapter 2

Smashwords (https://www.smashwords.com)

Lulu (www.lulu.com)

Scribd (www.scribd.com)

Project Gutenberg Self-Publishing Press (self.gutenberg.org)

Chapter 3

Oculus Rift (www.oculusvr.com)

Google Glass (www.google.com/glass/start)

NASA (www.nasa.gov)

Rolling Stones (www.rollingstones.com)

Esquire (www.esquire.com)

Layar (https://www.layar.com)

Wikitude (www.wikitude.com)

Chapter 4

Google (https://www.google.com)

Yahoo! (https://www.yahoo.com)

Bing (https://www.bing.com)

Chapter 5

Screenr (www.screenr.com)
Jing (www.techsmith.com/jing.html)

Chapter 6

Facebook (https://www.facebook.com)
Zynga (www.zynga.com)
New York Times (www.nytimes.com)
Bloomberg (www.bloomberg.com)
USA Today (www.usatoday.com
CNBC (www.cnbc.com)
TechCrunch (www.techcrunch.com)

Chapter 7

Udacity (https://www.udacity.com)
edX (https://www.edx.org)

Chapter 8

Harvard Library (www.library.harvard.edu)
HathiTrust Digital Library (www.hathitrust.org)
Internet Archive (https://archive.org/index.php)
New York Public Library (www.nypl.org)
Digital Library of Georgia (www.dlg.galileo.usg.edu)
Empire State Digital Network (www.ny3rs.org/projects/empire-state-digital-network)
Kentucky Digital Library (www.kdl.kyvl.org)
Minnesota Digital Library (www.mndigital.org)
North Carolina Digital Heritage Center (https://www.digitalnc.org)

Chapter 9

Diigo Education (https://www.diigo.com/education)

Chapter 10

Microsoft OneDrive (formerly SkyDrive) (https://onedrive.live.com/about/en-us)

Google Drive (https://drive.google.com)

Apple iCloud (https://www.icloud.com)

Amazon Cloud Drive (https://www.amazon.com/clouddrive)

Box (https://www.box.com)

Facebook (https://www.facebook.com)

Twitter (https://twitter.com)

Zynga (www.zynga.com)

Groupon (www.groupon.com)

Chapter 11

American Association of Publishers (www.publishers.org)

Douglas County Libraries (www.douglascountylibraries.org)

Chapter 12

Williamson County Public Library (www.lib.williamson-tn.org/index.html)

Chapter 13

Simplenote (www.simplenote.com)

Google Keep (https://keep.google.com)

Microsoft OneNote (www.onenote.com)

Fetchnotes (www.fetchnotes.com/#)

Chapter 14

Twitter (https://twitter.com)

Facebook (https://www.facebook.com)

Instagram (www.instagram.com/#)

Tumblr (https://www.tumblr.com)

New York Times (www.nytimes.com)

Politico (www.politico.com)

Vanity Fair (www.vanityfair.com)

Etsy (https://www.etsy.com)

Facebook Paper (https://www.facebook.com/paper)

Chapter 15

Microsoft OneDrive (https://onedrive.live.com/about/en-us)

Apple iCloud (https://www.apple.com/icloud)

Amazon Cloud Drive (https://www.amazon.com/clouddrive)

Box (https://www.box.com)

Chapter 16

Path (https://path.com)

Evernote (https://evernote.com)

CNN (www.cnn.com)

New York Times (www.nytimes.com)

Twitter (https://twitter.com)

Facebook (https://www.facebook.com)

Elle (www.elle.com)

Field Trip (www.fieldtripper.com)

TripIt (https://www.tripit.com)

Open Table (www.opentable.com)

Foursquare (https://foursquare.com)

Tumblr (https://www.tumblr.com)

Chapter 17

Facebook Messenger (https://www.facebook.com/mobile/messenger)

WhatsApp (www.whatsapp.com)

Apple's iMessage (https://www.apple.com/ios/messages)

Skype (www.skype.com/en)

Phil Bradley's Weblog (www.philbradley.typepad.com)

Chapter 18

WebEx (www.webex.com)

Adobe Connect (www.adobe.com/products/adobeconnect.html)

Chapter 19

Facebook (https://www.facebook.com)

LinkedIn (https://www.linkedin.com)

Twitter (https://twitter.com)

Google Plus (https://plus.google.com)

Foursquare (https://foursquare.com)

Tumblr (https://www.tumblr.com)

YouTube (www.youtube.com)

Virgin (www.virgin.com)

Sony Music (www.sonymusic.com)

CBS Interactive (www.cbsinteractive.com)

Chrysler (https://www.chrysler.com)

The Red Cross (www.redcross.org)

Tiffany & Company (www.tiffany.com)

H&M (www.hm.com/us)

IBM (www.ibm.com/us/en)

Chapter 20

Facebook (https://www.facebook.com)

Twitter (https://twitter.com)

Pinterest (https://www.pinterest.com)

Chapter 21

Facebook (https://www.facebook.com)

Twitter (https://twitter.com)

Tumblr (https://www.tumblr.com)

Flickr (https://www.flickr.com)

Pheed (https://www.pheed.com)

Vine (https://vine.co)

Chapter 22

Facebook (https://www.facebook.com)

Twitter (https://twitter.com)

Google Plus (https://plus.google.com)

Chapter 23

Dropbox (https://www.dropbox.com)

Google Drive (https://drive.google.com)

Microsoft One Drive (https://onedrive.live.com)

Facebook (https://www.facebook.com)

Twitter (https://twitter.com)

WordPress (www.wordpress.org)

Pinterest (https://www.pinterest.com)

Tumblr (https://www.tumblr.com)

Chapter 24

Google (www.google.com)

Nokia (www.nokia.com/us-en)

Pet Shop Boys (www.petshopboys.co.uk)

Chapter 25

Indiegogo (https://www.indiegogo.com)

GoFundMe (www.gofundme.com)

YouCaring (www.youcaring.com)

Causes (https://www.causes.com)

Giveforward (www.giveforward.com)

FundRazr (https://fundrazr.com)

Fundly (https://fundly.com)

Chapter 26

Pinterest (https://www.pinterest.com)

Chapter 27

Flickr (https://www.flickr.com)

YouTube (www.youtube.com)

Dropbox (https://www.dropbox.com)

Delicious (https://delicious.com)

SlideShare (www.slideshare.net)

Prezi (www.prezi.com)

Chapter 28

SparkFun (https://www.sparkfun.com)

K'NEX (http://www.knex.com)

Littlebits (http://littlebits.cc)

TekVenture (www.tekventure.org)

Chapter 29

Elsevier (www.elsevier.com)

Chapter 30

Google Docs (https://docs.google.com)

Zoho (www.zoho.com)

Open Office (https://www.openoffice.org)

Chapter 31

Amazon Appstore (www.amazon.com/gp/mas/get/android)

Apple App Store (https://itunes.apple.com/us/genre/
   mobile-software-applications/id36?mt=8)

Google Play (https://play.google.com)

Microsoft Windows Phone Store (www.windowsphone.com/en-us/store)

BlackBerry World (https://appworld.blackberry.com)

Chapter 32

Centre for Learning and Performance Technologies (www.c4lpt.co.uk)

Chapter 33

Apple iCloud (https://www.icloud.com)

Google Drive (https://drive.google.com)

Dropbox (https://www.dropbox.com)

Box (https://www.box.com)

Chapter 34

Twitter (https://twitter.com)

Facebook (https://www.facebook.com)

Google Plus (https://plus.google.com)

YouTube (www.youtube.com)

Chapter 35

Gap (www.pinterest.com/gap)

Chobani (www.pinterest.com/chobani)

Nordstrom (www.pinterest.com/nordstrom)

Etsy (www.pinterest.com/etsy)

Edudemic (www.edudemic.com)

Chapter 36

McDonalds (www.mcdonalds.com)

Google (https://www.google.com)

Starbucks (www.starbucks.com)

Virginia Tech University (https://www.vt.edu)

Duke University (www.duke.edu)

University of Notre Dame (www.nd.edu)

University of North Carolina at Chapel Hill (www.unc.edu)

Chapter 37

University of Minnesota Libraries (https://www.lib.umn.edu)

Chapter 38

Project Gutenberg (www.gutenberg.org)

Chapter 39

Simon and Schuster (www.simonandschuster.com)

Chapter 40

Apple's Safari (https://www.apple.com/safari)
Amazon Kindle (https://kindle.amazon.com)
Flipboard (https://flipboard.com)
Reeder (www.reederapp.com)

Chapter 41

Diigo (https://www.diigo.com)
Pinterest (https://www.pinterest.com)
Storify (https://storify.com)

Chapter 42

Netflix (https://www.netflix.com)
Smashwords (https://www.smashwords.com)

Chapter 43

Scribd (http://www.scribd.com)

Chapter 44

Facebook (https://www.facebook.com)
WhatsApp (www.whatsapp.com)
Instagram (www.instagram.com/#)

Vine (https://vine.co)

Wickr (https://www.mywickr.com)

Silent Circle (https://silentcircle.com)

Chapter 45

Diigo (https://www.diigo.com)

Flipboard (https://flipboard.com)

Paper.li (www.paper.li)

Pinterest (https://www.pinterest.com)

Scoop.it (www.scoop.it)

New York Post (www.nypost.com)

BET (www.bet.com)

Weather Channel (www.weather.com)

Detroit News (www.detroitnews.com)

Daily Beast (www.thedailybeast.com)

General Electric (www.ge.com)

Scholastic (www.scholastic.com/home)

Cinemax (www.cinemax.com)

University of California Berkeley (www.berkeley.edu)

University of Texas at Austin (www.utexas.edu)

Harvard University (www.harvard.edu)

Livefyre (www.web.livefyre.com)

Chapter 46

Netflix (https://www.netflix.com)

Chapter 47

Bubbl.us (https://bubbl.us)

Coggle (https://coggle.it)

FreeMind (www.freemind.sourceforge.net)

LucidChart (https://www.lucidchart.com)

Mind42 (www. mind42.com)

XMind (www.xmind.net)

Popplet (www.popplet.com)

Chapter 48

Twitter (https://twitter.com)

Chapter 49

Live Journal (www.livejournal.com)

Blogger (https://www.blogger.com)

WordPress (www.wordpress.org)

Facebook (https://www.facebook.com)

Twitter (https://twitter.com)

Chapter 50

Twitter (https://twitter.com)

Chapter 51

Georgia Department of Education (www.gadoe.org)

Harley-Davidson (www.harley-davidson.com)

Canadian Pacific Railway (www.cpr.ca)

Microsoft (www.microsoft.com)

Pearson (www.pearsoncanada.ca)

Chapter 52

Indiegogo (https://www.indiegogo.com)

Kickstarter (https://www.kickstarter.com)

Fundly (https://fundly.com)

Leddy Library, University of Windsor (www.leddy.uwindsor.ca)

University of Alberta Libraries (www.library.ualberta.ca)

Z. Smith Reynolds Library, Wake Forest University (www.zsr.wfu.edu)

Chapter 53

Twitter (https://twitter.com)

Facebook (https://www.facebook.com)

Chapter 54

SitePal (www.sitepal.com)

Chapter 55

Facebook (https://www.facebook.com)

Instagram (www.instagram.com)

Twitter (https://twitter.com)

Pinterest (https://www.pinterest.com)

Chapter 56

Blogger (https://www.blogger.com)

Google Sites (https://sites.google.com)

WordPress (www.wordpress.org)

Chapter 57

Facebook (https://www.facebook.com)

Instagram (www.instagram.com)

Snapchat (www.snapchat.com)

Chapter 58

Wikipedia (https://www.wikipedia.org)

Facebook (https://www.facebook.com)

YouTube (www.youtube.com)

Twitter (https://twitter.com)

Google (https://www.google.com)

Yahoo! (https://www.yahoo.com)

Bing (https://www.bing.com)

PBworks (www.pbworks.com)

Wetpaint (www.wetpaint.com)

Wikia (www.wikia.com/Wikia)

Google Sites (https://sites.google.com)

Chapter 59

Google Lunar XPRIZE (www.googlelunarxprize.org)

Chapter 60

Klout (www.klout.com/home)

GitHub (https://github.com)

Zendesk (www.zendesk.com)

Chapter 61

Recorded Books (www.recordedbooks.com)

Appendix IV

Tools by Type of Service

Audience Response/Polling Service

Poll Everywhere

Augmented Reality Service

Aurasma

Google Glass

Avatar Creation Service

Voki

Barcode Scanning and Generator Software

Kaywa

Cloud Storage/File Hosting/Sharing Service

Dropbox

Google Drive

Jumpshare

OneDrive

Course Management System

Udutu

Crowdfunding Platform

Kickstarter

Unglue.it

Digital Learning Board

Learnist

Digital Library

Digital Public Library of America

Digital Library/Self-Publishing Platform

Project Gutenberg Self-Publishing Press
Scribd
Smashwords

Digital Publishing Service

Issuu
Zinio

DIY Collaborative Workspaces

Makerspaces

Ebook Collections and Services

Ebooks

Ebook Reading Devices

Ebook Readers

Global Conference/Ideas Sharing Platform

Technology, Entertainment, Design (TED)

Infographics Creator

Infogr.am

Instant Messaging Service

WhatsApp

Massive Open Online Courses (MOOCs) Platform

Coursera

Microblogging Service

TodaysMeet

Tumblr

Mobile Applications

Mobile Apps for Libraries

Note-taking Software

Evernote

Online Education Platform

Codecademy

Online Reputation Management Service

BrandYourself

Philanthropic Competition

XPRIZE

Photo and Video Sharing Service

Instagram

Snapchat

Productivity and Creativity Tools

Adobe

Productivity Tool

Microsoft Office Online

QR Code Scanner and Generator

Kaywa

Reference Management and Collaboration Service

Mendeley

Screen Recording and Video Editing Software

Camtasia

Self-Publishing Platform

Amazon CreateSpace
Project Gutenberg Self-Publishing Press
Scribd
Smashwords

Social Bookmarking Service

Diigo
Evernote
LiveBinders
Pinterest

Social Media Management Service

Hootsuite
Netvibes
TweetDeck

Social Networking Service

Tumblr
Wattpad
Yammer

Social News Aggregator

Flipboard

Paper.li

Scoop.it

Storify

Video Conferencing Service

Google Hangouts

GoToMeeting

Video Sharing Service

Vine

Visualization Service

Popplet

Text 2 Mind Map

Wearable Technology

Google Glass

Web and Mobile Reading Application

Readability

Web Hosting Service

Weebly

Wiki Hosting Service

Wikispaces

Appendix V

Tools Availability by Mobile Device*

Amazon Appstore for Android

Adobe Connect

Adobe Reader

Amazon Kindle Reading App

Coursera

Dropbox

Evernote

Flipboard

GoToMeeting

Hootsuite

Instagram

Issuu

Kickstarter

Learnist

Microsoft OneDrive

Pinterest

Quick Response (QR) Codes (code readers and generators)

Readability

Scribd

TED Conferences

Tumblr

Vine

---

* This list was compiled in February 2015 and may not reflect apps for resources that were developed and released after this date.

Wattpad

WhatsApp

Yammer

Zinio

Apple App Store

Adobe Connect

Adobe Reader

Amazon Kindle Reading App

Aurasma

Codecademy

Coursera

Diigo

Dropbox

Evernote

Flipboard

Google Drive

Google Glass (My Glass)

Google Hangouts

GoToMeeting

Hootsuite

Instagram

Issuu

Kaywa QR Code Reader

Kickstarter

Learnist

LiveBinders

Mendeley PDF Reader

Microsoft Office Online (various apps)

Netvibes

Pinterest

Poll Everywhere

Popplet

Quick Response (QR) Codes (code readers and generators)

Readability

Scoop.it

Scribd

Smashwords (available in Apple iBooks app)

Snapchat

TED Conferences

Tumblr

Vine

Voki

Wattpad

Weebly

WhatsApp

XPRIZE

Yammer

Zinio

BlackBerry World

Adobe Connect

Adobe Reader

Amazon Kindle Reading App

Dropbox

Evernote

Microsoft OneDrive

Quick Response (QR) Codes (code readers and generators)

Readability

Wattpad

WhatsApp

Zinio

Google Play (Android)

Adobe Connect

Adobe Reader

Amazon Kindle Reading App

Aurasma

Coursera

Diigo

Dropbox

Evernote

Flipboard

Google Drive

Google Glass (My Glass)

Google Hangouts

GoToMeeting

Hootsuite

Instagram

Issuu

Kaywa QR Code Reader

Kickstarter

Learnist

Microsoft Office Online (various apps)

Pinterest

Poll Everywhere

Quick Response (QR) Codes (code readers and generators)

Readability

Scoop.it

Scribd

Smashwords

Snapchat

TED Conferences

Tumblr

Vine

Voki

Wattpad

Weebly

WhatsApp

XPRIZE

Yammer

Zinio

Windows Phone App Store

Adobe Reader

Amazon Kindle Reading App

Coursera

Dropbox

Evernote

Flipboard

GoToMeeting

Instagram

Kickstarter

Microsoft OneDrive

Pinterest

Quick Response (QR) Codes (code readers and generators)

TED Conferences

Tumblr

Vine

Weebly

WhatsApp

Yammer

Zinio

About the Author

Cheryl Ann Peltier-Davis is Digital Initiatives, Cataloguing and Metadata Services Librarian at the Alma Jordan Library at the University of the West Indies, St. Augustine, Trinidad and Tobago. She is the author of several refereed journal articles on public and national libraries in the Caribbean and in 2007 served as co-editor of the book *Caribbean Libraries in the 21st Century: Changes, Challenges, and Choices* (Information Today, Inc.), which received the Association of Caribbean University, Research and Institutional Libraries (ACURIL) Award for Excellence in Research and Publication. She is also the author of the blog Caribbean Connector (caribbean-connector.blogspot.com) created to connect Caribbean librarians and serve as a clearinghouse to deliver information directly to their desktops.

Cheryl has given conference presentations on a diverse array of library-related topics including Web 2.0 and libraries, core competencies for librarians, digitizing library collections, information management, and Caribbean public libraries. She is a member of both the American Library Association (ALA) and ACURIL, and her continuing interest in emerging technologies has led to the publication of two volumes of *The Cybrarian's Web*.

Index